A brazilian k edition of this book
has been published by
Berliner Verlag
Am glol 230, 52172 Berlin, Germany

& Foreign & Commonwealth Office

Crossroads
and
Roundabouts

Junctions in German-British Relations

by Thomas Kielinger

A hardback edition of this book
has been published by
Bouvier Verlag
Am Hof 28, 53113 Bonn, Germany

This book was designed and produced by
Sears Davies Limited
Unit A, 25 Copperfield Street,
London SE1 0EN

Printed in Germany by
Graphischer Großbetrieb
Pößneck GmbH
D-07381 Pößneck

Reprographics by
Data Layout, London

CHAPTER IV

Britain's role in building German democracy
Official and unofficial co-operation

CHAPTER V

CHAPTER VI

LAST BUT NOT LEAST

ANNEX

A word of thanks
and explanation

The idea for this book originally came from the British and German Governments. However, responsibility for the final manuscript lies entirely with the author.

I have drawn on several sources for the material in this book. Where appropriate, they are indicated in the text itself. But this has been done sparingly so as not to disturb the narrative flow. For the same reason, I have dispensed with footnotes, in the hope that the bibliography will provide sufficient information. It makes no claim to completeness although it does include numerous essays and articles from newspapers and magazines as well as lectures and interviews, since they were often the sole sources for some details on German-British relations.

The manuscript has benefited from intensive conversations with many German and British friends, some of whom are named as authors in the text or the bibliography. I am greatly indebted to them all. Some read the text at various stages of its development and contributed stylistic and substantive suggestions. In particular I should like to mention Angelika Volle, Rainer Dobbelstein, Manfred Schlenke and Rolf Breitenstein - all well-versed in the topic and the relevant literature. The External Department of the Federal Press Office and the British Embassy in Bonn have tirelessly collected and supplied me with material for this book. Ursula von Langermann and Carole Sweeney, Herbert Behrendt and Michael Smith deserve my special thanks. Hagen Graf Lambsdorff and Robert Cooper have displayed infinite patience with the author and the constant shifting of deadlines necessitated by significant last-minute developments. But the additional time was also used for valuable discussions on the pitfalls and nuances of the subject matter.

David Ward has not merely translated the book, he has re-created it for an English-speaking readership - and for that I cannot thank him enough. The decision to deviate occasionally from the original German text was taken jointly in a most enjoyable and fruitful collaboration. It should be noted that the term "Britain" is used to denote the United Kingdom of Great Britain and Northern Ireland, while "Great Britain" comprises only England, Wales and Scotland. As a rule, the German language does not make such fine distinctions. Germans often say "England" when they mean "Great Britain" or even "Britain" (in the English sense of the word). However, this book attempts to give the respective terms their precise topographical meaning.

Nowadays, texts are conceived at computer terminals. But computers are capricious creatures full of cunning and trickery. When I needed help, I could always rely on Maik Linke and Stephan Lorz. I therefore gratefully include them in the family which has made this project possible.

Bonn, 12 August 1996

Foreword

Since September 1979, visitors entering the inner courtyard of the Federal Chancellery in Bonn have been greeted by Henry Moore's monumental sculpture "Large Two Forms". There is an eye-catching fascination about this gentle giant, reposing solid as a rock in stormy times.

A gentle giant and a solid rock in stormy times - the Germans and the British would no doubt happily subscribe to these differing descriptions. That is the ideal world. But in real life, things never quite turn out that way.

In the 1840s, at the time of William Turner's trips to the Rhine and Neckar, people's view of Germany may still have been influenced by its portrayal in Madame de Staël's book "De L'Allemagne" (1813) - as a nation gently slumbering in seclusion. Bismarck's arrival on the European stage changed this perception, which was then radically altered by his successors. Indeed, the change was so dramatic that memories of this power-plagued Germany still occasionally resurface even now, 50 years after Germany's re-integration into the democratic western community.

Not surprisingly, today's reunited Germany has no greater wish than to be seen as just a gentle giant and yet it has to face the harsh realisation that trying to please everyone may not be the most appropriate response to its history.

By the same token, the image of stoic Albion calmly weathering the storms is also an embellishment of the truth. Britain has always keenly defended its independence. Yet beneath the calm exterior of its national discipline, the country's élite has struggled hard to maintain a balance in domestic and foreign relations.

Serene composure was certainly not what prompted John Major's government to boycott EU decision-making processes for a month in response to the export ban on beef and beef byproducts imposed by Brussels in the early summer of 1996.

So when you think you understand something about British fairness, you should always bear in mind that this virture has a natural ally: fighting spirit. On the other hand, withstanding a global barrage of criticism does require a high degree of composure and imperturbability which can be quite impressive even if it is merely feigned.

Are the British and the Germans increasingly getting on each other's nerves as European Union deadlines approach? It would be unhelpful to draw such conclusions. Surely no one really believes that European integration will remove all the differences which make the coexistence of nations so fruitful, albeit occasionally frustrating? Alexis de Tocqueville summed it up quite neatly: "The more alike people become, the more sensitively they react to differences." Paradoxically, we must expect the growing convergence of European structures to promote greater awareness of cultural individuality and independence.

Henry Moore's "Large Two Forms" dominates the inner courtyard of the Federal Chancellery in Bonn

At the same time, the process of exchange and cross-fertilisation continues unabated. This has long been a feature of German-British relations; in the post-war period it became a model example of the synergy which civilised societies can achieve through mutual relations. The degree of co-operation between the two countries would have seemed utopian to earlier generations steeped in lethal rivalry. But an intensive exchange in culture, life-style and business is now taken for granted.

A British architect, Sir Norman Foster, has been commissioned to free the future seat of German parliamentary democracy, the tradition-laden Reichstag, from the burdens of its past legacies in preparation for its new task. This underlines once again the important role which Britain has played in rebuilding German democracy since 1945 - perhaps the "finest hour" in Britain's recent diplomatic history. The modernisation of German society through contact with the Anglo-Saxon "way of life", the influence of fashions and language, is clear for all to see.

Yet the British tabloids take little if any notice of these remarkable changes. "Fritz", a name from the heyday of friendship between Britain and the Prussia of Frederick the Great, has degenerated into a pejorative code word in London's gutter press. The true picture of present-day Germany and the traces of British involvement are completely obscured by tired images of spiked helmets, monocles and goose-stepping soldiers. They also obscure such minor details as the fact that the United Kingdom has become Germany's favourite location for its foreign investment, creating thousands of British jobs.

No wonder many Germans see this as confirmation of their prejudice that Britain is still living in the past - a nation of antique-lovers and antiquated attitudes.

This book sets out to counter the caricatures and clichés on both sides of the Channel. No other two countries and societies in Europe have touched, inspired or rejected one another so often in the course of history as the British and the Germans. Neither could ignore the other, which is probably why they always found each other so fascinating. But each fresh controversy that comes along chips a piece out of the colourful mosaic of German-British relations.

What can a book like this do to help? Well, it can reassemble the mosaic and restore some of the faded fragments to their original lustre in an attempt to give a clearer picture of British-German relations past and present. If, at the same time, it also succeeds in challenging and dismantling some of the reader's preconceived ideas, so much the better.

British-German Stereotypes and how to evaluate them

The role of caricatures

Relations between peoples and nations are based on an odd mixture of ideas, comparisons and stereotypes. So it is difficult to speak of a uniform "picture" which people have of one another. Nowhere in Europe does this apply more than in relations between Germany and Britain. Both countries are enmeshed in such a dense web of historical and present-day ties that it is precisely the diversity of these contacts which occasionally leads to confusing judgements. It would therefore be quite erroneous to assert that any particular image was now "the true picture" the two societies had of one another today.

In geographical terms, Britain and Germany are classic opposites - the island on the one hand and the central continental location on the other. One could almost speak of two geographical stereotypes - fixed co-ordinates which have led to "typical" differences in the history and mentalities of the two countries.

Yet they share a similar "genetic cocktail", so to speak: Angles and Saxons are also of Germanic origin, having drifted across to Britain from Frisia. Germanic siblings, separated at an early age, the British and the Germans developed under different conditions and in different environments.

The German-British "cousins", as they have been called since Queen Victoria married her cousin, Prince Albert of Saxe-Coburg-Gotha, have not always behaved like friendly relatives. The two World Wars fought this century are sad testimony to this fact.

Although most people on both sides of the Channel felt no hatred whatsoever towards one another, they were driven into conflict firstly by a rivalry which escalated into hysteria and secondly by their reaction to Hitler's madness.

The hearts and minds of Britons and Germans today are full of conflicting images of the past and the present, personal and recounted memories, the documented history of enmity and reconciliation as well as today's media headlines. For each view there is an opposing view; everything we hear said about "the other" (or about ourselves) sounds familiar - and so does the contrary.

After Berlin's bid to host the Olympic Games in the year 2000 was rejected in autumn 1993, the mass-circulation daily tabloid *BILD-*

Zeitung spontaneously asked Europeans for their opinion of Germany. "Does nobody love us any more?", was the worried premise.

The result was confusing and by no means conclusive in answering the basic question. Here are two contradictory reactions obtained by the paper in London. Harold Smith, 51 years of age, clerk:

"I enjoy going on holiday to Germany. I like the ordinary people, their modesty. The Germans are liberal-minded and

The two cousins in apparent harmony like Tweedledum and Tweedledee ...

passionate Europeans. We English still have a lot to learn."

By contrast, Kevin Mully, 46 years of age, haulage contractor:

"The Germans are a sulky bunch. The only good thing about them is their Mercedes. I am always glad to get out of the country again."

Vox populi - what does it really tell us? Perhaps we should ask the cartoonists in the two countries whether they at least paint a more uniform picture of the other.

"Great Britain: Turning to Germany" was the title of Chris Riddell's cartoon in the *Economist* at the beginning of a new phase in German-British co-operation after the Gulf War (1991). The two fat cousins

stand arm in arm. They have swapped hats and everything is so harmonious, including the ancestral portraits of Queen Victoria and William II, her grandson, the last German Emperor. It is like a scene from *Alice in Wonderland* : Tweedledum and Tweedledee or the German-British symbiosis ...

But the family atmosphere is effectively ridiculed by Raymond Jackson (JAK) in the *Evening Standard.* Queen Elizabeth is paying her first State visit to the united Germany in 1992 and all the die-hard figures of the past are wheeled out on parade - the spiked helmets, monocles, lorgnons, tufts of chamois hair and Tyrolean hats, the fur caps of the Death's Head Hussars and the

... but British-German relations are plagued by stereotypes

walking sticks of the invalids and ancient war veterans. All old hat. Spectres from the crypt. Raves from the grave.

So no hope for Tweedledum and Tweedledee and the German-British symbiosis after all?

Not necessarily. Jackson's picture is simply a reminder of how much time has elapsed since the old "cousins" period. It bears no relevance to today's bilateral relations. Even nostalgia has an expiry date. The interesting aspect of this cartoon is that the stereotypes used to portray *"the"* German also reveal their own true nature - outdated, passé, pure masquerade.

But we all love masquerades, don't we? And none more so than cartoonists! Which probably explains the conspicuous fact that, to this day, British tabloids still employ caricatural epithets of *"the"* Germans. These may have been applicable one or two World Wars ago, but they should now be consigned to the theatrical prop store - the goose step, the Hitler salute, the Iron Cross, the spiked helmet, the monocle, the *Wehrmacht* boots, the swastika and all the other paraphernalia. And yet they aren't. Why is that?

If what the historian Harald Husemann wrote is true, namely that to be successful a caricaturist *"must share with his audience a common cultural background, a common iconography of (popular) mythology, literature, art, history, etc"*, then what we are encountering here is an "iconography" of the German which is deeply-rooted in the past and created from memories of the former wartime enemy and the emblems of that period. We could say of them what we say of certain stars: their light continues to reach us although they themselves have long expired.

Their light continues to reach us ... The cartoonist Franklin draws on this in the *Sun* for his comment on the collapse of Barings Bank in March 1995. *"Mein Gott, Fritz, you've been gambling with Nick Leeson"*, the caption reads with cutting irony. The three guards, two of them in full *Wehrmacht* uniform, look like the stupid German officers in the popular TV series *"'Allo, 'Allo"*.

Nick Leeson triumphs over his German gaolers in Franklin's cartoon

Stereotypes are the whispered asides of international relations and banner headlines are amongst their most loyal allies. In 1990, the year of German unification, the *Sun* produced one such revealing headline, with a play on words to boot, which triumphantly presented German-British relations like a freshly-taken scalp. The German Ambassador in London, Freiherr von Richthofen, had paid a visit to the newspaper's offices to explain Germany's position on unification. *"THE SUN MEETS THE HUN"* exclaimed the front page the following day. As this example shows, certain linguistic stereotypes are also employed to evoke old clichés of enmity in addition to the iconographic components. Incidentally, the interview with the "Hun" was conducted in a spirit of mutual respect, as readers learned when they turned to the paper's inside pages...

The "Huns": How Emperor William II helped coin the most famous term of abuse hurled at the Germans.

The Huns, Asiatic tribes of nomads, struck fear and terror into Western Europe under their leader Attila (Etzel) in the 4th century. How did the Germans gain this epithet in the First World War, an epithet which still haunts Anglo-Saxon cartoons to this day as the classic stereotype of contempt? Well, they probably have their last Emperor, William II, to thank for that. On 27 July 1900, the Hohenzollern ruler, notorious for his bombastic speeches, spoke the following parting words to the German contingent of an international force leaving to suppress the xenophobic "Boxer" uprising in Peking:

"No pardon will be given! Prisoners will not be taken! Anyone falling into your hands falls to the sword! Just as the Huns under their King Attila created for themselves a thousand years ago a name which men still respect, you should give the name 'German' such cause to be remembered in China for another thousand years, so that no Chinaman, whether his eyes be slit or not, will ever dare look a German in the face..."

Of course, the Germans and the British are no longer at each other's throats - although the Chancellor, Norman Lamont, was not the only person in London seething with anger at the *Bundesbank's* alleged "betrayal" of the British Pound when it was forced to devalue and leave the European Exchange Rate Mechanism in September 1992, just two years after joining. Horst Busse expressed in the *Rhein-Neckar-Zeitung* what was riling many Union Jack patriots at that time: He depicted Her Majesty, the Pound Sterling, curtseying to the overpowering figure of the DM-Chancellor.

Royal curtsey to the German currency

Such cartoons thrive on pet perceptions which are stripped of everything which does not fit the concept. For example, the fact that Germany's budget deficit had already reached dangerous proportions in the year in question and cracks were beginning to appear in Germany's fabled industrial performance. But does the same not apply to our stereotyped views? That, after all, is what makes them "stereotypes" or pre-judgements. They are set hard and fast in concrete, chiselled out of traditional images which do not readily adapt to a changing world. The American writer and journalist, Walter Lippmann, made a pertinent comment on this phenomenon in his book "Public Opinion" (1921):

"For the most part we do not see first and then define, we define first and then see. (...) We pick out what our culture has already defined for us, and we tend to perceive that which we have picked out in the form stereotyped for us by our culture."

Obviously with this caveat in mind, experts habitually warn against taking British stereotypes of Germans all too seriously. That is not *really* how the British see Germany, Lord Dahrendorf tells us:

"For one thing, the British love the outrageous and the eccentric, and positively relish being politically incorrect, without always appreciating that they may be taken more seriously abroad than they themselves take the world beyond the Channel which they insist on calling "Europe".

And Jonathan Steinberg, an American historian teaching in Cambridge, adds:

"The English are regarded in German eyes (...) as fundamentally anti-German. The fact that they are equally fundamentally anti-French is deliberately ignored in Germany."

When Nicholas Ridley, Trade Minister in the last Thatcher government, provoked a *cause célèbre* in July 1990, by claiming in an interview with the *Spectator* that European Monetary Union was just a German *"racket to take over Europe"*, the most remarkable reaction came from the German Chancellor himself - namely none at all. Kohl chose the British way: the stiff upper lip. He refused to be provoked, following the advice of the Austrian satirist Johann Nestroy: Don't even ignore it... His restraint was particularly remarkable since the *Spectator's* front-page cartoon by Garland left no doubt about the target of Ridley's broadside: it showed a poster of Helmut Kohl, his face painted over with a Hitler parting and moustache and Ridley the graffiti artist stealing away from the scene of the crime.

Helmut Kohl responded with equally disarming silence to the news (which broke in July 1990) of the Chequers seminar in March of that year. Margaret Thatcher had invited a group of historians to discuss German national characteristics (the newly uniting country had raised questions not just in London). Yet the newspaper reports contained strong stuff - the participants in the Chequers seminar allegedly agreed on the following German characteristics: aggressiveness, assertiveness, bullying, egotism, inferiority complex, sentimentality etc.

Xenophobia paints its own demons

This was too much even for some cartoonists. John Kent turned the tables in the *New Statesman*: The Foreign Secretary, Douglas Hurd, was depicted explaining whom those characteristics really fitted ... Very often it is self-deprecation which saves the day. Humiliation ruined it for Nicholas Ridley: he lost his Cabinet job as a result of his improvident interview.

Margaret Thatcher and the Germans: the cartoonist Kent turns the tables

If contemporary Germans supposedly have an unspecified "angst" about the future, fear of German hegemony is one of the equally dominant features of recent cartoon tradition in Britain. It plays on deep-seated phobias from the period around 1940, when the "blitz" indeed gave the British a scare, and transports these phobias into the present-day world with a mixture of new and old elements. This fear is obviously the basis for one of those Anglo-German clichés which Roger Berthoud describes as "slower to turn around than an oil tanker".

Nicholas Ridley appears in many different guises...

Emotional outbursts like Nicholas Ridley's on the allegedly threatening intentions of German policies sound like the theme tune of British "angst". In the early 1960s, when Franco-German rapprochement began to take shape and Walter Hallstein was elected first President of the European Commission, the 'Ridley' tune went as follows:

"There exists a conspiracy of silence ... designed to make people forget the unpalatable name and personality of the real boss of Brussels, who is neither smooth nor pleasant nor French but a German - none other than Dr. Adenauer's old and trusted crony, Professor Walter Hallstein (...) Where Hitler failed in war, Hallstein expects to succeed in peace (...) To Adenauer and Hallstein no economic sacrifice is too great if it helps to bring about an advance towards German-controlled political domination of Europe."

(Willi Frischauer in the Evening Standard of 20 January 1962)

Suspicion, fear, mistrust of an increasingly powerful Germany - these stereotypes soon reappeared with the German "economic miracle" of the 1950s. Witness a Cummings cartoon from August 1957. The background: in that month, the *Bundesbank* had been founded as the successor to the "Bank of the German *Länder*", the

German Mark was growing stronger, the French Franc had just been devalued and the British Prime Minister, Harold Macmillan, feared the worst for the Pound. What better way to portray the imperial German Mark than as a tank heading inexorably towards Britain.

1957: is the German economic miracle about to invade Britain?

1957 and 1996 - the years are virtually interchangeable! British Euro-scepticism is suffused with similar doubts, the only difference being that German preponderance is now feared in the guise of a common European currency. Stereotypes seem to bear out the French saying: "Plus ça change, plus c'est la même chose".

One can imagine Nicholas Ridley nodding his approval at a cartoon by Vicky in 1960 in which US President Eisenhower whispers the true message of Wagner's "Rheingold" into the ear of a dumbfounded Harold Macmillan: *"The story goes that he who's got the ring rules the world..."* Meanwhile, Konrad Adenauer and the "father" of the German economic miracle, Ludwig Erhard, are giving a self-confident performance on stage.

The Nibelungen treasure or how to become ruler of the world

Whether they like it or not, politicians must make allowances for such preconceived ideas or at least take them into account. Caricaturists may exaggerate - but most exaggerations contain an element of immutable fact. In the case of the UK, for example, insularity has produced a national frame of mind that defies attempts to impose rapid change. Islands are focal points of resistance to sundry adversaries and unwanted guests. Britain has not been occupied by a foreign power since 1066, which has created a national myth out of an historical and geographical condition as much celebrated as caricatured, the most cutting caricatures coming from the British themselves. Among a people tending to self-irony, one's very raison d'être may become the target of mockery, for irony sees through everything - particularly when it comes to the basics of one's national mythology.

But pride in insular independence has a way of surviving any attempt to ridicule it. John of Gaunt's message, in Shakespeare's "Richard II", has stood the test of time. His famous paean is one of the texts on which British self-confidence is founded:

> *" This happy breed of men, this little world;*
> *This precious stone set in the silver sea,*
> *Which serves it in the office of a wall,*
> *Or as a mount defensive to a house,*
> *Against the envy of less happier lands;*
> *This blessed spot, this earth, this realm, this England ..."*

However, there is a downside to classical quotations - they sometimes have the misfortune of sounding out of place in a modern context. Unwelcome connotations can easily surface, exposing any such unthinking transfer of cultural heritage into the present as a high-risk undertaking. One wonders if the majority of British people would still be happy to identify with metaphors like "this little world", "wall" and "defensive mount". Actually, the unease goes back quite a while.

Little Englander or the world is full of foreigners

EXPOSURE BY BLIMP

Gad, sir, Lord Beaverbrook is right. This League of Nations is a big sham. Why, it's nearly all foreigners.

After the First World War, when Britain was in danger of sliding first into its "splendid isolation" and then into appeasement, it was David Low who created the character of Colonel Blimp, the typical conservative "Little Englander" who entrenched himself behind his island defences as well as behind his own prejudices and xenophobia.

In a celebrated cartoon of 1937, Low depicted the late Colonel seated on a cloud and commenting on an article in a newspaper owned by the baron of Fleet Street, Lord Beaverbrook: *"Gad, sir, Lord Beaverbrook is right. This League of Nations is a big sham. Why, it's nearly all foreigners."*

When the now late Nicholas Ridley attacked alleged German plans for hegemony in 1990 and called the French "the poodle of the Germans" (he too was a caricaturist *sui generis!*), many felt they could hear the familiar strains of this insular resistance to foreigners. In *Punch*, Paul Thomas depicted Ridley the chain-smoker and amateur painter with a vision of Europe containing a host of undesirable nationalities rising in the cloud of smoke from his cigarette.

Nicholas Ridley's pipe conjures up ghosts

But long before that, Carl Giles had created his famous British grandmother, a cult figure drawn with typical self-irony: a distortion of the original Britannia, seated on her sea chariot and a bit of cliff-top, armed not with a trident but with an umbrella and a rather anxious-looking mongrel, grimly determined not to allow anyone or anything to pass. "Britannia rules the waves" - and pokes fun at herself in the process.

This tongue-in-cheek cliché later appeared a perfect fit for Margaret Thatcher - much to the delight of the cartoonists, who lovingly cultivated the image of Maggie / Britannia fighting the rest of the world as if there were some collusion between the

Mother Britannia guards her island armed with just an umbrella and her mongrel ...

11

... while Margaret Thatcher resorts to more traditional weapons

cartoonists and their subject. Just a few days prior to the Prime Minister's political demise, Fritz Behrendt summed up once again just what it was about the "Iron Lady" which so impressed - and dismayed - the Germans. (cf. also SPOTLIGHT 50)

But who takes these masquerades of fantasy, these exaggerated caricatures, seriously anyway? Surely even the most distorted portrayals in the rainbow press are just a joke? Not laughing at them would indicate a deficient sense of humour and nobody wants to expose himself to an accusation like that. The noble thing is simply to ignore the jibes and put on a brave face. This is probably why the British intelligentsia and many German observers have long deemed it beneath them to pay particular attention to the underlying anti-German feelings in the British tabloid press. German-British relations were and are regarded as much too sound and thick-skinned to be disturbed by such fleabites.

Until the summer of 1996, when this reserved attitude was abandoned with a vengeance and - a unique event - by the British general public themselves. What had happened? Football fever had gripped the nation. It was "EURO '96", the European football championships, and a remake of the classic showdown between England and Germany was scheduled for Wednesday, 26 June. This time the clash came in the semi-finals, not the final as in the 1966 World Cup. But the venue was once again Wembley - a crucible where fans are consumed by the passions of partisan frenzy.

Two days before the match, as expectations were bubbling up to boiling point, the *Daily Mirror* contained what it probably considered no more than just a prank: five pages of jingoistic praise for "England's Glory", accompanied by stories about the German opponents over whom victory was as certain as in wartime. "Achtung! Surrender!" was the front-page headline - the "Krauts" were not expected to put up much of a fight. Beside the headline were pictures of players Pearce and Gascoigne wearing First World War helmets and laughing. Inside, *Mirror* reporters had masqueraded as "spies behind enemy lines" making sure that the message of Germany's imminent capitulation would weaken Fritz' willpower to fight.

Seldom has Fleet Street created such a furore as the *Mirror* unleashed with this issue. Even the Prime Minister, John Major, spoke out in the House of Commons to warn against nationalist excesses and xenophobia. The British people were also not amused. Their patience was exhausted. The German Embassy in London was deluged with messages of goodwill and the letters pages of British newspapers expressed the general public's sense of shame and indignation.

But this incident has to be put in the context of another simmering debate immediately prior to EURO '96. It would not have surfaced quite so vigorously without the BSE crisis that had driven a mighty wedge between Britain and the Continent.

Griffin: how Helmut Kohl and his generals stop the invasion of Mad Cow Disease

Cartoonists had a field day with the subject which they treated as if the European dispute over the export ban on British beef and beef byproducts were something of a replay of German-British animosities. Anyone who saw Griffin's cartoon in the *Daily Express* in May 1996 (*"Who is that keeps muttering 'Just like ze old days, mein Führer'?"*) must subconsciously have thought the Germans were trying to achieve with "Operation Bull Semen" what they had failed to do 56 years earlier with "Operation Sea Lion": the capitulation of the

British Isles... All the old favourites are dusted off and put on parade. Naturally, war is the source of inspiration. But this time the emblems of the enemy are borrowed from the Brussels props room.

It is tempting to compare this with a German cartoon on the same subject, say to one of Horst Haitzinger's celebrated products. *"I knew the British would strike back some time!"* - we read in the Munich newspaper "tz". Here too, a war metaphor is used but only as a humorous background, whilst the "war" in question is held up to ridicule: cows being parachuted into enemy territory...

"Ich hab's geahnt, irgendwann würden die Briten zurückschlagen!"   tz-Zeichnung: Haitzinger

Haitzinger: John Major drops mad cows on the EU

One could argue, as many have done in the past, that it's all very well for Germans and German cartoonists to be so sensitive about evoking the war. For one thing, they cannot pin swastikas on the British... For another, Germany's belligerent past completely rules out any such backward-looking, bellicose metaphors which are the standard fare of the British tabloids. In Germany, they would damage newspaper sales figures rather than enhance them.

But that is neither here nor there, for as far as the subconscious perception of Germany in Britain is concerned - despite the evidence of excellent bilateral relations - it continues to be overshadowed by images of war and a presumed German threat. It takes a dose of excessive indulgence to jolt the public into conscious awareness. Could envy have something to do with it? Is it perhaps *"more comfortable to live with the images of the past and our moral superiority to Nazi Germany than to look seriously at the reality of the present and Germany's material superiority today?"* (Robert Cooper)

But to repeat: why should we be influenced by published images? Is "published" synonymous with "public" opinion? Indeed, how many of the impressions which influence us are gained from personal experience, as another important source of potential enlightenment?

Some analysis of current data may be useful here. Anyone comparing the number of cross-Channel travellers might conclude that Germans take the opportunity more frequently than the British to learn from personal experience. According to a MORI opinion poll conducted in November 1994 (cf. also p. 74), 24% of the Germans interviewed said that they had visited Britain the previous year; by contrast, only 6% of the British interviewees had been to Germany during the same period. In a poll commissioned by BBC TV in June 1995, every second British person still regarded himself as non-European and only 7% felt "close to Germany".

Yet we should not be lulled into hasty conclusions by these (for the Germans) flattering statistics. The high frequency of visits to Britain does not automatically remove all the clichés from German minds. There is obviously still much to be learned if, in the words of Lord Dahrendorf, *"German visitors come to Britain to find a gigantic museum of past glory"* and then discover that *"the British live and work in their museum and even read books in the Bodleian"*.

Matters become more serious when, as recent opinion polls show, critically-minded Germans regard Britain as a backward country where social justice, prosperity, the economy and even basic human rights are not in particularly good shape. Such perceptions may arise from superficial knowledge of the discussion in Britain about the constitution and "the State we're in". They also smack time and again of a certain attitude for which the Germans are frequently criticised: they don't know everything, but they do know everything better.

On the other hand, many German views are aided and abetted by the British themselves. At the Young Königswinter Conference in Berlin in August 1995, for example, the Federal Republic of Germany was praised as more flexible, more modern and more democratic than Britain's central government because of its decentralised Länder structure. As a result, the argument went, Germany might be much better placed than Britain to resist the overweening Brussels' bureaucracy.

Jokes about the Germans and the British: a parade ground for national stereotypes.

In Europe, it is the "multinational" joke which has flourished best. Obviously, Europeans have their own ingrained experiences with one another - one says nice things about immediate and close neighbours whilst using mockery to keep them at a distance. Bilateral jokes are rare. It is the family context which makes for the most popular jokes and within this grouping the British and the Germans get their legs pulled most. Sometimes an American or even a Russian joins the scenario. Such comparisons thrive on every conceivable stereotype. It is like a large single market: there are no national frontiers. And they all come home to roost.

A few examples:

In Heaven and Hell, Europeans are allocated certain tasks according to the capabilities they are best known for.

In Heaven, the chef is French, the policeman is British, the mechanic is German, the organiser is Swiss and the lover is Italian.

In Hell, the chef is British, the policeman is German, the mechanic is French, the organiser is Italian and the lover is Swiss.

A new book about elephants is published in several languages. The French version is called: "The elephant cook-book". The German version: "A short natural history of the elephant, in five volumes". The English version: "How to keep elephants as pets."

A group of condemned men appear before a firing squad and each is granted a final wish. The Frenchman wants to sing the Marseillaise one last time - and is then shot. The Englishman asks for a cup of tea - and is then shot. The German asks if he may make one last attempt to explain the overall concept for European security - at which point the American asks if he could please be shot before the German.

Or the classic situation: two men and a woman cast away on a desert island. If the woman is French, she marries one of the men and has an affair with the other. If she is Russian, they all sit around on the beach and bemoan the futility of human existence. If she is English, they do not speak to each other - they have not been formally introduced. If she is German, she marries one of them while the other is busy completing the necessary application forms for the Registry Office.

When the end of the world comes I should prefer to be in England. Why? Because there everything happens 100 years later ... (This joke travels well. Germans often hear it told about themselves and their reluctance to introduce reform).

But beware of final judgements. Just as beauty is in the eye of the beholder, so the ability of the British and the Germans to rise to future challenges often depends on the commentator's point of view. As Anatole Kaletsky reminded his audience during the Königswinter Conference in March 1995, Britain was now leading Germany in many areas - such as privatisation and deregulation. Charles Powell, Margaret Thatcher's former adviser, concurred in his review in the *Financial Times* of Giles Radice's new book "The New Germans". He bemoaned the lack of flexibility of the German labour market, unfavourable German cost structures and Germany's slow response to the Asian challenge.

All famous last words. Amid the chorus of voices you may also detect that of the author Will Hutton ("The State We're In"). Like Radice, Hutton holds up numerous German institutions and management traditions as examples for the British to emulate, e.g. co-determination, the "dual system" of training skilled workers, the role of small-and medium-sized businesses etc.

A constant to and fro. For their part, German companies have discovered Britain's advantages as a place to invest, something unthinkable just a few years ago. Whether BMW (acquisition of Rover), Siemens (new semi-conductor plant near Newcastle), Bosch (car components industry in South Wales) or the major German banks, which are increasingly shifting their global financial transactions to London: they all regard Great Britain as an ideal investment market. As a result, one of the oldest German stereotypes about Britain - the allegedly poor work ethos - has quietly been laid to rest.

So are we right in concluding that the preponderance of national stereotypes causes no more than minor damage, if that? The picture varies. It is no surprise to find that young people, those with little or no direct personal experience, are particularly vulnerable to the influence of constantly regurgitated prejudices. In June 1996, the company Gestetner conducted a poll among 10 to 16-year-olds in Britain asking them about their views on Germany. The result was startling (according to a report in the *Independent* of 10 June): 78% think of the Second World War when they hear the name Germany. No wonder Germany is voted the country they would least like to visit: the verdict of 43%. Even Bosnia fares better (only 26% voiced a negative opinion). In the list of "most boring countries", Germany again leads the field (57%), ahead of France (26%) and Italy (10%).

This should remind us that one of the prime tasks for people in open societies today is learning how to liberate and emancipate themselves from the mass media and their influences. That, however, is easier said than done. The international nature of the modern world offers mixed blessings: as interlinking networks grow, so too do our opportunities to expand and deepen our knowledge. On the other hand, we are confronted by the mass industry of slogans and prejudices. In the final analysis, however, progress is determined by the practitioners, not by the spin doctors and their clichés. When the right moment arrives, the two sides overcome their prejudices and meet in a skilful *pas de deux* - interests, after all, are not determined by friendships nor enmities, as Talleyrand noted (cf. p. 157ff, Talleyrand "defused").

Yet that fabled dictum, in turn, undervalues the German-British partnership and its high degree of compatibility. Division of labour in today's world also means defining what each society can do best, the areas in which it excels - whether it be the flexibility of the British, the scrupulous precision of the Germans or other qualities which invite mutual exchange. (cf. also final chapter)

Both countries have now reached this very point in their relations. Excesses like the tabloid canards about Germany in the summer of 1996 also have their good side. By overstating the point, they can concentrate the mind in their own fashion. After all, the British undoubtedly *do have* a problem with Europe. It is equally clear that Germany is part of this problem because the recently reunited country has highlighted its renewed opposition to the concept of the old-style sovereign nation state which the United Kingdom (among others) holds up as a virtue not to be surrendered.

So much for the grain of truth in the caricaturist's view of the world. On the other hand, every excessive outburst is followed by a cathartic period of coming back down to earth. Which is what happened in June 1996 when the waves of anti-"Hun" feelings had subsided. People shook their heads at so much folly and turned their attention again to the future. That could have pleased no one more than Monica Harper, former head of the German desk at the Foreign Office. When interviewed by a German journalist in late 1993, she said that her greatest hope for German-British relations was that there would be *"less looking back and more looking forward"*.

If we can agree on a premise like that, we might even be able to accept the archetypal exaggerations of our best cartoonists... Admittedly, they say too much, yet much of what they say is accurate. For example, two British cartoons of 1987 and 1992 which have since become classics. They treat their German subject with demonic humour, in a mocking yet by no means unamusing tone. Perhaps this chapter is best concluded with a look at these two cartoons.

[Zeitungsschlagzeile.] Die "Krauts" [Schimpfwort für Deutsche] sind Rüpel im Urlaub

Holiday enjoyment on Spanish beaches: Achtung! Operation Sunbed!

To refresh your memory: The legendary German habit of rudely jumping the queue gained unexpected media coverage some years ago when it was claimed that German holiday-makers in Spanish resorts had cheated their fellow British guests out of the best sunbeds - by getting up at the crack of dawn to reserve the most coveted places with their towels. An incident which has all but entered British folklore about the Germans by now. How peaceful our obsessions have become by comparison with an earlier era!

Although Bernard Cookson could not resist the temptation of resorting to the standard repertoire of Nazi Germans in the *Sun* in 1987 to make his point, the message - how disagreeable it is when people jump the queue, but how much more disagreeable when they do it systematically! - was not totally obscured by the eccentric stereotyping. The prejudice came in an old guise to make a modern comment: I still don't like the Germans, they haven't changed except that their desire for conquest and occupation is now focused on something much more innocuous like sun-beds...

This typecasting re-emerged five years later in a cartoon by Bill Caldwell in the *Daily Star* which used a few rich clichés about Germany to mark the acquisition of the traditional British holiday tour operator Thomas Cook by the *Westdeutsche Landesbank* and the German tour company LTU.

Isn't it rather strange that we still laugh at such caricatures although we know that they now have virtually nothing to do with the society at which they are aimed. Or do they? There's the rub. They do - if only in a very remote, oblique way. Such as when we contemplate what the over-fastidious quest for a "place in the sun" (albeit only on a holiday island) may still tell us about die-hard national habits.

Thomas Cook under German leadership: "At least there is a guaranteed sunbed", Caldwell writes

Some German tourists may unintentionally add a few extra touches to the picture of the "ugly German" just as - in a different sphere - the emergence of football hooliganism has kept the image of the "ugly Brit" alive.. (Much to everyone's surprise, though, the hooligans maintained a very low profile during the EURO '96 football championship in England). But goose-stepping precision is just about the last characteristic with which to identify today's emancipated Germans - permissive, hedonistic and democratically unruly as they have become, not least of all under the influence of a more relaxed way of life practised by the British. If the police had to find the "culprits" on the basis of stereotype identikit pictures like these, they would have a long search.

And yet, if something is entertaining, like the two cartoons mentioned above, we are willing to forgive all the inaccuracies. As a rule, this is true of all stereotypes about the supposed idiosyncrasies of different nations. People love them like familiar and well-worn jokes. But they have to be funny to avoid becoming self-defeating. As Heinrich Heine realised when forced to discard some of his own prejudices following a trip to England in 1827:

"The old stereotype characteristics we find in learned manuals and ale-houses can serve us no more and lead us only to hopeless errors."

("English Fragments", 1828)

Like some we find in cartoons, too.

Off to Germany! Thomas Cook invents package tours to the Continent.

The fact that Thomas Cook is now under German management must be a stroke of providence. Cook, born in 1808, was the first European tour operator - and Germany the first country visited by the package tours he invented. The first "Continental Tour" of this kind took tourists to Cologne, Mainz, Mannheim and Heidelberg. It was the romantic Rhineland which most attracted the British; Lord Byron had enthused about it in his epic verse "Childe Harold". And it was from this long poem that a certain Mr. Green read aloud to his fellow travellers as they passed the Drachenfels near Bonn.

Thomas Cook and Sons founded their first overseas subsidiary in Cologne. No less a person than Emperor William II later commissioned the British company to organise a gigantic imperial expedition to Jerusalem in 1898. The expedition boosted Cook's business - but seriously damaged Anglo-German relations, since it helped to increase London's suspicions of German activities in the Middle East.

Thomas Cook smiles as his company passes into German ownership

Culture: German-British cross-fertilisation

Pop and classical music, social behaviour, literature, science, education

I. *"Yeah, yeah, yeah!"*

On 23 August 1963, Britain experienced a musical revolution which spread rapidly from the British Isles throughout the whole world. Germany was one of the countries most powerfully affected. The musical revolution was to become a cultural revolution, a caesura which cut deep into modern life. This was the day on which the Beatles' fourth single appeared in Britain's record shops. A million copies of *"She Loves You"* were sold in the first four weeks, an unprecedented indication of the mass appeal of popular music.

The Beatles had already won the adulation of their fans with previous songs, but *"She Loves You"* became the tune to end all tunes, supported by the hammering rhythm of the three-word refrain: *"yeah, yeah, yeah!"*. It seemed as if the era had found its byword, its new creed, as it were - the affirmation of complete cultural freedom.

Germany was the cradle of another global culture, classical music, which had begun its triumphant advance 200 years earlier, also captivating Britain with composers like Handel, Beethoven, Mendelssohn and Brahms. Now it was Germany's turn to be swept along by another cultural wave, albeit of a less high-brow but no less significant kind. It added to German high 'Kultur' with a capital 'K' the meaning of mass 'culture' with a small 'c' and opened up a gateway to a whole new life-style.

A politician helped the Beatles to their breakthrough but ...

People talk a great deal about pop culture and the influence it had on Germany, too. But whom do the Beatles really have to thank for their breakthrough and the basis of their world-wide success? The British Chancellor of the Exchequer, Selwyn Lloyd, of course. Lloyd, a Cabinet member in the then Macmillan government and formerly Foreign Secretary (until 1959), had introduced an important innovation in 1960: the hire-purchase law - payment by instalments or the 'never-never', as it was popularly called. Suddenly, people in the music "scene", on Liverpool's Merseyside for example, could afford the latest and most sophisticated guitars and drum kits, which had previously been beyond even their wildest dreams.

Gone was the cheap skiffle style with its standard sound. One small down-payment and you were up there competing with Elvis Presley on the same level. This inconspicuous but pioneering step by the politicians turned Britain's pop music scene overnight into a spawning ground for future talent.

... it was Hamburg where they served their apprenticeship.

Then came Hamburg... the Beatles' "incubation period". They made guest appearances at various beat clubs and cellar bars on or near the Reeperbahn: at the "Indra", "Kaiserkeller" and "Top Ten" from mid-August to mid-October 1960 and from April to June 1961; at the better-known "Star-Club" for seven weeks from mid-April 1962 and again, for the last time, from 18-31 December 1962. Even if all that was required of them was the standard repertoire, Hamburg was nevertheless a valuable test of the group's stamina, cohesion and impact on audiences. As George Harrison stated in a 1969 interview:

"I am quite certain in my own mind that we reached our peak as a live band in Hamburg. Because we weren't yet famous, people would be attracted purely by our music or by the kind of atmosphere we were creating (...) And we had to be very good as a band to be able to play for eight hours every night. (...) As a group we grew very close together in Hamburg."

It was during the Beatles' second trip to Germany in 1961 that the photographer Astrid Kirchherr decided to give her fiancé, Stuart Sutcliffe (the group's drummer in those early days), a new hair-style. This later became the famous Beatles' "mophead". In late 1961, while still in Germany, the group also released its first record ("My Bonnie" and "When the Saints go Marching In"). When the Liverpool record-shop owner, Brian Epstein, was unable to obtain this single for a customer, he was so annoyed that he went in person to the "Cavern Club" where the Beatles were playing - and ended up as their first manager.

35 years later, the dream of a lifetime is coming true for Volker Schuster, a 26-year-old clerk from Hamburg, who also knows his way around a drum kit, guitar and piano. Together with 52 other young artists, he has been selected from among 3,000 candidates world-wide for a 3-year course at the Liverpool Institute for the Performing Arts (LIPA), founded by Paul McCartney. The Hamburg wheel thus turns full circle and pop history encounters its own roots - 1996 salutes 1961.

It was the allied liberators who, as occupation forces and later as friends, had acquainted post-war Western Germany with the democratic life-style. But it was via pop music and the all-pervading influence of English that the process of Germany's internationalisation reached new heights. Now a distinct *way of life* entered not only the German language but also the hearts and minds of a whole generation.

The ground for this revolution had already been prepared. Rock 'n' roll, Elvis Presley, Bill Hailey - that was the American wave of liberation in the 50s. While eagerly received, it was still restricted to a relatively small section of the younger generation. English singers, such as Helen Shapiro and Cliff Richard, soon followed and with them came the Hit Parade, that magical barometer of success, the chart one had to know to be part of the in-crowd.

Chris Howland, originally from the "British Forces Network" (BFN), established himself at the Cologne studio of *Nordwestdeutscher*

Rundfunk as Germany's first radio disc jockey - and another term of the new pop culture celebrated its German première. Howland had a witty charm about him enhanced by a pronounced English accent when he spoke German. He used to delight his listeners by signing off with the catch phrase *"Ihr alter Freund Heinrich Pumpernickel"*

Pumpernickel? That sounds somehow familiar...

Well yes, perhaps to literary experts, but to Chris Howland's radio audience this very German and very strange word simply sounded funny coming from an Englishman's mouth. They were not interested in William Makepeace Thackeray - the allusion was too "insidig" (to borrow the jargon of a later generation). In chapter 63 of his novel "Vanity Fair" (1847/48) the great Victorian novelist transports his characters to the Duchy of Pumpernickel, a typical minor German principality of the time, which Thackeray mocked to his heart's content. It was modelled on the Duchy of Weimar which the author had visited in 1831 and where he had also met Goethe. Was the intention - to come back to Chris Howland - to compare post-war German federalism with this caricature of old German particularism? Hardly. The disc jockey was not one for making political statements: he felt far too much at home in the cosy world of German federalism and, by invoking the name Pumpernickel, his aim was to drag this world into the modern era rather than to poke fun at it.

Idyllic early days - which exploded with the phenomenal success of the Beatles. This was more than just entertainment for a select social group. A whole generation of young Germans identified with the rhythmic scream of *"Yeah, yeah, yeah!"*. Elvis had electrified the dance-halls, but the Beatles captured the heart and soul. Where Rock had been an invitation to depart from the traditions of everyday life, the Beatles transformed the very way of life itself. The 1960s opened with a bang.

Groups sprouted like mushrooms in the fertile ground broken by the Fab Four from Liverpool and gradually set Swinging London alight. Among them were the Rolling Stones, who first caused a sensation in 1964. King's Road and Carnaby Street soon emerged and in 1965, the cult film of the period was born: "Blow up" starring David Hemmings and the German actress Gräfin Veruschka; the British Motor Corporation brought out the "Mini", Mary Quant invented the "mini-skirt" and Twiggy became the fashion model with the "mini-bosom"...

British entertainment together with a relaxed British attitude to clothing, posture and life in general, especially sexual mores, became a compass with which an entire generation took its bearings. People said "mini" and actually meant "maxi" - maximum permissiveness and individual self-fulfilment. While it modelled itself politically on the protest movement in the USA, the 1968 student revolution in Germany also derived important socio-cultural inspiration from Britain. The "sit-ins", "walk-ins" and "love-ins" were borrowed from across the Atlantic, the permissive society from across the Channel.

Warming up for international success: the Beatles in Hamburg, 1960/61

A.S. Neill: A Scot who left the British cold but kindled German enthusiasm

Although it did not reach the Federal Republic of Germany until 1969, a single book by A.S.Neill, translated from the English under the German title "theorie und praxis der anti-autoritären erziehung / das beispiel summerhill", played an important role in Germany's social revolution begun the previous year. (The fact that the German title was printed in lower case was a socio-political statement in itself.) It appeared in December 1969 and gave Germany its slogan - one could even say, its marching orders - for the next decade. The concept of "anti-authoritarianism" turned traditional ideas on education, schools and children as thoroughly upside down as the student rebellion had previously done with the German university system. Alas, the thoroughness with which the Germans assimilated and implemented these theories was to create great difficulties for an entire generation of young people.

Summerhill also provides a fascinating case study of the cultural divide between Germany and Britain. The book and even Summerhill boarding school itself, situated near Leiston in Suffolk, 150 km north-east of London, were virtually unknown in Britain. As indeed was the school's founder, the Scot, Alexander Sutherland Neill (1883-1973), who had been permitted to test his somewhat extreme ideas on difficult children in Summerhill since 1921. The British are customarily tolerant towards people with different views but maintain their own critical distance. They are anti-authoritarian without renouncing discipline (which was Neill's idea). At any rate, the Scot had virtually no followers in Great Britain to speak of. Consequently, the first English edition of "Summerhill - A Radical Approach to Child Rearing" was published not in the UK but in the USA (1960).

For a long time, the German cultural scene had also remained unmoved by the book and its explosive contents. 1960 was ten years too early for the intellectual climate which was later to spark on Neill's ideas. Even in 1965, when the Munich publisher Szczesny Verlag brought out the German edition in hardback under the rather laboured title "Erziehung in Summerhill - Das revolutionäre Beispiel einer freien Schule" ("Education in Summerhill - The Revolutionary Example of a Free School"), the time was still not ripe. It sent no seismic shock-waves through society. In *fact, it was not until Rowohlt-Verlag bought up the remaindered copies and re-launched the book as a paperback with a new programmatic title that it caused a sensation. The concept of total liberation from all pedagogic ties was obviously the missing link in the long chain of emancipation in the 60s - after the Beatles, swinging London, the anti-Vietnam protests, the student rebellion and sexual liberation. All the elements of the permissive society were now in place. With the exception that Britain had allowed this final chapter to pass by unheeded - and thus saved itself a lot of future problems.*

2. *English and German: unequal competition*

The irony of intellectual peregrinations: in the early 1960s, *passé* was still an acceptable term for something old-fashioned or outdated. But if you wanted to be up-to-date, you now had to use an English word: "in". These two letters became the fashionable term of the era and are now a permanent feature of everyday German. (Deciding what was "in" or not later provided great scope for propagators of political correctness).

Passé and *in*: this pair of words also marks the increasing gap in preference between the two leading European cultural languages. At the end of the 18th century, the founder of German idealist philosophy, Immanuel Kant, wrote in the essay "The Character of the People": *"French is the general language of conversation, principally among women in genteel society, but English is the most widespread commercial language in the world of trade."*

That was 200 years ago. Thanks to the advent of modern communications technology, Kant's "world of trade" has turned into the ubiquitous global village. Conversely, international "conversation" - not only "among women in genteel society" - has largely shifted from French into English. Even *passé* is now passé - it has been replaced by "out". Similarly, nobody in Germany nowadays uses the word "mannequin" - everyone says "model".

None of this seems to trouble the majority of Germans. Unlike France, where the advance of the English language is regarded as a threat to the primacy of French culture (although just what steps could be taken to combat this virus remains unclear), Germany has long since made its peace with this development, apart from the occasional expression of concern. Indeed, Germany has accepted the influx of the English language more widely, and apparently irreversibly, than other countries and societies.

Germans have always been dedicated followers of foreign fashion...

At an anniversary meeting of the "Franco-German Society for Trans-national Co-operation" held in the southern German town of Offenburg on 16 October 1995, the historian and philosopher Joseph Rovan, complained that the Franco-German cultural summit of 1986, which had agreed inter alia an intensive linguistic exchange between the two countries, had produced virtually no concrete results. His rebuke:

"If things continue along the present course, we shall soon have to conduct Franco-German relations in English."

Goethe had already noted the German tendency to copy foreign trend-setters when he told his "Boswell", Johann Peter Eckermann, on 10 January 1825:

"It is in the German nature to appreciate everything foreign and to adopt foreign characteristics."

170 years later, a British expert on the Germans is even more critical. Stuart Pigott, 35 years of age and a wine connoisseur par excellence - he is the author of the standard work "The great German Riesling wines" - gave the following answer when asked why so many Germans do not drink their own finest wines:

"Many do not know that they exist. Or if they suspect it, they are not interested because prejudices and the tendency to regard one's own produce as plain and second-rate, block these people." (Frankfurter Allgemeine Zeitung, 10.11.95)

Immanuel Kant's terse comment on this subject taken from the essay quoted above:

"Germans (...) have no national pride."

... much to the annoyance of some upright citizens.

A 75-year-old pensioner from Nuremberg decided that this poisoning of German culture with the English language had to stop and threatened in turn to poison the products of a German sweet manufacturer if the company did not stop using the word "kids" in its advertising. He also sent threatening letters to a coffee manufacturer which used the expression "Night and Day" and to a brewery which was guilty of calling its beer "light". . .

The court had no sympathy with this form of expressing indignation and gave the old man a suspended sentence of five years' imprisonment for threatening behaviour.

This became apparent quite early on, when young musicians starting imitating the Beatles. In 1964, one of the first German groups to copy the Beatles' sound, the "Lords", won top prize at Hamburg's legendary "Star-Club" in a competition entitled *"Who can play like the Beatles?"* The prize: a recording contract. However, their first single, recorded in German, was a flop. It was only when they switched to English that their 1965 song *"Shakin' All Over"* made it into the hit-parade.

The English language seems to be unrivalled in all those areas where succinctness and brevity are paramount: sport, finance, computers, the entertainment industry, leisure culture, aeronautics. In short: all aspects of modern life. On the other hand, no 20th century Heinrich Heine has attempted yet to find concise and vivid German terminology which could hold its own in today's information technology revolution.

Germans are all the more willing to accept English since the whole world has meanwhile adopted it as the new "lingua franca", the new universal language. Add to it the fact that Germany is one of the world's leading trading nations and has always cultivated intensive cultural exchange, then the position of English in German life today is a plausible reflection of German psychology.

This inclination towards a more international life-style is also a clear rejection of purely national ideas which the Germans have totally abandoned following their traumatic experiences earlier this century. But again, the political failure of nationalism is not the sole explanation. Rather Germany has reverted to traditional patterns of behaviour which were established in this country, with its decentralised history, long before it went astray following unification in 1870.

Once again, Goethe provides us with the best testimony. He saw through his fellow countrymen better than anyone else. Witness the "Xenien", a collection of witty distiches written together with Friedrich von Schiller, which contains the following famous two-liner (under the title "German national character"):

"Germans, you hope in vain to form yourselves into a nation;
You should instead educate yourselves to be freer human beings."

Illuminated the Germans with their intellect: Goethe and Schiller in Weimar

The difficulties of the German language
- are they predetermined by the mode of thinking?

Many people have observed and commented on the fact that the German tendency to abstract thinking matches the complex characteristics of the German language (and vice versa). To quote a few examples:

"A Frenchman always has something to say even if he has no ideas; a German always has more ideas in his head than he can express."
(Madame de Staël, 1803)

"On the whole, philosophical speculation is an injury to the Germans, as it tends to make their style vague, difficult and obscure. The stronger their attachment to certain philosophical schools, the more they write. (...) Schiller's style is at its most splendid and effective when he is not philosophising."
(Goethe, Conversations with Eckermann, 14 April 1824)

But it was precisely the possibilities of the German language for philosophical expression which attracted a writer like Samuel T. Coleridge, a contemporary of Goethe and the German Romantic movement. Coleridge even considered how the German prefixes "ver-" and "zer-" might be incorporated into English:

"Why not verboil, zerboil; verrend, zerrend? I should like the words verflossen, zerflossen, to be naturalised:

And as I look
Now feels my soul creative throes,
And now all joy, all sense zerflows."

The most vociferous complaint about German syntax came from Mark Twain in his amusing essay "The Awful German Language":

"An average sentence in a German newspaper is a sublime and impressive curiosity..."
... is how he opens his famous tract. He goes on to parody a German sentence with never-ending syntax and castigates the delayed use of the verb as the most unpardonable idiosyncrasy of the German language.

The distress caused by the remote position of the verb in German sentences also plays a role in the following anecdote recounted by Gordon A. Craig, the doyen among American experts on German history, in his book "The Germans" (1982):

"In the days when Bismarck was the greatest man in Europe, an American visitor to Berlin, anxious to hear the Chancellor speak, procured two tickets to the visitors' gallery of the Reichstag and hired an interpreter to accompany her there. They were fortunate to arrive just before Bismarck intervened in a debate on a matter of social legislation, and the American pressed close to her interpreter's side so as to miss nothing of the translation. But although Bismarck spoke with considerable force and at some length, the interpreter's lips remained closed, and he was unresponsive to his employer's nudges. Unable to contain herself, she finally blurted, "What is he saying?" "Patience, madam," the interpreter answered, "I am waiting for the verb!"

British visitors to Germany today are astonished to find their own language staring back at them from billboards and newspaper ads, in press headlines and the jargon of radio presenters. Is Germany in the process of introducing English as its second official language, they may wonder? Things have not gone quite that far, but one cannot deny that Germans have a certain desire to Anglicise their everyday language.

"Thanks Bill, together we're opening a new window" was how German Telecom announced the introduction of "Windows 95" in Germany. *"Spirited by nature, cowboy by choice"* was the *"slogan"* (another English word) used in a major German advertising campaign for a brand of cigarettes in November 1995, together with the corresponding *"action"* photo. (Although it should be noted that Germans habitually pronounce the "t" in "action", just like they insist on saying *"life"* when in fact they mean a *"live"* TV broadcast. Germans are no longer conformists...)

A foreign communications company attempts to lure customers with the phrase "You too can make a *turnaround"* (accompanied by the photo of a giant tanker on a calm sea); a German clothing chain store uses the photo of a female fashion model and the discreet pun: "Your Sixth Sense". If that were not enough, a national daily praises its own financial *"service"* (a word now totally assimilated into the German language) with the comforting news "The latest on *swaps* and *warrants* before breakfast!", which is obviously supposed to guarantee enhanced breakfast enjoyment for "in" readers. Provided, of course, that the person concerned has no *"cash flow"* problems.

Germans say *"Have fun!"* to one another so often now that surely the last glum face will soon disappear from the German streets. One particular bank has obviously concluded that a pun on this phrase will attract young customers. The caption to a photo of a young couple frolicking on a beach reads: *"Let's Have Fonds"* (a play on the word *"Aktienfonds"*, meaning stocks and shares, with the implication of a higher return if offered in English). A special award should go to a language which promises Germans so much enjoyment and profit!

The latest craze on German motorways:
English verbs of one syllable!

The masterstroke of Anglicisation was played in spring 1995 when BMW launched its new model on the crest of four waves of advertising posters. But - and that was the stroke of genius - nobody realised to begin with that the posters had anything to do with a car: the dominant themes were sport scenes with dynamic young people against a backdrop of lively land and seascapes suggesting additional energy. This is the sequence of posters, each containing a series of mono-syllabic English verbs in capital letters:

1. ROW, PUMP, PUSH, GLIDE, RUN, SWEAT, KICK, SWIM,
   (Illustration: jogger in the forest, appearing out of a clearing)
2. BIKE, SWEAT, RUN, SPRINT, SURF, DIVE, CLIMB,
   (Illustration: cyclist in front of a waterfall)
3. CAMP, RACE, SKI, SPRINT, SKATE, JOG, RUSH, GLIDE,
   (Illustration: mountain scenery with a tent by a lake)
4. SAIL, PRESS, SKATE, JOG, FLY, SPRINT, MOVE, WIN,
   (Illustration: close-up on board a sailing yacht)

The secret was not revealed until the last poster appeared depicting the new BMW model against a breath-taking sea-shore view. At the same time, the crucial and operative verb was added and, unlike in the previous instances, the series of words was concluded with a full stop:

5. SERVE, RUN, CLIMB, RIDE, PUSH, SWIM, JOG, SKATE, DRIVE.

This campaign, according to the company spokesman, was aimed at customers in the upper income bracket who saw themselves as dynamic, active, sophisticated, athletic - and intelligent.

It would appear that a certain group of consumers cannot be reached with long German words any more. English is fun and fast-moving. Such adverts are a rich source of material for students of comparative synergy: the effect is not only to enhance the appeal of the product and its implied qualities but also the appeal of the foreign language used. In fact, the language becomes part of the qualities being overtly praised and thus ceases to be "foreign". In successful advertising everything is mutually enhancing.

Incidentally, the English language has become so attractive to Germans that they have even started inventing entirely new English words of their own - for example, the all-pervasive *"Handy"*. No one in Britain uses this word - they have to make do with the longer phrase *"mobile phone"*. (cf. also SPOTLIGHT 11)

Of course, people use English to demonstrate that they are "in", that they are worldly-wise. So no reader should be surprised to open a weekly paper which regards itself as a *"trend-setter"* and encounter headlines such as "prosperity *light*" (in the context of cuts in the welfare state) or *"opposition as usual"* (on the subject of a crisis within a German opposition party). Being surprised would be a give-away, a form of "coming out" and confessing that you are not "in"! The English language is like the German identity card - something you must constantly be prepared to display.

As a result, it has virtually ceased to be a foreign language. English is gaining *"momentum"* and *"drive"* by the day; its compactness and economy make it irresistible. Rail travel is 50% cheaper with a hybrid "Bahn*card*", just as Anglo-German relations run much more smoothly in a spirit of good *"Team*geist", that's just *common sense!* The two countries have *"gefightet"* long enough (sorry for alluding to that unspeakable "w" word again, as in *"Fawlty Towers"*, don't mention the w..). But all that is now *"gecancelt"* once and for all. Nowadays it just has to be correctly *"gemanagt"*, our opposite number regularly *"abgecheckt"* to ensure that our wires do not get crossed. And if a bit of polishing is required - just stay *"cool"*! We simply drive to the *"COSY WASCH"* car-wash in Bonn and the Anglo-German *"image"* will soon be sparkling again. Which is not bad for *"business"*, as everyone knows.

Beware: when everyone thinks they can speak good English, it is easy to slip up ... A selection of clangers.

- The sloppiness began with Handel... He had the habit of signing even his German correspondence with the English spelling of his Christian names, but had a slight problem with his middle name which constantly turned up as "Frideric" (sic) instead of Frederick.

- In 1992, the punk-rock group "Die angefahrenen Schulkinder" lost an action for damages brought by Steffi Graf before the Higher Regional Court in Karlsruhe; the group had called one of its songs: "I want to make love with Steffi Graf". The fine: DM 60,000. (If one considers the fact that the incorrect use of the preposition meant that the tennis player was literally untouched by the presumed libel, this verdict strictly ought to be regarded as a miscarriage of justice ...)

- In a TV chat-show in late September 1995, a municipal councillor wished asylum-seekers "a happy welcome" in Frankfurt.

- The expression "shooting star" has established itself in the German language to describe a show-business star who has achieved overnight success. Unfortunately, this has exactly the opposite meaning in English. A "shooting star" is a "falling star", a short-lived and ephemeral phenomenon. Two examples: "Most university lecturers are around 40 when they take up their first post. But there are also "shooting stars" who show that it can be done faster." (Die Woche , 21 June 1996).

And: "With her long black curly hair (...) - that is Maria Grazia Cucinotta (26). The fiery Sicilian is Italy's new shooting star." (BILD-Zeitung, 17.10.1995, p.1). Such is life! Creative people smugly insist on their right to be wrong. And why not? It was Alexander Pope back in the 18th century who wrote of "the divine right of Kings to govern wrong"... In a democracy everyone has the right to sing out of tune.

- "The fall in the exchange rate of the French Franc requires an intensive brainstorming by the Paris-Bonn axis." (Süddeutsche Zeitung, 11.10.1995, p.24)

- The magnetic railway at Frankfurt airport, which travels to the new terminal C, makes an automatic announcement as it departs from each station: "The train is leaving the station. Please hold on".

(What is actually meant is then revealed by the subsequent German version of the announcement: "Bitte festhalten" - the small but important difference between "hold on" and "hold tight")

Vorsprung durch Englisch ? Or examples of "Dummdeutsch" ? (E. Henscheid)

Compared with the ground English has gained in Germany and among the Germans, the inroads made by the German language in Britain appear relatively modest. But at least words like *tannenbaum* and *kindergarten* have been permanently adopted.

It was Prince Albert who brought the 'tree of German inwardness' to Britain, whilst the émigrés Johannes and Bertha Ronge - who like many of their compatriots set sail for England in the wake of the failed revolution of 1848 - opened the first English kindergarten in Hampstead in September 1851. The pedagogic principles of the kindergarten, where children are supposed to grow and flourish like flowers, were familiar to Bertha Ronge from her Hamburg days when she had studied them at first hand under Carl Fröbel, nephew of the kindergarten pioneer Friedrich Fröbel. In less than ten years, the

Ronges trained fifty British teachers in the Fröbel method. Widespread success soon followed.

The first German word to be popularised in England was *hock* - a German wine. The Cologne "Hanseatic" merchants in 13th century London had a penchant for this wine from the Franconian town of Hochheim (as the British today have for *Liebfraumilch*).

But "Hochheim" proved too complicated for the English to pronounce, so it was shortened, or rather Anglicised, to *hock*. (The "ch" continues to be a tongue-twister for non-Germans. Most do not even attempt it. They get round it by pronouncing a name like that of the tennis player Michael Stich as "Stitch" or "Steetch".)

Steps in the fertilisation process: Some early examples

Irish monks brought Christianity to the British Isles, from where an Englishman, Wynfrith of Devonshire, better known as Boniface, set out to convert the Germanic peoples, becoming Archbishop in 732. He and his companions died as martyrs in Frisia in 755. As Angelika Volle wrote: "The organisation of the Franconian-German Church according to the Anglo-Saxon model and its subordination to Rome by St. Boniface and St. Kilian were crucially important for German history. The monasteries founded and run by Anglo-Saxons, for example in Fulda, became focal points of the island's cultural influence."

Alcuin, head of the cathedral school in York and probably Europe's greatest academic of the 8th century, was summoned to court by Charlemagne in 782 where he soon rose to the position of the Emperor's closest confidant and adviser. Alcuin's importance lies above all in the fact that he brought knowledge of classical antiquity to the Carolingian Empire.

Duns Scotus ("the Scot"), probably Britain's most outstanding philosopher of the Middle Ages, went from Oxford via Paris to Cologne to measure himself against Albertus Magnus, his scholastic opposite number. Incidentally, in those days, the term "nation" was used to designate communities of students with related ethnic backgrounds - for example, the English, Scottish, Irish and German students at the Sorbonne in Paris formed the "Germanic nation".

Cologne merchants - "the merchants of the Hanseatic League of Alemannians" - had been demonstrating international business success in London since the 12th century. The free trade alliance of the Hanseatic League included towns such as Hamburg, Lübeck, Lüneburg, Bremen, Stralsund, Rostock and Wismar; commercial centres in Brabant, Scandinavia and the Baltic states joined later. Sadly, the German merchants were not scrupulously fair in their business practices, insisting on their monopolies while refusing similar privileges to English traders who wanted to establish themselves on the continental markets of the Hanseatic League. "The persistent refusal to grant English traders reciprocity" (A. Volle) led to the expulsion of German merchants from England by Queen Elizabeth I in 1597. The London headquarters of the Cologne merchants was the Stalhof, which survived until 1853 when it was demolished to make room for Cannon Street railway station.

Words like *strafe* and *blitz*, or *blitzkrieg*, entered the English language through the two World Wars. *"Gott strafe England"* ("May God punish England"), the Kaiser commented grimly during the First World War - which for a long time Germans and British alike referred to as the "Great War", before the subsequent "most unnecessary" war (Winston Churchill) changed their vocabulary. In their practical way, the British transformed the central word of the Kaiser's curse - *strafe* - into a dynamic verb to describe machine-gun fire ... The word *blitz* is also most commonly found in the English language as a verb, transmuted from its historical usage as a noun in 1940, namely for Hitler's *'Blitzkriege'*.

Why did *schadenfreude* make it across the Channel? There are countless examples of such compound nouns in the German language with nuances of meaning which even English, with its talent for brevity, cannot always match. The British have simply borrowed some as "loan words", although they have not yet adopted the concise

"Tierschutzverein" (literally: "Animal Protection Association"). They still prefer the more convoluted: "Royal Society For the Prevention of Cruelty to Animals"...

In Britain, the term *abseiling* is now a vital part of the vocabulary of both mountaineers and jail-breakers, just as linguists cannot do without the word *umlaut* to describe the two dots over certain German vowels. The *lied* has become an indispensable feature of musical terminology, as has *leitmotif* - although the latter has a considerably broader application in English, as the following sentence from a newspaper article demonstrates: *"These are the leitmotifs of our national design for rural living."*

The greatest linguistic breakthrough was achieved with the car advertising slogan: *Vorsprung durch Technik*. Seldom has a foreign phrase been so readily accepted in the United Kingdom. The campaign strategists stopped at nothing to put their message across: in one of their TV commercials (or *"spots"* as they are called in Germany), they portrayed German humour as lagging way behind other countries - so the real German advantage, namely the *Vorsprung durch Technik*, stood out even more clearly by contrast. A clever play on national stereotypes - one upstaged by the other.

Political and economic analyses are now unthinkable without such terms as *ostpolitik, mitbestimmung* and *Bundesbank*, even if Britain is unlikely to adopt the concept of *mitbestimmung* in a hurry and despite the fact that the Pound Sterling still has a bone to pick with the *Bundesbank* over the events of September 1992... *Realpolitik*, on the other hand, is a different matter; although coined in Germany and popularised by Bismarck, its most faithful practitioners were to be found in Britain.

The English language has also adopted numerous German terms of a philosophical nature. Such words have always given the British a special insight into the German soul and character. They include *weltschmerz, weltanschauung, zeitgeist, gemütlichkeit* - and of course *angst*, for many the hallmark of modern German society.

"Der Freischütz" becomes "The Black Rider" .
The result is a kind of "Germglish"

It had rave reviews in New York and drove audiences wild for three years at the Thalia theatre in Hamburg. In the 1995/96 season it played to full houses in Bonn: "The Black Rider", a musical full of black humour, adapted from the "Freischütz" story, which gained international fame through Carl Maria von Weber's opera of the same name.

This product of a pop-inspired cultural mixture lives entirely off the symbiosis of the German and English language. Songs and spoken text switch constantly between the two and sometimes the libretto jumbles them up into a synchronous hotchpotch.

In the process, the American authors - William S. Burroughs, the grand old man of beat poetry, pop star Tom Waits and impresario Robert Wilson - have highlighted a fascinating cultural phenomenon.

To give you a taste of the lyrics:

"Feder weg... Und Flinte her... Leicht gesagt... Und ist doch schwer...
Put down a pen... Pick up a gun ... Easy said ... Und schwer getan..."

"Der, und mein?... das kann nicht sein... He is such a piece of slime... stinkt nach Zwiebeln und nach Wein... er schlägt mir auf den Magen... dieses Wildschwein will mich frei'n and be mine... in guten und in schlechten Tagen... I say 'no!' and 'nein!'... O Wilhelm, lerne jagen!"

"Verkaufe nie dein Ich... Denn dann verlierst du dich... So whatever you do... Don't sell your You... Denn: if you do... You got no You... Remember what I'm telling you."

(It might not be quite how Coleridge would have imagined the marriage of German and English, but after all this is no longer the year 1800...)

3. *University College London*

On 28 March 1828, Goethe again broached the subject of "the English" in conversation with his assistant Eckermann. He was particularly partial to this topic - the country had exerted a strong fascination on Goethe since his youth and influenced his artistic development. This time he made yet another comparison between the islanders and his dear German countrymen. The wise man of Weimar sighed:

"If one could only teach the Germans less philosophy and more initiative, less theory and more practice, like the English, it would go some ways towards our salvation."

But Goethe's plea went unheeded. For shortly after he had made his otherwise quite accurate comparison, something exciting happened. In autumn 1828, the University of London opened its doors for the first time and inverted Goethe's dictum - the export of German theory and philosophy to English academia, to the great benefit of the latter, if not exactly its "salvation". The exception which proves the rule.

However, nobody in Germany coerced the British into accepting this piece of cultural enrichment; in fact, it was two Scots, the journalist Henry Crabb Robinson (1775 - 1867) and the essayist and poet Thomas Campbell (1777 - 1844), who were full of praise for Wilhelm von Humboldt's ideal of "academic freedom" and urged their compatriots to adopt it. Robinson had travelled around Germany in 1800, had met Goethe and Schiller and enrolled at Jena university. He was thus at the heart of German classicism, witnessed the birth of the Romantic movement and gained first-hand experience of the "education boom" which seized German intellectual circles at the time. (Robinson later became the *Times* foreign correspondent, one of the very first in his profession, and was subsequently appointed the paper's foreign affairs editor.)

After a visit to Göttingen University in 1801, he wrote to his brother back in England:

"The German university is not at all like the English, a Seat of Discipline, a sort of School for grown Gentlemen. They are mere places of assembly where Professors are nominated to give lectures on all the Sciences and branches of learning. They have no prayers, no Costume, no obligation to attend lectures, no Tests, few Examinations and then only when Degrees are conferred, and they deserve the name of University much better than the English Colleges (...) They are cheap, hence there are very many poor students."

Some years later, Robinson's friend Thomas Campbell came to the same conclusion after visiting Bonn, whose university had been founded in 1811. (Prince Albert, it will be remembered, was later to enrol at Bonn University too, from where he sent his cousin Victoria polite congratulations on her accession to the throne in 1837...).

In those days, curricula at British colleges would only allow for the study of classical languages, theology and law. The world of modern science, especially natural science, was excluded. Potential students also had to pass an entrance test, the traditional examination questions of the Anglican Canon - in his "History of Europe", H.A.L. Fischer called it the "enslavement by religious test". (Oxford and Cambridge retained the test until 1871.)

The University of London, which was finally made possible thanks to the initiative of William Brougham (another Scot), did away with all that. Many more "redbrick universities" were to follow. London was the first British university to establish a natural science faculty and a professorship for English Literature. Intensive exchanges with German universities such as Berlin and Göttingen became the rule.

"University College" - the name itself symbolised Anglo-German synthesis ...

What's in a name? Sometimes a great deal. London University, founded in 1828 and free of theological stewardship unlike the other British colleges of the period, was renamed "University College" in 1831 when its Anglican rival "King's College" appeared on the scene. The name "University College" was a perfect marriage of the English and German spirit - "College" described the traditional and pragmatic approach, whilst "University" stood for the German input, the speculative thinking and academic freedom of research and teaching.

John Mander sums it up neatly in his book "Our German Cousins" (1974):

"The more 'idealist' German ideas could be gently transformed by the more pragmatic spirit of the English"

... yet it retained its British character !

In one respect, however, enthusiasm in London for the German way of doing things did not last long: the abolition of the test system, an innovation when London University began, was soon overturned. The primacy of career-oriented objectives, of teaching over research, quickly reasserted itself. The right to spend an unlimited time at university proved too much academic freedom for the British way of thinking.

Equally, strong emphasis continued to be placed on teaching the young to take up the trading professions. As Thomas Campbell wrote in a letter to the editor of the Times on 9 February 1825:

"Knowledge of foreign languages, domestic and foreign statistics and of political economy ought to enter fully into the education of a British merchant of superior grade."

Campbell had the "youth of our middling rich people" in mind - which Mander, in the above-mentioned book, called a "decidedly un-Humboldtian" idea. Certainly, to make the innovations attractive to the general public, Campbell had no option: he had to appeal first to the dominant sectors of his society, the landed gentry and the upper middle classes of the early industrial era.

4. *A German in England: Prince Albert*

During this period of intellectual upheaval, Albert of Saxe-Coburg-Gotha, the personification of German belief in progress and cultural commitment, arrived in Britain. He was initially viewed with suspicion and regarded by the British aristocracy as an incorrigible foreigner on account of his "Prussian virtues". *This* German was not eccentric like the Hanoverian Kings, primarily the four Georges, who had played the role of constitutional monarchs in London whilst remaining absolute rulers in Hanover.

As John Mander writes, Albert was *"didactic, self-righteous, a zealot for progress, and a bigot for improvement... a regular pedagogue. Added to this was the assumption that Germany had rather more than her fair share of these good things and Great Britain rather less."* To which George Gillespie adds: *"The fox-hunting country squires who ruled the country regarded him as cold, boring, unsporting and far too serious - and furthermore abstract, a stickler for principles and uncompromising."*

Only when he was with his family, in the company of his wife and nine children, did Albert thaw out and diffuse an atmosphere of the art-loving, paternal bourgeois, with German as the informal language spoken at home. The members of the royal family were the first true Victorians ... *"Papa is an oracle and what he decides must be correct,"* wrote Vicky, the eldest daughter, full of admiration. (She later married the Prussian crown prince, the so-called "90-day-Emperor", Frederick III.) "Your perfect Papa", was how Queen Victoria described him in a letter to her daughter on the occasion of her wedding on 25 January 1858.

Prince Albert: not eccentric enough for the English

Queen Victoria was also of pure German stock. But how did Germans accede to the British throne in the first place?

In short, through their links with the Protestant Stuarts. It's quite a simple story really... In the "Glorious Revolution" of 1688/89, the English had driven out the much-despised last Stuart King, James II, who wanted to re-catholicise the country by force. At the insistence of Parliament, succession passed to the Protestant William of Orange and his wife Mary, a daughter of James II, and subsequently to her younger sister, Anne. Both had chosen Protestantism. (The union of England and Scotland to form "Great Britain" was finally sealed during Queen Anne's reign in 1707.)

William and Mary remained childless, whilst Anne and her husband, Prince George of Denmark had seventeen children - still not sufficient to maintain the dynasty. Twelve died shortly after birth and the other five did not survive their mother. The newly installed succession was in danger of collapsing - Parliament had to step in once again with the Act of Settlement of 1701. This ignored the claims of James II's two Catholic Stuart sons and transferred the rights to the throne to the closest Protestant relative of the Stuarts - to Sophie, the widow of Elector Ernst August of Hanover, who had died in 1698, and their heirs.

Why Sophie? Well, she was the fifth and only Protestant daughter of the unfortunate "Winter King" Frederick V of the Palatinate and his wife, Elizabeth of Bohemia, a daughter of James I, the first Protestant Stuart to reign over Scotland and England. But Sophie, James I's granddaughter, never acceded to her intended place on the throne - she died even before Queen Anne. In accordance with the "Act of Settlement", succession thus passed to her son, Elector Georg of Hanover, who was crowned King George I of England on 1 August 1714 without being able to speak a single word of English (he refused ever to learn it). He embodied the personal union between the House of Hanover and the British monarchy.

All four Georges and William IV preserved their German stock. Instead of marrying members of the British aristocracy, they all chose wives from among the German nobility: George I married Sophie of Celle; George II married Caroline of Ansbach; George III married Charlotte of Mecklenburg-Strelitz; George IV married Caroline of Brunswick-Wolfenbüttel and William IV married Adelheid of Saxe-Coburg-

Meiningen. Since the latter two marriages produced only daughters who died before their parents (although William IV also had ten children from a liaison with the Irish actress Dora Jordans...), it was William's 18-year-old niece, Princess Victoria, who succeeded him on the English throne in 1837. This ended the personal union with the House of Hanover - but not the family connections with Germany. On the contrary.

Victoria was the only child of the Duke of Kent (the fourth son of George III and brother of George IV and William IV) and Princess Victoria of Saxe-Coburg-Gotha. Following her father's early death, her Coburg uncle Leopold (later king of Belgium) became her guardian. A further uncle, Duke Ernst I, Prince Albert's father, was head of the House of Coburg.

Victoria's marriage to her cousin Albert on 10 February 1840 meant that the British monarchy became even more "Germanified" than it already was. Incidentally, both had been delivered into the world by the same midwife in the same year, 1819 - Victoria on 24 May and Albert on 26 August. They always spoke German together.

The couple had nine children (four sons and five daughters) who were later to produce offshoots of the Anglo-German monarchy with all of Europe's dynasties. But the Coburg name was dropped in 1917, during the First World War, when George V cut the ties at the height of anti-German animosities and adopted the name Windsor - which has remained to the present day.

It is interesting to note that the British royal family has retained one German tradition. Contrary to the custom throughout Britain of offering gifts on Christmas morning, the Windsors follow the old German tradition of distributing presents on Christmas Eve.

Victoria and Albert - the love match of the century

The Prince was always happiest when planning something. There was a long tradition of collecting, building and preserving works of art among the Princes of Saxony - the Dukes of Coburg, also of Saxon descent, were no exception. Patronage of the arts was one of Albert's passions. His philanthropy displayed signs of a strong social conscience which was rare at that time and did not become more widespread until much later in the industrial era.

The promotion of art and education in Albert's adopted country was in a sorry state. One royal patron, Charles I, had ended up on the scaffold in 1649 and George IV (1820-1830), whose excesses were legendary, "paid the artists with money he did not possess" (Gillespie). By contrast, Albert approached his new tasks with high-minded ideals instilled in him by his tutor, Baron von Stockmar: liberalism coupled with responsibility; sensitivity for the enlightened bourgeoisie; a monarchy with a sense of duty, yet open to technology and other innovations.

Unlike the Establishment sceptics, the Prime Minister, Sir Robert Peel, was quick to recognise the German Prince's talents and seriousness of purpose. As early as 1841, he appointed him President of the Fine Arts Commission. The Commission's first task was to take forward preparations for a new Parliament building. This was one of many honorary offices into which Albert was able to channel his energy in the following years. By the age of 22, he was convinced that the State should assume patronage of the arts.

There was something of an "ingenious entrepreneur" (Gillespie) about him. This not only assisted the Queen in performing her State business, it was also to prove beneficial to Cambridge University inter alia, whose Chancellor Albert became in 1848. What the three Scots, Robinson, Campbell and Brougham had meant for the founding of University College London (UCL), Albert brought in person to the Cambridge Colleges: a breath of fresh air.

His ideas closely mirrored the German educational concepts so dear to the founders of UCL. In a letter to Lord John Russell (1853), and with conditions at Cambridge in mind, Albert stated:

"In general, universities should not just be institutions of learning and tuition but also places of erudition where the savants of this country may find a home which at present is absolutely denied to them, and they themselves being driven to join the mere money-making pursuits or to starve."

The new University Chancellor also brought his influence to bear on reform of the curricula. Until then, theology, classical languages and mathematics had been the only courses of study on offer. Under Albert, the range of subjects was broadened to include geography, foreign languages, history of art and aesthetics.

Prince Albert: Patron of the Arts, social reformer, open to technical innovations.

Victoria's husband lost no time in implementing his ideas. A few examples...

... of his promotion of art and architecture:

July 1843: First exhibition of the frescoes commissioned for the planned Parliament building. ("Cartoon", the technical name for these drawings on cardboard, subsequently became the popular word for "caricature").

1845: Work began on a new royal castle at Osborne on the Isle of Wight (later Victoria's favourite residence; she died there in 1901). Mixed Italian style, large gardens. A further royal residence was built in Northern Scotland: Balmoral Castle, in Scottish baronial style.

At Windsor Castle, the archives and graphics collections were secured and reorganised.

With the aid of the new technology of photography, Prince Albert compiled the first complete catalogue of Raphael's works.

Commissions for German and British painters, including Franz Xaver Winterhalter's "The First of May". Purchase of works by Lukas Cranach and Albrecht Dürer.

spotlight 16

... of his social commitment:

Albert's first public office was as chairman of the "Society for the Extinction of the Slave Trade" (in the British Empire).

He also designed construction plans for more humane workers' housing estates (which can still be seen today in London's Battersea Park.) Each house was fireproof and equipped with running water and a flush toilet for each family - an unprecedented idea in 1851. "The goal of all humanitarians," he wrote, "should be to show how each person can help his neighbour, despite the complexities of civilisation and modern society; it is particularly the duty of those who are blessed by Providence with social standing, wealth and education."

In his standard work on Prince Albert, "The Prince Consort", Roger Fulford summed this up as follows:

"In no sphere of activity in England did the Prince make a better impression than in his careful leadership of Cambridge University. His progressive spirit, supported by good common sense, shone with refreshing clarity in contrast to the narrow-minded partiality of the extreme reformers on the one hand and the intellectual port-soaked backbenchers on the other."

Crystal Palace, 1851: Prince Albert's dream is fulfilled

But Prince Albert is probably remembered best, in his adopted country and throughout the world, for the "Great Exhibition", London's international fair of 1851 - an event which was designed to display Britain's pre-eminence as an industrial and colonial power. He was chairman of the committee which succeeded in pushing the idea through against initial resistance in

Parliament and the scorn of the press. However, Albert's interest in the project, which he initiated, went far beyond national apotheosis. It incorporated many of the ideas with which the Prince Consort hoped to influence his era.

Peaceful international co-operation, an enlightened belief in the power of the links between art

Victoria and Albert Museum in Kensington: the jewel in the crown

and science and finally the embodiment of these ideas in the architectural design - in the exhibition pavilion itself, the "Crystal Palace", designed by the famous landscape gardener and greenhouse engineer Joseph Paxton. This bold construction of glass and ornamental iron girders, flooded with natural light, was like a demonstration of Albert's thinking, a progressive way of thinking in "synergies", as people might say today.

The Great Exhibition was an enormous success and achieved something which is usually just a dream for cities competing to host such events today: a huge profit of 186,000 Pounds Sterling (the equivalent of £12 million at today's value), which Albert immediately reinvested. He purchased the best exhibits from the Fair as the basis for a new complex of spacious museums to be built in the London district of South Kensington, which is still lovingly referred to as "Albertville" or "Albertopolis": the Victoria and Albert Museum, one of the world's best museums for the applied arts, the Natural History Museum and the Imperial College for Natural Science founded at the same time (and where August Wilhelm von Hofmann, whom Albert brought over from Germany, built up the chemistry department). Title to all this property is still held by the Commission of the World Fair of 1851, today administered by a foundation.

In Albert's day, the Germans and the British were also linked by technology, transport and tourism.

19th century Europe was not about a single treaty designed to create a European Union but rather a matter of agile minds and dextrous hands united by progress, inspiration and mobility.

Four examples:

In 1845, Queen Victoria and Prince Albert made their first joint trip to Germany, also visiting Coburg where a public festival was held to celebrate Albert's 26th birthday on 26 August.

What route did the royal couple take for their return journey? The railway line from Gotha to Eisenach, where they greeted English workers who were helping to construct this new rail link...

Six years later, a German "communicator" came to London, a certain Paul Julius Reuter, proprietor of a news agency founded in Aix-la-Chapelle in 1849 which was famous for the fact that it used carrier pigeons for the section from Aix to Brussels which had no telegraph wires...

Paul Julius Reuter: carrier pigeons brought him fame

He moved to England because the country already had a "Vorsprung durch Technik" and, as the centre of a world empire, promised communications opportunities on a global scale. Reuter, the son of a Rabbi from Kassel, rented two rooms in the City of London in 1851 and rapidly built an empire of his own - news about industry and politics, above all stock exchange quotations, but also general news for European and then world-wide subscribers.

"Follow the cable", was Reuter's motto. By 1872 he had already expanded his branches as far as Japan. But his country of birth did not forget him either: in 1871, the Duke of Saxe-Coburg-Gotha elevated him to the nobility and he became Freiherr Paul Julius von Reuter! In 1915, on the death of Herbert von Reuter, the founder's eldest son, the business was converted into a

private limited company, in which the British Press Association acquired a majority shareholding in 1925. In 1984, the company was listed on the London Stock Exchange as "Reuters Holdings plc". One of the many German-British success stories.

Travelling around the Continent of Europe was already part of the "Grand Tour" undertaken by young British aristocrats in the 18th century. In the early decades of the 19th century, prosperous members of the bourgeoisie also gradually began to partake of these delights. Only one thing was missing: books about the countries to be visited.

Interest in Germany had grown considerably as a result of Madame de Staël's book "De l'Allemagne" (1813). But when the son of her London publisher, John Murray III, travelled through Germany in 1829, he felt inadequately equipped with the then customary but very flawed brochure by a certain Mrs. Stark. This prompted him to write his own travel guide - the start of an entire series of new-style "Handbooks". They were to become the most popular reference works for the well-travelled Victorians. Murray wrote the first three "Handbooks" himself: "Holland, Belgium and Northern Germany", "Southern Germany and Switzerland", "France". (1836)

One notable visitor to Germany was the painter William Turner (1775-1851), who characteristically applied the eye of a landscape visionary to the hills and valleys of Germany's highlands and created a unique panorama of his host country in hundreds of sketches as well as the drafts for many later oil paintings. Turner visited Germany seven times altogether - in 1817, 1824, 1833, 1835, 1839, 1840 and 1844 - with the river landscapes of Rhine, Moselle, Neckar, Nahe and Danube among his favourite haunts. Reviewing his large Heidelberg painting exhibited in the Tate Gallery, the art historian Doris Schmidt wrote that it revealed Turner's "principle of colourful transparency which turns every 'view' into a vision."(Süddeutsche Zeitung, 4.11.1995)

The Albert Memorial
in Hyde Park

There is a certain element of tragedy in the fact that, despite his commitment to British patriotism, Albert never felt completely at home in his adopted country. He simply could not deny his "Germanness". He loved England's forward-looking energy, the material progress and all the liberal ideas of his day - but where was the "Gemüt", this warm sense of sentimental homeliness? The English had no proper term in their language for this concept because they had no corresponding feeling. It was with a certain sarcastic melancholy that he wrote to his brother:

"Gemüt is a plant that cannot grow in England ... An Englishman, should he find himself entrapped in this sentiment, becomes frightened at the thought as at having a dangerous illness - and he promptly shoots himself... I think this seedling is smothered by reading too many newspapers."

When he died of typhoid fever at the age of 41 on 14 December 1861, Prince Albert nevertheless left behind a distressed nation and an inconsolable Victoria. She was to survive him by forty years, permanently attired in mourning. His unexpected death (after an illness of only five weeks) *"was experienced like a national disaster"*, as the Brockhaus Encyclopaedia of 1893 records. Several monuments were erected in Albert's memory, such as the Prince Albert Memorial in Hyde Park and the magnificent Prince Albert Hall. In Germany, the Prince Albert Society in Coburg has long devoted itself to academic research into this period of the 19th century. At Albert's funeral, Benjamin Disraeli delivered a eulogy on the Prince which, even allowing for pious exaggeration, still contains a great deal of truth:

"This German Prince ruled England for twenty-one years with a wisdom and vigour which none of our Kings have ever displayed."

5. *An Englishman in Germany: Shakespeare*

I f one had to choose a single common denominator for Anglo-German ties, there could only be one - William Shakespeare. More than any other, he inspired the German mind and liberated it from the shackles of rationalism. German literature not only learned true poetry from Shakespeare, the gracefulness of imagination, but also the self-determination of the artist. At a time when absolutism and autocracy kept political Germany a long way from democratic renewal, *literary* Germany experienced something verging on a democratic revolution under Shakespeare's influence. The Bard of Stratford reassured Herder and the *"Sturm und Drang"* writers, and via Herder confirmed the young Goethe in his vocation as a poet. It was Shakespeare who gave German literature the self-confidence to discover itself.

And it was Shakespeare who enriched the German language with the greatest stock of quotations after Luther's Bible, the Latin poets and Goethe. This was due in large measure to the brilliant translation by August Wilhelm Schlegel and Ludwig Tieck (assisted by Schlegel's daughter Dorothea and Graf Wolf von Baudissin), which was begun in the early 19th century in the mature classic idiom of Goethe. "The milk of human kindness" - what Muse inspired the authors to render this as *"die Milch der frommen Denkungsart"*? This masterly translation, as much a recreation as a translation, full of empathy and eloquence, quickly became popular and virtually turned the Elizabethan Englishman into a German author *sui generis*. Even today, Shakespeare's plays are still performed in Germany more than the works of any other dramatist. One theatre in Bremen has devoted its entire repertoire solely to Shakespeare.

**Leo Tolstoy quipped: "Shakespeare is a German invention".
How right he was...**

*He arrived late on the scene but his career was meteoric. Thanks to the brilliant
Schlegel/Tieck translation, the Bard was so monopolised by German sentiment
in the 19th century, his world considered so Germanic, that people seriously
began to question the Renaissance author's spiritual and cultural roots. August
Wilhelm Schlegel had set the tone when he called the poet "a fellow
countryman born abroad".*

*As German-British rivalry intensified in the 1860s and the profoundly
philosophical German character began to assert itself against what was
disparagingly called the small-minded British "nation of shopkeepers", Shakespeare
was drawn into this dispute over cultural superiority, too. German intellectuals simply
could not accept that he was a product of British "civilisation", he must have been
shaped by German "culture"!*

*It was called a "nostrification campaign" - clearly a case of cultural adoption by
conceit... In 1867, Hermann Ulrici, the first President of the German Shakespeare
Society, actually wanted to "de-Anglicise" and "Germanify" Shakespeare. Eventually,
when the harsh tones of nationalism gained the upper hand in the First World War,
even the playwright Gerhart Hauptmann could resist no longer. In 1915, he jumped
on the bandwagon of German attempts to monopolise Shakespeare:*

*"There is no nation, not even the English, which has acquired such a right to
Shakespeare as the Germans. Shakespeare's figures are a part of our world, his soul
has become united with ours; and despite the fact that he was born and buried in
England, Germany is still the country where he truly lives."*

But a lot of ground had to be cleared before this imported English rose could take root in Germany. The biggest obstacle was the Germans themselves. Or rather, for a long time there was a bottleneck in communications which just would not let Shakespeare pass. This blockage took the shape of a professor at Leipzig University, Johann Christoph Gottsched, who presided over his aesthetic rules until the middle of the 18th century like the very incarnation of infallibility. Gottsched was an extremely orderly person, uncompromising to the point of intolerance, and supported by powerful allies, above all by French Classicism, or to be more precise the senior censors of the *"Académie Française"*. They had elevated the Greek philosopher and art theoretician Aristotle (who had been dead for 2,000 years...) to the highest authority on everything which was and was not permissible on the stage.

Was William Shakespeare a German poet?

They were fastidiously insistent on their notorious "three unities": unity of action, place and time. A play could only present a single basic theme, without episodes or sub-plots; it had to have a single geographical location; and it was not permitted to portray more events than could take place within 24 hours. Sound familiar? Of course. A "Maastricht II" in 18th century Europe. A "Stage and Drama Union" with strict conditions on candidates for accession...

Naturally, Shakespeare's dramas had no chance against such rigid "convergence criteria". They were the living contradiction of these rules, a grand cultural "opt-out" from so much aesthetic absolutism long before its time.

Shakespeare's early days in Germany: harmless, silly - but "typically English".

The first people to import Shakespeare into Germany were English actors in the 16th and 17th century. As England's rich theatre reservoir overflowed, these itinerant troupes travelled to the Continent and were hired by German Princes to entertain the people with cheap fun, musical processions and mime shows. In the process, Shakespeare's original texts were changed beyond recognition and reduced to their bare bones. From "Hamlet" only the comical or spine-chilling scenes were played, "Titus Andronicus" lent itself to horrible grimaces, while "Romeo and Juliet" was performed as a soap opera... "Katherina", as "The Taming of the Shrew" was called, was given a particularly raucous reception.

In a cultural environment of fearful bigotry and unquestioning belief in authority, the English actors and their slapstick plays provided a form of "comic relief" for the Germans (initially only in English but then gradually, as they stayed for longer periods, also in German). An English contemporary described what was otherwise traditional fare on the German stage at the time: "German actors are much too devout - on every fairground stage they recite what should be left to the preacher to proclaim from the pulpit."

This situation was relieved by the Monty Pythons of their age. "The comic figure they brought with them actually served the audience as an outlet for all the silliness of which they would otherwise have been ashamed," Friedrich Gundolf wrote in his monograph "Shakespeare und der deutsche Geist" (1911), which is still the best work ever written on this subject.

Even John Milton, whose poetry had begun to be appreciated in literary circles from Zurich to Göttingen and Frankfurt to Hamburg, was shown no mercy by the strict Gottsched. These unruly Englishmen! As the self-styled authority on culture wrote to the Zurich Professor Johann Jakob Bodmer in a letter dated 17.11.1732:

"*I admit that I am curious to know what rules can excuse such an unbridled power of imagination as that of Milton.*"

"Excuse"! It is difficult nowadays to imagine how suffocating the strait-jacket must have been which the pedantry of rationalist aesthetics - prescribed by Gottsched - had placed on the German mind for such a long time.

But the counter-attack eventually came with a vengeance. Its thrust was no less powerful than the shock it caused. Gotthold Ephraim Lessing, critic and playwright, had the intelligence, the impudence and the linguistic skills to demolish the arguments of Leipzig's literary despot. His "17th letter on literature" of 16 February 1759, published in Friedrich Nicolai's Berlin magazine "Letters concerning the latest literature", delivered the final blow. The opening sentences of this polemical tract, their power and wit were to secure the 30-year-old a firm place in the history of German literary criticism:

"Nobody (...) will deny that German drama owes much of its early improvements to Professor Gottsched.

I am that nobody; I categorically deny it. I wish Herr Gottsched had never become involved with the theatre in the first place..."

Gottsched was hoist by his own petard: it was the French, Lessing countered, who were the real rule-breakers! What is a Corneille compared with Shakespeare, compared with his unique depiction of human nature and behaviour! Is it not precisely the Englishman, despite all the "disorder" of events in his plays, who best fulfils Aristotle's most important criterion: catharsis, the emotional upheaval we experience in the face of human passions and the concomitant purification through fear and compassion? Shakespeare's dramatic form, Lessing concluded, is far more akin to the German character than the overrated French models.

This line of argument triggered one of the most momentous changes in German cultural history. The French ideals were replaced by English ones. Not only Shakespeare was released from exile. There now followed an unprecedented "English invasion". German literary society was swept along on a wave of enthusiasm for English novels; the cult of sentimentality in poetry and prose (Lawrence Sterne's term "sentimental" became a household word) caused quite a stir; the young Goethe polished his English by reading Edward Young's "Night Thoughts"; Ossian's epic ballads touched everyone's emotions and virtually every paper written by the English and the Scots on the theory of art between 1760 and 1780 was translated and subjected to critical review. J.G.Herder wrote: *"With the aid of the kindred English mind, I appeal to the German mind to come to its senses and take stock of itself!"*

Shakespeare: yes, but in moderation - said Goethe, who himself constantly returned to the Bard for inspiration.

Shakespeare, the creator of living worlds, competing with Divine Creation itself - these were the ideas which Herder used to stimulate the young Goethe's creative processes during his Strasbourg period. And quite successfully, too. In 1771, at the age of 22, the Frankfurt firebrand published his first essay, "On Shakespeare's Day", in which he proclaimed his own vocation as a poet, stating that he wanted to follow the "gigantic steps" taken by this "greatest wanderer". He moved fast ... in November 1771, he produced the first version of "Götz von Berlichingen", after a thorough reading of Shakespeare's Histories. (When Walter Scott published the translation in 1799, one reviewer in Edinburgh immediately situated the play "in the Shakespeare tradition" - "Götz" as a Shakespeare playback...)

Goethe subsequently found further inspiration in "Hamlet" for his "Werther" (1774). In his novel "Wilhelm Meister" (1796), he describes Shakespeare as the "most exceptional, most wonderful of all writers". The intellectual and emotional education of the novel's hero, which takes him into the theatrical world, reaches its climax in the assimilation of Shakespeare, above all in the description of a performance of "Hamlet". This play is described as representing an absolute value, a self-contained creation with its own reality. This view, first proposed by Goethe, has guided an entire generation of art critics in Germany.

spotlight 20

In his correspondence with Schiller (1794), however, Goethe's admiration for Shakespeare is less evident - "Iphigenia" and the principles of Classicism had caught up with him. In the much-maligned essay "Shakespeare and no end" (1816), he even doubts whether one ought to bring the Bard's plays "in their entire breadth and length to the German theatre". He sees Shakespeare's place more in the history of poetry than that of the theatre.

But that was not to be Goethe's last word on the subject. He admitted to Eckermann on 3.12.1824: "Our own literature is largely derived from the English. Where do our novels and tragedies come from if not from Goldsmith, Fielding and Shakespeare?" And again on 25.12.1825: "Shakespeare is too rich and overpowering. A productive nature ought not to read more than one of his plays every few years, if it would not be wrecked entirely." Finally, referring to the review of an English edition of "Hamlet" (1826), he expresses his conviction "that Shakespeare, like the universe he portrays, offers ever new aspects and yet remains inscrutable to the end; for none of us, whoever we may be, can match either his writings or his mind."

This change even affected German garden architecture: Le Nôtre and the Baroque geometry of French gardens were out, Lancelot "Capability" Brown and English landscape gardening were in. Nature and freedom - these were the new aesthetic principles. The gardens in Wörlitz created by Prince Friedrich Franz of Anhalt-Dessau represented the first of their kind dedicated entirely to the English style (cf. also "SPOTLIGHT" 27). Lord Rumford gave Munich its English Garden (1789).

6. *Jewish Émigrés or the Continent comes to Great Britain*

In the 1920s and 30s, Berlin exerted a powerful influence on the British intelligentsia. The effervescence of the German capital stimulated the imagination of writers such as W.H. Auden, Stephen Spender and Christopher Isherwood. Despite the dark clouds on the political horizon, these authors could not resist the melting pot that was Berlin and Germany.

People clung to the vision which Berlin represented - despite a growing sense that the vision was doomed to end in disaster. This

Fascinated by Berlin
of the early 30s:
W. H. Auden and
Christopher Isherwood

mixture of excess energy and melancholy is the subject of "Good-bye to Berlin", Christopher Isherwood's moving report on his experience of Berlin in the early 30s. It is the finest record of the strong Anglo-German attraction of that period. By now, everyone is probably familiar with the story and its heroine, Sally Bowles, if not from reading the book then from seeing *"Cabaret"*, the musical which Liza Minelli immortalised in the film version.

When *"Good-bye to Berlin"* was first published in 1939, on the eve of the Second World War, disaster had already struck a significant section of the German-speaking bourgeoisie: the Jews. The catastrophe was soon to spread throughout Europe. No author could have imagined a "good-bye" on such a scale.

But in the first few years after Hitler assumed power, many Jews still managed to leave Germany and seek refuge in other cultures. Among them were some of the greatest Europeans in the fields of art, science and economics. Britain was at the forefront of those countries offering asylum and it was here that many of the exiles, from Vienna, Berlin, Budapest, Hamburg and Leipzig, made a fresh start or, like Sigmund Freud, found a dignified final resting place.

From Siegmund G. Warburg, the banker, to Eric Hobsbawm, the sociologist; from Norbert Brainin, the co-founder of the Amadeus-Quartet, to André Deutsch, Victor Gollancz and George Weidenfeld, the publishers; from Karl Popper, the philosopher (who came to London via New Zealand), to Ernst Boris Chain, the biochemist; from authors like Arthur Koestler, Elias Canetti and Erich Fried to art historians like Nikolaus Pevsner and Ernst Gombrich or the cartoonist Victor Weisz ("Vicky"): all victims of persecution, yet each and every one a pioneer in his own field, with the courage to make a new start and the creative ability to adapt in Britain's multicultural environment.

Some of them went on to win the Nobel Prize (Chain, Friedrich von Hayek). But all of them, together with many more not mentioned here, enriched the life and society of their host country more than virtually any other migratory movement across the Channel before them. *"It is impossible to imagine British culture in the late 20th century without them"*, is the succinct and accurate verdict of Paul Johnson. This is a unique chapter in the annals of Anglo-German ties and one uniquely related to an historical accident: on the verge of extinction, a significant section of Europe's intelligentsia was not only saved but presented to the receiving State, Great Britain, as an unexpected gift.

Two names stand out which demonstrate this German-Jewish-British fertilisation in a particularly vivid way. Ernst Gombrich (b. 1909) and Nikolaus Pevsner (1902-1983), from Vienna and Leipzig respectively, were both art historians, experts in a field which had led something of a Cinderella existence in Great Britain until their arrival. However, thanks to their untiring dedication, their host country's eyes were re-opened to art, which in turn revolutionised the way the British saw themselves in cultural terms.

In 1848/49, London was already the capital of a united Europe of the persecuted.

The British Isles have traditionally been a haven for political asylum-seekers from the Continent. The reason being that Britain's parliamentary system had created civil liberties long before people living under absolutist and authoritarian regimes in Europe even dared to think about freedom of speech or freedom of the press.

England witnessed a large influx of refugees after the failed popular uprisings of 1848/49 - mostly politicians, writers and revolutionaries oppressed and persecuted by the authorities in their home countries. London became something of a centre of a united Europe - a united Europe of the persecuted. Here Germans such as Carl Schurz (who later emigrated to the USA), Arnold Ruge, Ferdinand Freiligrath, Gottfried Kinkel or Malwida von Meysenbug met the Italians Garibaldi and Mazzini, the Hungarians Kossuth and Pulsky or the Russian Alexander Herzen.

Curiously, among the refugees there were two men who embodied what people had fled to London to escape - Crown Prince William of Prussia, later to become Emperor William I (in London from March to June 1848) and Prince Metternich, Chancellor of Austria (in London from March 1848 to November 1849), who gave his name to the system of European restoration, which Liberalism had fought so long in vain. The Hohenzollern Prince and the Prince in the service of the Hapsburgs had been advised to seek temporary refuge in London from the upheavals in their own capitals.

Meanwhile, in the Reading Room at the British Museum, Karl Marx, another refugee, was immersed in his studies on the revolution of the proletariat... The very idea is fascinating: Metternich, repression personified of the "Holy Alliance" and Marx, father of a system which was later to produce even great repression - both briefly in London at the same time, unbeknown to one other, their paths crossing somewhere on the streets of the metropolis ...

Hitler's accession to power drove not only *people* to the Diaspora - entire libraries of books, which the new barbarians neither tolerated nor appreciated, had to flee the country, too. One of the most famous was Aby Warburg's "Cultural Science Library" at Heilwigstraße 116 in Hamburg, which had opened as a centre for research into the "influence of Classical Antiquity on post-Graeco-Roman cultures" but had only been able to operate for seven years. At the end of 1933, the 20,000 volumes were shipped to London. As the newly founded Warburg library, it developed over the years into the now internationally renowned Warburg Institute at the University of London. (Warburg's house in Hamburg has since been restored and was opened in September 1995 as a new centre for research into the history of art.)

In 1936, this London institute-in-exile, which was committed to the methodology of a scientific approach to art history originally developed in Vienna, engaged Ernst Gombrich as a research assistant. He had recently fled from Austria. It was like a spark igniting a creative process. Gombrich, possessed with an encyclopaedic knowledge, was to become a byword for art appreciation and interpretation in Great Britain. His publications were world premières of a different kind: Gombrich's ideas on viewing and understanding paintings not only became an integral part of the relevant university syllabuses, they also sold well in book form, thus reaching a wider public and changing the way people perceived art.

Books like "The Story of Art", "Art and Illusion", "Perception and Reality" and "The Image and the Eye" read like phases of Gombrich's peaceful revolution in Great Britain. Experts are agreed that his legacy will be perpetuated through his many pupils well into the 21st century.

Nikolaus Pevsner was 31 years of age when the Nazis came to power. He had already made a name for himself at the *Staatliche Gemäldegalerie* in Dresden and as a lecturer on the history of art at Göttingen University, above all for his interest in the history of church architecture, still a young discipline in those days. Pevsner had written his dissertation on "Leipzig's Baroque Architecture" - and Baroque is certainly the word to describe Pevsner's life achievement. It bridged much of the cultural divide between Britain and the Continent and showed the British ways to discover their own architectural heritage and its European dimension.

Pevsner himself became the greatest surveyor and recorder of Britain's architectural treasures. In 1951, he began his monumental encyclopaedia "The Buildings of England", which finally grew to 46 volumes - a complete stocktaking of all the nation's buildings with even the slightest claim to architectural merit. 32 of these 46 volumes were compiled by Pevsner himself, combing Britain county by county, a tireless explorer. No other German-speaking person has ever made a finer, more important or more expansive declaration of love to his adopted country.

How Marx and Engels hoped in vain for the revolution in Great Britain.

Marx and Engels took a much different view of their host country to that of the refugees of the 20th century! They were far more critical and probably also more confused about the repercussions of what Friedrich Engels came to call "the industrial revolution" in the preface to his epoch-making work "The Condition of the Working Class in England" (published in Leipzig in 1845). Engels was still only 25 at the time and not politically persecuted like his friend Marx, but instead undergoing a business apprenticeship in Manchester. His father, a textile manufacturer in Wuppertal, had sent him there in 1842 to study with business partners. Written with a captivating gift for observation, "The Condition of the Working Class in England" was the first book of its kind devoted specifically to the approaching industrial era, the horrendous "pauperisation", as the Socialists rightly called it, of a large section of the "wage-dependent" population in the slum-ridden industrial towns of the world's leading trading nation: England.

If only Engels and Marx (who arrived in London in 1849) had stuck to their analyses instead of straying into prophecy! The sight of so much actual poverty led them to the conclusion that a place where such outrageous injustice was possible also had to be the place where the disfranchised, the proletariat, would rise up to unseat the ruling system and cast off their chains. "England is the classical ground for these upheavals" - even this sentence from the preface to Engels' book "The Condition ..." totally

misunderstood the British mentality and distorted a distressing plight of the time into a pattern for predestined developments. "Upheavals" and "classical ground" - that was pure wishful thinking, the hope that England would do him the favour of confirming his and subsequently Marx's theory of the inevitability of the proletarian revolution. Yet England, stubborn as ever, refused to oblige.

Karl Marx and ...

Engels should have followed his first impressions. Soon after arriving in Manchester in 1842, his summary in a letter was better than in his book three years later: "The English are still held back from violent revolution by their innate respect for the law". Incidentally, this view was echoed ten years later by Theodor Fontane, the greatest authority on England of his day, who never tired of proclaiming his "extreme disbelief in an English revolution from the lower or even the lowest levels".

But to no avail. Marx and Engels continued to lie in wait for the proletarian revolution in England. In July 1866, at a workers' demonstration in Hyde Park, Marx's heart began to beat faster. Will there be a confrontation this time? Will the revolutionary spark ignite? Alas, once again nothing. No blood was shed, he wrote in an ill-tempered letter to Engels: "These stubborn John Bulls, whose skulls appear just made for the constables' truncheons, will achieve nothing without a really bloody clash with the ruling forces." But he is still hopeful: "First the Englishman needs a revolutionary education ... and two weeks would be enough for that."

... Friedrich Engels: the condition of the working classes correctly observed but wrongly evaluated

Two weeks! Two millennia would not be long enough... The two revolutionaries cannot have been very pleased by the fact that the anticipated revolution failed to materialise in their host country. At any rate, the German scholar George Gillespie from Cardiff has pointed to one fact which he himself calls "embarrassing": the entire works of Marx and Engels do not contain a single favourable judgement or kind word about England or the English... Were they just bad losers?

Pevsner summarised what it was he found unique about his host country, and what he wanted to offer as a present in return, in his no less famous series of lectures "The Englishness of English Art", later published in book form. The popular success of Pevsner's writings was also aided by the fact that his publisher, Allan Lane, was in the process of building Britain's first paperback empire. He had launched the two series "Pelican" and "Penguin" and was looking for opportunities to popularise educational topics. With Pevsner as author and editor, he began to publish the "Pelican History of Art" in 1953, an undertaking of tremendous scope which is still adding ever more volumes today.

The refugees wanted to be "living interpreters between different cultures", as one of them, the political scientist Karl Mannheim, once put it. *"They certainly helped to make Britain a less insular place,"* Paul Johnson summed up.

And a more European place as well. After Aby Warburg's death, a reference was found amongst his papers to the dedication which had been inscribed on the foundation stone of his Institute in Hamburg in 1926: *"To the good European"*. It is hard to imagine a better epitaph for this chapter of Anglo-German relations, born in dark times yet shining through to the present day.

London's institutions of higher education, which had acquired an international reputation long before Hitler appeared on the scene, included the "London School of Economics (LSE)", founded by the Fabians Sidney and Beatrice Webb around the turn of the century. The Vienna-born economist Friedrich von Hayek was already teaching at the LSE in the early 1930s. A radical Liberal, anti-interventionist and anti-Keynesian, von Hayek was a pioneer of free-market economics alongside Röpke, Eucken and (later) Müller-Armack.

During his London period (1931-1950), he published what was probably his most influential work "The Road to Serfdom" (1944). Margaret Thatcher was later to prove not only an ardent admirer of his theories but also a politician with the determination to base her own economic programme on Hayek's ideas. In the final analysis, the battle for "Thatcherism" was also a battle for von Hayek and his philosophy, which was honoured with the Nobel Prize for Economics in 1974.

Another Viennese academic, the philosopher Karl Popper, was appointed to the LSE after the war, further strengthening the European links of this renowned institution. He was made head of the LSE's philosophy department, whilst continuing to teach logic and scientific methodology at the University of London (1945-1969).

Popper had also just published his main work, "The Open Society and Its Enemies" (1945), while still in exile in New Zealand. It became something of a standard work for all critics of Marxism, the most important refutation of Socialist promises of salvation. It also had a lasting influence on the *realpolitiker* Helmut Schmidt, among many others. In his obituary on Popper, the former Federal Chancellor confessed:

"I have him to thank for the rational justification of my instinctive aversion to all forms of political utopias and visions - including the various forms of Marxism." (*Die ZEIT*, 23.9.1994)

Popper, like von Hayek, was regarded as a leading Liberal. Yet he preferred to describe himself as a moralist, a sceptic and a rationalist in the tradition of Kant and the English Enlightenment, above all of the Empiricism of Shaftesbury or Hume. Indeed, Popper's conviction that human reason was basically fallible and that progress could only be achieved by subjecting reason to constant checks, so-called "fallibility tests", had little in common with the Hegelian branch of German Idealism, from which Marx had derived the despotic code of infallible theories.

Honoured: Karl Popper receives the Federal Cross of the Order of Merit with Star and Sash

It had more in common with the British philosophical tradition of "trial and error", of *Trial and Compromise*, as Herbert Spencer called it in the 19th century. But did the Germans not also once possess in Lessing, Friedrich Nicolai and Moses Mendelssohn thinkers of a like persuasion? What was the "ring parable" in Lessing's "Nathan the Wise" if not an early "fallibility test" à la Popper which any claim to absolute truth would automatically fail? After the Second World War, Karl Popper thus became the most important interpreter of this European cultural legacy - a mediator with the best credentials - a Jew from Vienna, expelled by National Socialism, a British national by choice and a friend of the new democratic Germany. He was also an important adviser to the SPD in drafting the reforms in its 1959 "Godesberg Programme", with which the German Social Democrats confirmed their western orientation.

Germany: Where political reforms were lacking, intellectuals soon sought refuge in theory and speculation ...

To what extent is a nation's character mapped out a priori and to what extent is it shaped by history, by the "social superstructure", as Marx would have called it? The answer could fill libraries. One thing is certain: political systems and their development are partly responsible for the way a society thinks and behaves. On the other hand, there must have been a certain predisposition before the political system was applied, something like a national trait, which favoured one particular system above all others and allowed it to flourish. Consequently, one would have to conclude there was an apriorism in the national character...

Be that as it may, "domination from above" in England had disappeared with the "Glorious Revolution" of 1688/89. From then on, it was the political will anchored in Parliament "which was not yet that of the people but nevertheless spoke in the name of the people" (H.D. Gelfert: "Typisch englisch - Wie die Briten wurden, was sie sind", 1995). The evolution of English philosophy was its mirror-image: empiricism, pragmatism and political self-determination were its catchwords.

In Germany, however, a different reality prevailed - authoritarian, inclined to restoration, opposed to civil rights reforms. And so philosophy also took a different direction - into "inwardness". This is where the Germans finally found the only unchallenged field for their free development. Faced with a reality of crude suppression, abstract thinking was the path to salvation - but unfortunately also to intransigence, rigid absolutism and isolation.

The text of a song performed with great fervour by German male-voice choirs since the 19th century says it all:

" Thoughts are free / who can guess them?
They fly by / like shadows in the night,
No one can see them / no hunter shoot them
With powder and shot, / thoughts are free!

I think what I please / and what pleases me,
But all on the quiet / as it should be...

"All on the quiet" - the expression of a society which had been politically silenced for all too long. "Deliberate as much as you want, but obey!", Frederick the Great - otherwise a progressive spirit - had drilled into his subjects. Censorship, imprisonment and submissiveness to authority ensured that indeed only thoughts remained free.

So politics and philosophy went their separate ways. This was soon noticed by visitors, like Madame de Staël, whose irritation is apparent from this comment jotted down during her first journey to Germany in 1803:

"Germany's greatest minds indulge in the fiercest arguments about the world of ideas and no one may interfere in their speculations. But when it comes to the real world, they are only too willing to bow to authority."

It was probably more a question of having to than wanting to... Even Goethe had complained:

" Germany? But where does it lie? I cannot find the country,
Where erudition begins, politics stop."

"The thing-in-itself", the fundamental concept of idealistic philosophy, "the preoccupation of the best minds" (Friedrich Gundolf), became the substitute for a reality in which active political participation was impossible. Instead of the real world, from which people were excluded, the world of ideas and the untried imperative became an even more important litmus test for the German intellect.

... but also soon learned to joke about it

Political constriction leading to abstract thinking as a way out: this dialectic endured long enough. But as if by way of compensation, the Germans learned occasionally to mock their excessive speculation and their lack of down-to-earth realism. While Professor Hegel was still explaining his philosophical theories in Berlin, the following joke was already doing the rounds:

A young philosophy student, 20 years of age, writes to his father:
"Now I know how the world should be; consequently, it is not worth making an effort to discover how it really is."

While we are on the subject of Hegel - there was also a standard joke about him which has since become a stereotypical joke about the Germans in general:
Someone asks the famous man of learning: "What happens if your theories do not correspond with reality?" To which Hegel replies: "More's the pity for reality!"

In a similar vein, Goethe mocked the Germans by praising the British:
"Whilst the Germans torment themselves solving philosophical problems, the English make fun of us with their great practical sense and gain the world."
(Conversations with Eckermann, 1 September 1829)

One of the best put-downs on the subject comes from Heinrich Heine in "Deutschland - Ein Wintermärchen" ("Germany, A Winter's Tale", 1844):

" The land belongs to the French and Russians,
The sea belongs to the British,
But we have undisputed control
In the lofty regions of the dream.

Here we exercise hegemony.
Here we are whole;
The other nations have
developed on flat and shallow earth."

Some time ago, the Oxford historian Timothy Garton Ash wondered aloud why British people say:

"What on _Earth_ is the matter here?"

whereas a German would express the same frustration by saying:

"Was um _Himmels_ willen (for _Heaven's_ sake) ist hier los?"

Curious - or symptomatic?

What is the heritage of the school of German speculative thinking? Well, perhaps there is still a reluctance among Germans to step out into the real world. At any rate, no other society spends so much time discussing how to break down rigid social structures, without ever actually reaching any concrete decisions on what steps to take. Instead, there is a further conference, yet another seminar, a new panel of experts. The debate about reforming the law on ìshop-closing hoursî, for example, went on for several decades while a whole generation of potential late-night shoppers slipped gently into retirement. Finally, in summer 1996, the debate produced a "mini-reform".

But this German aversion to taking the first step in case one tramples on a thousand potential objections was already the subject of a joke 170 years ago. It goes like this:

After his death, a German is on the path to Eternity and reaches a crossroad. One sign points in the direction "Heaven", the other in the direction "Lectures about Heaven". There is no doubt which path the German takes: to the lectures, of course...

But the generation of the Poppers and Hayeks, those born around 1900, was not the end of the LSE's "German connection". On the contrary, the head of the institute from 1974 to 1984 was none other than the German-born Ralf Dahrendorf, one of the most famous sociologists and social scientists of his day. Dahrendorf drew on an exceptional breadth of professional experience - Professor in Constance, Minister of State in Bonn, a formative influence on Germany's Liberal Party and EC Commissioner. By appointing Dahrendorf as its Director, the LSE maintained its reputation as a seat of non-conformist thinking. As it states in the handbook given to all new applicants: *"If you want to spend a few years in the company of like-minded people, this is not the right place for you ..."*

Dahrendorf, meanwhile Warden of St. Antony's College, Oxford and a naturalised British subject, wrote <u>the</u> history of the LSE for

Oxford University Press in 1995, to mark the LSE's 100th anniversary. It is a book rich in both stories and history, virtually a guide to the past 100 years of political and intellectual development in Britain. An English newspaper recently described Lord Dahrendorf as *"the most influential German in Great Britain since Prince Albert"*. That is also a compliment to

Debating with the generation of 1968: Ralf Dahrendorf

Germany itself which must indeed have a wealth of talent to spare if it can afford to make Britain a present of a mind like Dahrendorf's.

Kurt Hahn is further evidence that the interaction of theory and practice can generate a special creativity. He left Germany in the 1930s because of his ideological opposition to the Nazis and founded Gordonstoun School in Scotland, a place with its own individual character and philosophy of life. It combined a love of outdoor activities and adventure, self-discipline and service to the community with ideas on character formation and personality development. The German elements complement the British - even Salem, Hahn's first school in Germany, was based on a mixture of traditions from the two countries. Both the Duke of Edinburgh and Prince Charles were educated at Gordonstoun, although Charles, by his own account, did not enjoy the experience as much as his father.

The books they write about one another have often been cultural "eye-openers" for the British and the Germans.

Dahrendorf's standard history of the London School of Economics is typical of the intellectual intimacy in Anglo-German relations: the author with an "outside" view closes a long-standing gap in his "host country" or helps people see things from a different perspective. The achievements of German-speaking émigrés in Britain are impressive evidence of this pattern of events. Friedrich Engels' work on "The Condition of the Working Class in England" was also an "eye-opener" for the British at that time (1845). But Britain was often ahead in the process of reciprocal enlightenment - above all in biographies and monographs, a literary genre which developed among the British earlier than anywhere else.

Who wrote the most interesting book about the German Bundesbank? An Englishman, David Marsh, for many years the Bonn-based correspondent of the Financial Times: "The Bundesbank - The Bank That Rules Europe" was the provocative title of his book which appeared in 1992, just in time to give an insight into the Sterling crisis of September 1992 ... Before Marsh, former colleagues had also provoked much comment in Germany with their books on German politics. Terrence Prittie, for example, the Bonn correspondent of the Times who in 1965 wrote one of the earliest comprehensive biographies of Germany's first Federal Chancellor entitled "Adenauer". (The German version appeared in 1971 under the title: "Konrad Adenauer. Vier Epochen deutscher Geschichte"). Or Jonathan Carr, who reported from Germany for the Financial Times and the Economist, with the first monograph on Germany's fifth Federal Chancellor: "Helmut Schmidt" (1985/1993).

And no book on German ostpolitik has been quite so widely discussed in recent years as "In Europe's Name" (1995) by Timothy Garton Ash.

But who would have thought that the standard work "The Great German Riesling Wines" (1994) had been written by an Englishman, Stuart Pigott, born in London in 1960? The Germans must have been waiting for him ... At the age of 23, Pigott wrote his first specialist article for the wine magazine "Decanter", took a flat in Berncastel on the Moselle in 1989 and has been living in Berlin since 1993 where he paints and writes. In 1995, Stuart Pigott and Hugh Johnson also published a revised edition of "The Atlas of German Wines".

Stepping back into the 19th century, one immediately encounters Thomas Carlyle and his great influence on Germany, extending beyond his own time, with books like "Life of Schiller" (1825), "On Heroes, Hero-Worship and the Heroic in History" (1841) or the six-volume(!) "History of Frederick the Great" (1858-65). Carlyle expanded his studies of German culture and history into encyclopaedic dimensions, far exceeding what Thomas de Quincey had bemoaned as a deficit among the British: "German literature is at this time (...) the wealthiest in the world. It is a mine the riches of which are scarcely known by rumour in this country." But it was his ideology about the hero which later helped him to dubious fame in Germany: the National Socialists regarded him as a welcome source of ideas for their own ends. In March 1945, Adolf Hitler even read Carlyle's biography of Frederick the Great in the bunker of the Reichskanzlei in the hope that he might experience the same miracle as the Prussian King, whose luck in the Seven Years' War began to turn following the death of the Russian Empress Elizabeth (on 5.1.1762). Carlyle had embellished this chapter with particular enthusiasm.

A brief survey like this would be incomplete without mentioning George Henry Lewes and his two-volume "Life of Goethe" (1855) - the first successful Goethe biography. For a long time it adorned the book-shelves of the bourgeoisie across the Continent and Germany in particular. Germany's first Federal President, Theodor Heuss, affectionately recalled the author's name during his State visit to Britain in 1958. Speaking at a reception in London's County Hall on 22 October 1958, Heuss reminisced: "The first 'true' biographer of Goethe was an Englishman, George Henry Lewes. In my youth, his book, published in 1855, was the most widespread life history *of the man even in Germany itself." No less a person than Rainer Maria Rilke (1875-1926) was liberated by Lewes from his fear of Goethe, to whom he had previously attributed the traits of a "personality cult and Olympian inaccessibility".*

140 years later, another Englishman, the Oxford literary scholar Nicholas Boyle, has caused a stir with a new Goethe biography - especially in Germany, where reviewers were unanimous in their praise for the first volume of his magnum opus: "Goethe - The Poet in His Time" (Volume I: 1749 - 1790).

7. *Educational exchange across the Channel today*

Travel broadens the mind, or so the saying goes, even if we often carry the baggage of preconceived stereotypes around with us on our travels. That is precisely one of the problems facing the official youth and educational exchange programmes organised by Germany and Britain. People are influenced by countless factors and may already have ingrained images and preconceptions of the respective partner country which are often completely outdated (cf. also the latest poll of 10 to 16-year-olds in Britain, Chapter I, p. 20). Which traveller to Britain or Germany can honestly claim that they are totally free of biased preconceptions about the "Tommies" or the "Huns", the "Krauts" or the "hooligans", British Euro-sceptics or the *Bundesbank*?

But we have an advantage over earlier generations: the pace and mobility of our way of life enables us to jettison many of these stock images more rapidly than before. There is even reason to hope that national stereotypes will become increasingly less relevant in today's interactive world.

Many, especially young people, have practical reasons for travelling. They want to improve their knowledge of foreign languages. Command of a second working language is becoming increasingly important and could be the crucial factor in career advancement. But this immediately highlights a discrepancy. It is a well-known fact that Germans want or have to learn English, but does the opposite also apply? No, on the contrary. Just as in "Macbeth" Birnam Wood once came to Dunsinane Castle, so too the entire world seems to be descending on Britain eager to learn English, the international language. So why should the "islanders" bother with foreign languages, especially this *"awful German language"* (Mark Twain)?

The statistics speak for themselves: only about 120,000 British schoolchildren took German to GSCE level in 1995 - although this nevertheless represented an increase of 20,000 since 1991. However, there are 3.75 million pupils learning English at German schools. Approx. 80 grammar schools in Germany currently offer bilingual tuition; there are no such courses in Britain yet.

Such imbalances are also reflected in the general volume of travel between the two countries. According to the MORI opinion poll conducted in November 1994 (already quoted in the opening chapter, p.17), only 6% of the British population had visited Germany in the previous 12 months, whereas 24% of Germans had been to Britain. Tourism is potentially one of the main sources for obtaining a more realistic understanding of the way the other half lives, as it were.

But further research is required to determine what effect this "recreational migration" actually has in terms of changing stereotypes (great? moderate? insignificant?). Furthermore, the direct German-British comparison chosen by MORI is also deceptive. Germans may travel more extensively in Europe than their British cousins and regard Britain in any case as a "must" for learning English. On the other hand, very few Europeans spend as much time living and working abroad as the British.

Commonwealth countries continue to play an important role here. And in many cases they are not that "foreign" since they display familiar elements, left behind by the former colonial power - from English as the legal language to cricket and bowls...

But to come back to the situation in schools and universities. On the German side, many different organisations are involved in promoting the German language in Britain. There are currently 55 German "assistants" from the German Academic Exchange Service (DAAD) teaching at British universities and a specialist adviser looks after German at school level. The Goethe Institute offers scholarships for further education courses, assists with pedagogic liaison work and advertising campaigns and is at present collaborating with the BBC on a new language-teaching film.

"That is what pleases our womenfolk!"
What the ageing Goethe thought about the young British...

Goethe himself never visited Britain - but his employer, Duke Carl August von Weimar, had a first-class agent in London by the name of Johann Christian Hüttner, who also kept Goethe the Privy Councillor up to date on events and obtained for him all the latest literary publications. Among the up-and-coming literary geniuses of his later years, Goethe was particularly impressed by Lord Byron (whom he eventually immortalised in "Faust II" in the figure of "Euphorion" - a son of Faust and Helena). Goethe also had contact with Britain through his extensive correspondence.

But in Goethe's later years, Britain came knocking at his door - a never-ending stream of young visitors, mostly scions of noble families, who were determined to visit Weimar and pay their respects to its most famous son. (Henry Crabb Robinson, whom we have already met in connection with the founding of University College London, was among these visitors). Feigning irritation at being distracted and yet also showing great respect for his visitors and what they revealed to him about the British character, Goethe gave several detailed and amusing accounts of these encounters. For example to Eckermann on 12.3.1828:

"In some respects, the English seem to be ahead of many others (...) They arrive here at the tender age of 17, yet they do not feel ill-at-ease or embarrassed in this foreign atmosphere; on the contrary, their deportment in society is as confident and relaxed as if they were the lords of the manor everywhere they go and the whole world belonged to them.

That is also what pleases our womenfolk and how they wreak so much havoc in the hearts of our young ladies. As a German paterfamilias, who is concerned for the tranquillity of his loved ones, I often feel a tinge of dread when my daughter-in-law announces the imminent arrival of some fresh young "islander". In my mind's eye, I can already see the tears which will flow on his account when he departs. They are dangerous young people; but admittedly, this very quality of being dangerous is precisely their virtue."

"Actually, the Irish receive the greatest approbation in my house." (to Sulpice Boisserée, 12 October 1827)
"If no other nation plagues me so much with visitors (...) as the English, I also have to concede (...) that no other countryman can surpass the Englishman's splendid sense of decorum."
(to Friedrich Förster, 16 October 1829)

Each year, about 30,000 British and German schoolchildren take part in exchange programmes. These are often organised by the counties and the *Länder*, but also by municipal and rural authorities through their respective twinning arrangements. There are currently about 400 such twinning schemes in operation between the two countries (cf. also chapter IV (4)). However, that is far from sufficient to meet demand on the German side: throughout Germany there are long waiting lists of German schools seeking partners in Great Britain.

It is therefore hardly surprising to learn that the British Council is having problems keeping up with demand for language projects in Germany. English is "in", also in the new *Länder*. The British Council has recently opened a new branch in Leipzig. A series of four readings in English by contemporary British authors attracted over a thousand visitors to the Council's main office in Cologne. Asymmetrical statistics as far as the eye can see.

The picture looks slightly better at secondary school level. The "Educational Exchange Service" of the Standing Conference of the Ministers of Education of the *Länder* and the "Central Bureau for Educational Visits and Exchanges" swap about 800 German foreign-language assistants who teach German in British schools for about 500 British teachers of English in Germany - paid by their respective host country. The discrepancy in these figures is due to the simple fact that the German *Länder* have less money at their disposal.

A comparison of the number of young people in higher education produces an equally asymmetrical pattern: in 1995, there were 8,000 German students enrolled at British universities, against only 2,500 British students in Germany. The high number of Germans is actually quite surprising when one considers that by no means all of them are on free scholarships. These young Germans therefore also have to be prepared to dig into their own pockets for the "educational advantage" of a limited course of studies at a British university. It is interesting to note that foreign students do not have to pay fees if they enrol for an entire undergraduate course, only for one, two or three terms.

Of course, there are scholarships to enable the gifted to study in Britain - the DAAD currently awards 265 such annual scholarships. Together with the British Council it also runs a project-related exchange programme for research scientists. In the period 1995/96, 700 researchers from both countries were engaged in 300 such projects.

The European Union is gradually also introducing its own exchange programmes - such as SOKRATES and LEONARDO ("Youth for Europe III"), which include vocational training. Around 2,000 German "trainees" received EU sponsorship for a period of vocational and linguistic training in Britain in 1995.

Vocational training: A German-British joint venture.

One cannot expect the State to do everything. Taking this as their motto, some major British companies and their German counterparts, represented by the German Chamber of Industry and Commerce, founded the "German-British Vocational School" in London in 1988. Based on the German "dual system" of practical training and day release, this school offers a two-year course with a diploma recognised in both countries (which is important because there is still no mutual recognition of qualifications e.g. in the university sector): the "Higher National Diploma in Business and Finance" and the German "Industriekaufmann" or "Bankkaufmann". The project is also a pace-setter for further German-British economic integration (cf. Chapter III).

Exchange and migration is the name of the game. A wealth of ideas which unfortunately collide with shrinking funds. Well, at least we have the media, which claim to be able to inform us about one another as we sit at home saving money, pick up the newspaper, surf the Internet or switch on the TV... But who, one may legitimately ask, is educating the media, no longer the "hidden persuaders" (Vance Packard) they used to be. Can a drop in the ocean make a difference?

That is indeed the hope of all those who are attempting the impossible - to sow the seeds of a new media awareness of the pitfalls, complexities and profile of national characteristics. A project along these lines was launched in the External Department of the Federal Press Office in 1995: five journalists from each country will be given the chance to spend two months in the editorial office of their counterpart in Britain with the aim of looking beyond the rim of their proverbial tea-cup and discovering new opportunities for understanding, away from all the usual clichés.

German-British relations will also be boosted by three recent media projects, each presented in a different form: in print, on video and on CD-ROM. The video *"If only we all played cricket"* was produced in 1995 and has already won two international prizes. It looks at how the British and the Germans both enrich and misunderstand each other and presents a candid view of mutual prejudices and half-truths.

The video was commissioned by the Foreign Office which has also published the brochure *"Scenes from a relationship - Britain's German heritage"* by Michael Jenner, that recently appeared in both a German and an English-language version. Jenner is a true pioneering spirit. He persevered where more faint-hearted predecessors gave up and thus uncovered some astonishing traces of British-German symbiosis both past and present. This book has also benefited greatly from Jenner's research and draws on many of his findings.

Last but not least, the CD-ROM project "Stop Press", which is being sponsored jointly by the British Council, the Goethe-Institut, the German Foreign Ministry and the British Foreign Office, is breaking completely new ground. The CD-ROM will contain a bilingual data base on German-British relations and allow the possibility of interactive dialogue and surfing. The planners certainly know how to reach their target audience of 16 to 25-year-olds.

If the quality of international or bilateral relations were measured in terms of the technical perfection with which information is presented, the German-British partnership ought to be flourishing better than ever.

But you can never be too sure because there is also the human factor to consider... So traditional forms of education and further education will remain an essential ally to these new learning opportunities which technology has to offer. In this context it is important to mention one of the most significant educational moves in German-British relations in recent years - conceived in parallel: the new "Institute for German Studies" at Birmingham University, which opened in autumn 1994, and the "Centre for British Studies" at the Humboldt-Universität in Berlin, which was inaugurated by Prince Charles during his visit to Germany in November 1995.

This adds two more study centres to an already illustrious list - such as the German Historical Institute in London, the Centre for Research into Contemporary German Literature at Swansea University in Wales and the "Wiener Library" in London, with its documentation on the Nazi era. Institutions of this kind shine like light-houses in a sea of distractions and forgetfulness.

How Prince Pückler went to England in search of a bride.

Planning a trip to Britain to learn English? Or a holiday in Wales, Scotland or the Lake District? Or just a shopping expedition? All good reasons to cross the Channel. But Prince Hermann von Pückler-Muskau had a different reason: he went to England in search of a bride - prompted by a lack of funds caused by his personal passion for things English. Prince Pückler loved gardens and parks, he surrounded his family home with landscape gardening. But the cost threatened to bankrupt him. So in September 1826, at the age of 41, he left the family estate at Muskau (not far from the border between Saxony and Silesia) and his wife Lucie to "pick up" a rich heiress in England and stabilise his rocky finances. A shopping expedition of sorts... wife-shopping! How shocking!

Lucie, née von Hardenberg (the daughter of the famous Prussian State Chancellor Karl August Fürst von Hardenberg), gave her consent. In fact she went a step further and agreed to a pro forma divorce to give her Hermann a free hand among England's rich and beautiful.

But it was not to be, despite every conceivable effort on the part of our adventurer who devoted over two years intensive travelling to the search. In 1827 alone, he clocked up one thousand four hundred morning calls in just eight months! The Germans have always been thorough - and the English nobility, from the landed gentry to the aristocracy, were regarded as the wealthiest of the period. But our Prince was not too proud to go fishing in bourgeois waters - the size of the dowry was all that mattered to him.

He came close on two occasions. Miss Gibbins, a doctor's daughter from Brighton, attracted him greatly. She was beautiful and had £50,000 to offer - the lowest Pückler was prepared to go. "But oh!", he sighs in his letters to the "sweetie-pie" he had left behind ("Schnucke" was his pet-name for Lucie), Miss Gibbins was also "soulless" and perhaps just a bit "too common" by birth and upbringing. He subsequently became engaged to a jeweller's daughter, Harriet Hamlet - or perhaps one should say to her dowry: the proud sum of £200,000. But somehow Harriet caught wind of the plot - the circumstances of the Prince's divorce seemed suspicious. No proper divorce? What was going on here? Religious scruples finally persuaded the girl to withdraw her promise of marriage.

Prince Pückler needed a rich heiress to finance his passion for gardens

Pückler-Muskau became a notorious man about town in London. His morning and evening dress could easily stand comparison with "Beau" Brummel and the coterie of dandies around the profligate George IV. His letters from this period, which he published anonymously in 1830 under the mysterious title "Letters of a Deceased Man", brought him instant fame throughout Europe.

8. *Songs without words: German-British relations are alive with the sound of music...*

The Lord Mayor of London could not suppress his enthusiasm. It was the gala dinner at the Guildhall on 21 October 1958 in honour of Theodor Heuss, the German Federal President, and the speaker was in full swing:

"Your country has for generations been the cradle of music and the birthplace of musicians. As a Past Master of the Musicians' Company of the City of London, may I say how much pleasure and inspiration the compositions of your countrymen have given to millions of people in every part of the globe throughout the centuries. It is an export which has over the years bypassed international boundaries and united people of all nationalities in a common bond and universal language. For this great inheritance we are all most deeply grateful and appreciative."

The words were friendly, full of admiration and like music to the ears of the German visitors. The first State visit to Britain by a German Federal President since the war was overshadowed by critical reminiscences and undisguised reservations in some quarters of the host country. There were still too many obstacles, too many painful memories. But with these few sentences the Lord Mayor of London diverted attention in a completely different direction - to the universal and timeless allure of German culture: music.

This was not a tactical compliment but the expression of a long-held view in Britain. It echoed a comment made by a former Prime Minister, Arthur James Balfour, back in 1904:

"If the music of all other nations were destroyed, we should be many masterpieces the poorer, but musical life would go on. If Germany's music were destroyed, musical life itself would cease."

Today, as we approach the end of the 20th century, Britain has long since repaid this esteem - through the riches of its own music culture, linked in a fruitful exchange with German musical tradition.

British conductors are now a permanent feature of German opera houses and concert halls while the renowned Bavarian State Opera has enjoyed a new heyday since Peter Jonas was appointed Director in 1994. Four conductors stand out in particular:

Sir Colin Davis who led the Bavarian Radio Symphony Orchestra and taught a new generation of musicians at the Musikhochschule in Munich for nine years until 1995; Sir John Eliot Gardiner, who was principal conductor of North German Radio for many years and co-directed the Handel Festival in Göttingen with Nicholas McGegan; Sir Neville Marriner, whose name was linked with the Stuttgart Radio Symphony Orchestra over a long period; and last but not least, Simon Rattle, Head of the Birmingham Symphony Orchestra, who is a regular guest conductor with the Berlin Philharmonic Orchestra and in autumn 1995 gave an impressive performance of all Beethoven's symphonies in Frankfurt's *"Alte Oper"*. (The *Frankfurter Allgemeine Zeitung* wrote at the time that the *Alte Oper* could *"record (this event) as a glorious page in its annals"*).

The maestro:
Ludwig van Beethoven

The "Beethoven marathon" held in Bonn in December 1995 had a British beginning: with Sir Edward Heath as introductory speaker and Roger Norrington as conductor. Norrington had been signed on with the BBC Symphony Orchestra and the BBC Choir for Beethoven's "Missa Solemnis" - that too a great compliment to British music.

But why stop at classical music? Are today's musicals not true successors to what classical music was originally, before we started idealising it and putting it on pedestals - namely, entertainment? This leads one directly to a name like Sir Andrew Lloyd Webber. Not only do the Germans find his musicals irresistible, they have even built special theatres for two of them: in Bochum for "Starlight Express" and in Wiesbaden for "Sunset Boulevard".

The "Philharmonic Society" and Beethoven: a great symphony - and much warmth of feeling...

Two attempts, in 1815 and 1817, failed. Then finally, in 1822, success. Ludwig van Beethoven promised to write a symphony commissioned by the "Philharmonic Society of London" within the space of a year. The fee: 50 Pounds Sterling. The piece was not actually delivered until April 1824 and Beethoven personally signed the receipt for his fee. It was the Ninth Symphony... On the copy sent to London he noted: "Great symphony written for the Philharmonic Society in London by Ludwig van Beethoven".

Just a few years later, news of Beethoven's serious financial hardship reached London. A donation of 100 Pounds was promptly dispatched to the composer in Vienna. It was the year of Beethoven's death. Severely ill, he wrote an emotional letter of thanks to London saying that the Society's generosity "touched my innermost soul". He promised a new symphony "the sketches of which are lying on my desk". Eight days later, on 26 March 1827, he was dead.

A generation later, Felix Mendelssohn-Bartholdy repaid Beethoven's debt of gratitude in his own way. In 1844, the conductor from Leipzig, back in London once again and responsible for the "Philharmonic", used his great administrative skills to improve the Society's reserves by 400 Pounds, thus wiping out an alarming deficit at a single stroke. Incidentally, on 27 May 1844, Mendelssohn presented the then 13-year-old Joseph Joachim in London as the new violin virtuoso - playing Beethoven's violin concerto.

The "Philharmonic Society of London", founded in 1813, received its Royal Assent in 1913. It is Europe's second oldest concert-giving society after the Leipziger Gewandhaus.

But box-office success is not the only criterion. Karlheinz Stockhausen's music is well-received by a knowledgeable British audience; the Berlin director Peter Stein made a name for himself with several productions for the Welsh National Opera Company in Cardiff; as did Pina Bausch with her Wuppertal Dance Theatre. On the other hand, the works of Benjamin Britten, Michael Tippet or Peter Maxwell Davies are an established part of the contemporary repertoire in Germany; and it was Sir Thomas Beecham who brought the music of the German-born composer Fritz ("Frederick") Theodor Albert Delius (1862-1934) to British audiences. This intensive give and take found perhaps its finest expression in the partnership between Dietrich Fischer-Dieskau and his piano accompanist Gerald Moore.

The great British voices of this century include the contralto Kathleen Ferrier and the tenor Peter Pears, the latter unforgettable in the première of Benjamin Britten's "Peter Grimes" (1945). The mezzo soprano Caroline Watkinson and the baritone Bryon Terfel are their internationally acclaimed successors. Terfel, born in North Wales in 1965, has already appeared on stages throughout the world, most recently as Leporollo at the 1995 Salzburg Festival. But he is also becoming indispensable as a *Lieder*-singer. His recording of Schubert's "Swan Song" (SAIN, North Wales, SCDC 4035), with its combination of powerful and tender musicality, has received enthusiastic reviews.

The British are also proud of their long history of musical criticism, even if present-day practitioners would probably be more reserved than George Bernard Shaw, who wrote:

"Music is a European, if not global language. This language is my mother tongue. I may understand nothing of Klopstock or Herder, but of Bach, Haydn, Mozart, Beethoven, Wagner and Richard Strauss I understand more than most Germans."

"That is quite a claim, but it is surely not without some justification",

Rudolf W. Leonhardt commented with laconic approval on Shaw's statement. Shaw's enthusiasm for Wagner, eloquently defended in his essay "The Perfect Wagnerite", reached heights which Germans might almost find embarrassing today.

Britain, Germany and music - of course it all began with Georg Friedrich Händel - sorry, George Frederick Handel - (1685-1759), who was born in Germany but effortlessly transmuted into England's most famous composer of all times... Let us put it this way: Handel was a great European who brought the musical traditions of his time together to a unique climax.

The newly appointed Electoral Conductor of Hanover came to London in 1711 at the invitation of Queen Anne, who had offered the famous musician a handsome monthly allowance in return. Shortly after his arrival, Handel gave the première in London of his opera "Rinaldo", which he had composed in just a fortnight. It was a triumphant occasion. It is hardly surprising that he was in no particular hurry to return to Hanover - much to the annoyance of his German employer, Georg Ludwig von Braunschweig-Lüneburg, the Elector of Hanover. But Parliament in London removed all the composer's worries. Three years later it placed this German Prince on the British throne as George I. Handel did not have to return to Hanover - Hanover came to him in London!

Whereas George I remained a stranger to his new home country and never learned to speak English, his "double" subject Händel was soon in his element. He dropped the *umlaut* in his name, adopted British nationality in 1726 and set about making London a major centre of European music. Under his direction, the Royal Opera House Covent Garden experienced its first great season in 1734.

London's freshly acquired musical reputation prompted Bach's youngest son, Johann Christian, to move from Milan to London in 1762 - a step which ushered in his mature creative phase and produced the symphonic works which later exerted such a powerful influence on Mozart.

**Great Britain, a "country with no musical tradition":
one of the oldest clichés around.**

*It is an inherent feature of stereotypes that they are based on judgements almost
entirely removed from reality - like the claim that there is no tradition of music and
musicality in Britain. Is that really the case? What about the festivals in
Glyndebourne, Aldeburgh, Bath and Edinburgh, London's opera and music scene,
the Welsh National Opera, the country's symphony orchestras and choirs.
Everywhere one looks one finds evidence of a music culture which could not have
grown up without the enthusiastic support of the British people. It is not for nothing
that Lord Yehudi Menuhin, Sir George Solti and Alfred Brendel chose Britain as
their adopted country.*

*The German adage about "the islands without music" originates, like most of our
mutual stereotypes, from the 19th century and the period of increasing rivalry
between the two countries. "It is a great pity that the English nation is so unmusical.
Never mind! Tonight you shall hear something...", a German trombone-player, the
"Herr Professor", condescendingly boasts to his English interlocutor. Katherine
Mansfield's first collection of short stories "In a German Pension" (1911), from which
this scene is taken, is a treasure-trove of such prejudices which the author illuminates
with subtle sarcasm.*

*But we are free to believe the evidence of our own ears. And music is not
restricted to so-called "serious music". We live in an age with a broader concept of
"culture" which grants us access to composers such as John Lennon and Andrew
Lloyd Webber as well as to other forms of musical entertainment.*

Handel made the same discovery as those who fled to England to
escape Nazi persecution 200 years later: by immersing himself in the
life of his host country, the immigrant opens up new horizons and is
spurred on to make breakthroughs in his chosen subject. Handel, for
example, harnessed Britain's budding choral culture, gave it a fresh
challenge in the form of his oratorios and thus established its
European status.

And also its popularity in Britain. After the première of the "Messiah" in Dublin (1742), the London performance developed into an overwhelming tribute to the composer. At the opening notes of the "Hallelujah Chorus", King George II and his entourage rose to their feet and gave him an enthusiastic ovation.

During his two visits to England in 1791/92 and 1794/95, Joseph Haydn was also spellbound by Handel's oratorios which he first heard in London. His own great compositions in this genre, both the "Creation" and the "Seasons", although not completed until after his return to Germany, can be traced back to English influences, namely the magnificent performances of Handel. In addition, the twelve "London Symphonies" were testimony to the artistic maturity which Haydn achieved in Britain. Four decades later, the British oratorical tradition founded by Handel gained a further master in the shape of Mendelssohn.

In a review of the London "Proms", the music critic Rick Jones neatly summed up Handel's achievement:

"The great German émigré observed Britain with the objective eye of the outsider. He saw things big. He envisaged fantastic royal pomp and heard heavenly choirs. Where Purcell's royal music had been intimate and composed for cathedral choir-sized outfits with small palace chapels in mind, Handel's oratorios were grand and conceived for huge forces of instrumentalists and singers in such modern architectural wonders as St. Paul's Cathedral." (*Evening Standard*, 15.9.1995)

Felix Mendelssohn-Bartholdy (1809-1847) fell in love with Britain on his first visit in 1829. The feelings soon became mutual. He was particularly enamoured of Scotland. He crossed the Channel ten times during his short life, often for prolonged sojourns.

We all know and love the "Scottish Symphony", the "Hebrides" overture and "Midsummer Night's Dream". But it was the oratorical culture, brought to the European consciousness by Handel, which was to link Mendelssohn and the British in a very special way. *"The country with a long tradition of choirs had produced no outstanding composers since Handel and welcomed Mendelssohn with open arms."* (Uwe Krämer in the CD programme notes to Mendelssohn's "Elijah" - "maestro", M2YK 46455)

The Leipzig Gewandhaus conductor came to Britain with the best credentials for this task. At a performance with the Zeltersche Singakademie in Berlin on 14 April 1829, he had rescued Bach's "St. Matthew Passion" from oblivion one hundred years after it was written, instilling new interest in this genre in Germany and beyond. His own first oratorio "St. Paul" was a great success in Düsseldorf in 1836. Mendelssohn himself conducted the English première in Liverpool in September of the same year. In the period 1840-46, he paid almost annual visits to England where his equally enthusiastic and knowledgeable fans warmly received "their Handel".

George Frederick Handel: of course he was an Englishman - wasn't he?

How Victoria and Albert once unintentionally drove their dear friend Felix to the point of exhaustion ...

Queen Victoria and her Prince Consort were great music-lovers: they sang, played skilful piano duets and repeatedly invited Mendelssohn-Bartholdy to Buckingham Palace to make music with them on the piano or the organ. They particularly liked the "Lieder ohne Worte" ("Songs without Words"), some of which Mendelssohn played for the first time in their presence, much to the royal couple's delight. Mendelssohn himself had a genuinely high opinion of his hosts' musical abilities.

Queen Victoria, untiring diarist that she was, recorded a delightful episode from her first meeting with the then 33-year-old musician on 16.6.1842. Mendelssohn had just finished playing and asked his audience to pick any theme at random on which he would then improvise. Victoria describes in her diary how he tackled the subjects proposed: "We gave him two, 'Rule Britannia' and the Austrian National Anthem (...) At one moment he played the Anthem with his right hand and 'Rule Britannia' as a bass with his left. Poor Mendelssohn was quite exhausted when he had done playing."

There were no such acrobatics scheduled at his next visit on 30.5.1844. But Victoria speaks of her continued pleasure in his company. To quote from her diary once again: "We went to the Drawing Room to see Mendelssohn and talked to him for some time. He played to us beautifully - music from the 'Midsummer Night's Dream' and two of his 'Lieder ohne Worte'. He is such an agreeable and clever man and his countenance beams with intelligence and genius." And again on 10 June 1844: "We played some of the 'Lieder ohne Worte' which Mendelssohn has kindly arranged for us as duets..."

... and why Mendelssohn has enjoyed undiminished popularity in Great Britain since Victoria's time.

Mendelssohn's great success in Victorian England and to this day is characteristic of the then fertile relations between Germany and Britain. Peter Lamb summed it up in these words: "The handsome young German had so many attributes that Victorians admired - personal charm, enormous drive and industry, great organising ability and a Jewish background that was totally acceptable in London where Nathan Rothschild was a leading financier and Disraeli was to become Victoria's Prime Minister. This was in marked contrast to his own country where the young Mendelssohn was once spat upon by a so-called nobleman and called a 'Jew-boy' (...) His private life seems to have been as well-ordered as was his music. No breath of scandals sullies his memory."

(Programme notes to a CD recording of the "Songs without Words" - "hypérion", CDA 66221/2)

In Victorian England, Chopin and Schumann were regarded as "too modern and emotionally somewhat unstable", Lamb continues. Brahms and Wagner were scarcely known, whereas Mendelssohn's piano and orchestral style "was, in contrast, well-mannered and likeable within its expressive limits of tender appeal and exhilarating spirits - spirits which never descended into tasteless exuberance. (...) It is clear that however much opinions and tastes fluctuate, Mendelssohn's art will continue to appeal to the Anglo-Saxon temperament."

The darling of the Royal Family and the Victorians: Felix Mendelssohn-Bartholdy

Mendelssohn's oratorical festivals generated even greater enthusiasm in England than the earlier performances given by Handel. Consequently, it was only natural for both sides of this fruitful 'elective affinity', that Mendelssohn should be commissioned to write a new oratorio, this time by the Birmingham Music Festival. For four whole days, from 25-28 August 1846, Birmingham was to host a music festival dominated by mass choirs, with Haydn's "Creation", Handel's "Messiah", parts of Beethoven's "Missa Solemnis" - and the première of Mendelssohn's "Elijah".

During the performance there was a silence and profound emotion which virtually made one forget the presence of the 2,000 people in the hall - that at least is how the celebrated guest later recorded it himself. The audience called for numerous encores and the entire scene from the beginning of the rain miracle to the end of the first part had to be repeated. (Eberhard Rudolph in the CD programme notes to "Elijah", Philips Classics, 420 106-2.) The size of the choir at the "Music Festival" was unique: 396 singers, comprising 204 sopranos, 60 contraltos, 60 tenors and 72 basses. (At the previous largest choral performance, the Handel memorial concert held in Westminster Abbey on the eve of the anniversary of Handel's 100th birthday in 1784, there had been "only" 300 voices.)

While still in Birmingham, the composer received an official letter of thanks from Buckingham Palace. Mendelssohn was hailed as *"the Elijah of the new art"*, who *"through genius and study"* was able to prevail against the false priests and *"accustom the ear once more to the pure tone of lawful harmony."*

"Lawful harmony" - has there ever been a more apt expression for the aspirations of the *Biedermeier*, of the early Victorians, than the name Mendelssohn?

How Carl Halle became Sir Charles Hallé
and a stroke of luck for Manchester ...

Händel dropped his umlaut. Carl Halle - not exactly a typically British thing to do - gave himself a French acute accent. The knighthood, more the English style, came later. So is it that easy for Germans to become British and famous sons of their adopted country? No. The process of German-British symbiosis (nowadays one would say "synergy") is much more complex, although there are certain patterns of a recurring nature. One astonishing and quintessential point stands out above all others: the two "cousins" seem so naturally matched in some areas that one wonders how they ever came to wage war against one another...

Carl Halle, born in the Westphalian town of Hagen in 1819, a pianist and piano-teacher, came to England - like many liberals of his generation - for political reasons. Things became too hot for him on the Continent during the upheavals of the 1840s, so he made his way to London via Paris in March 1848. That same year, he accepted an invitation to Manchester - a city renowned not only for the "Industrial Revolution" (Friedrich Engels) but also for its considerable music culture. Hallé, as he now called himself, helped raise this to international level. He became conductor of the "Gentlemen's Concerts", founded the "St. Cecilia Society", gave piano recitals in numerous English towns and later on the Continent, edited classical piano works, worked as a guest conductor throughout the Commonwealth - and founded Manchester's Hallé Orchestra, the oldest permanent orchestra in Britain.

The idea was triggered by the Manchester Music and Theatre Festival of 1857, for which Hallé had specially assembled a symphony orchestra, due to be dissolved when the festival was over. However, Hallé decided to make it a permanent fixture. On 30 January 1858, the orchestra gave its first concert in Manchester's Free Trade Hall. This marked the beginning of an illustrious career which has been continued by Hallé's successors - conductors such as Hans Richter, Hamilton Harty, John Barbirolli.

Charles Hallé maintained friendly contact with the music and art-loving royal family. The Queen invited him several times to Buckingham Palace and Osborne House on the Isle of Wight. He became a naturalised British subject in 1852, was knighted in 1888 and died in 1895 during a concert tour of South Africa. The Royal Manchester College of Music, which he established in 1893, is still one of Britain's most renowned colleges of music.

Another German
adopts Britain:
Sir Charles Hallé

The Economy:
money knows no bounds - nor does
German-British co-operation

I. Britain as a place to invest - more attractive than ever

John Bridge, head of the Northern Development Corporation in Newcastle-on-Tyne, rubs his hands with glee: *"This will give the North-East a tremendous boost"*. His colleague John Morrison from Newcastle's Chamber of Commerce agrees: *"These jobs are the best thing we could have hoped for. They will really help us make a fresh start."*

Can this really be the Germans they are talking about - the goose-stepping, sunbed-occupying Germans of the cartoons? No, obviously not those Germans. Nor "the Germans" in general. But rather Germans from Munich, from Siemens to be precise, the technology corporation which is now providing some confidence and a future for northern England. In August 1995, Siemens announced that the planned semi-conductor plant of the next generation - the generation of smart logic chips - would be located at the Hadrian Business Park in North Tyneside. This represents an investment of two billion Marks and jobs for 1,500 people, in addition to the 10,000 which have already been created by Siemens subsidiaries and holding companies. No sign here of the Huns and their spiked helmets...

Remarkable things happen in today's international division of labour. Among other examples, German industry has discovered Great Britain as one of its most important investment locations: in 1994, the United Kingdom overtook the USA as Germany's number one investment partner with 14.7% of total German investments going to Britain compared with 10% in 1993.

And the trend is upward. The figure of DM 3.5 billion for 1994 appeared small just a year later. The German-British Chamber of Commerce in London puts German investment for 1995 at DM 10.6 billion - an absolute record. Britain also occupies a leading position if one takes an overall look at the years since the Berlin Wall came down. Money writes its own history.

After the Americans and the Japanese, German companies are gradually becoming the largest foreign investors in Britain. 150,000 British jobs already depend on German subsidiaries and holdings.

Vorsprung durch Technik (I):
What Sir William Siemens, Audi, Steffi Graf and Bosch have in common.

In the 19th century, it was common practice for countries to send their young business talents abroad for training in what was then the leading industrial nation: Great Britain. Friedrich Engels was packed off to Manchester by his father to study the local textile industry. Julius Reuter went to London in 1851 to found his news agency. And Wilhelm Siemens (1823-1863), one of the ten Siemens brothers, was also curious to discover the capital of the Empire, where he arrived in 1843 with nothing in his pocket but a patent for an electro-plating invention, which he sold for 1,600 Pounds Sterling.

He returned to London in 1844 with more inventions in his luggage - one of them, the "chronometric governor", won a prize at the Great Exhibition of 1851 - and opened his business just off the Strand in 1852. Business was so good that William Siemens, as he now called himself, was able to start up a small factory near Lambeth Bridge in 1858 manufacturing products such as refrigerating machines, pyrometers, ohmmeters etc. At the same time, he continued work on his regenerative gas furnace, which he had invented in 1857 and which was to revolutionise the entire field of pyrotechnics.

Siemens was a dab hand at "Vorsprung durch Technik". A total of 1,13 patents were registered in his name. In 1870, he teamed up with his brother Carl to form the "Siemens Brothers". They were soon commissioned to supply electric lighting to prominent places in London: the Royal Albert Hall, the British Museum, the Thames Embankment, Waterloo Bridge, the Savoy Theatre. It was like the repayment of an old German debt: in 1827, an English company had installed the first gas lighting equipment in Berlin... The construction of the telegraph line from London to Calcutta, 11,500 kilometres, was also the work of William Siemens. Queen Victoria knighted him in 1883. He died later that same year.

In 1994, the "Sir William Siemens Medal" was inaugurated - an award scheme aimed at encouraging young British people to develop their interest in science and technology.

The slogan "Vorsprung durch Technik" (cf. also Chapter II/2), used by marketing strategists in the 80s to promote Audi cars in Britain, must go down in advertising history as a stroke of genius. The exotic "aura" was intensified by deliberately leaving the text in German; the message behind the text described a quality which foreigners identified with Germans but with which Germans themselves could also identify. (For more about this, see David Head's book: "Made in Germany - The Corporate Identity of a Nation", 1992).

Vorsprung durch Technik:
Steffi Graf

When Steffi Graf first won Wimbledon in 1988, her sponsors Opel put out whole-page adverts under the motto MADE IN GERMANY, printed in huge letters above a photo of the tennis star and the long version of the Audi slogan: "In Wimbledon Steffi Graf has proven once again: reliability, flawless technique and precision lead to the greatest successes. We at Opel agree." So even Steffi at Wimbledon was paraded as a textbook example of "Vorsprung durch Technik".

"In London, Bosch communications go underground." Bosch-Telecom has been using this slogan since 1995 to point out that the Central Line is now equipped with the company's latest digital communications system: "Dikos" - improved communication between the individual stations and improved options for responding to any kind of emergency. Vorsprung durch Technik - now in the London underground too?

There's no business like business - much to the delight of the Chancellor of the Exchequer. But one man's joy is another man's sorrow. British investment in Germany is rather meagre by comparison: DM 600 million to be precise (1994). Admittedly, the British are not alone in their reluctance to invest in Germany. This reluctance is only less apparent in the field of fixed assets and shares held by British and German companies in the other country: DM 23.1 billion in Britain, DM 17.8 billion in Germany (figures for end of 1993).

There are many factors which make Britain attractive to German investors. In the case of Siemens, it was a "market proximity" analysis which favoured England - Europe's third largest market for semi-conductors and the sixth largest in the world. The Munich corporation is thus continuing the global expansion of its chip-manufacturing plants. The Newcastle factory will be the fifth, the other locations being Regensburg, Villach (Austria), Paris and Dresden. There are also assembly plants in Singapore and Malaysia with a further plant planned for the USA.

But Britain has genuine location advantages to offer German companies (and not just them):

- lower wages and non-wage costs,
- more flexible working hours and shift regulations,
- investment grants for needy regions,
- low corporation tax,
- lower profit tax and - an important factor,
- shorter approval and licensing periods.

A comparison of just four of the above points shows: wages in Britain are about half those in Germany, non-wage costs about 67%; taxation of retained profit accounts for approx. 62% in Germany, 33% in Britain; licensing procedures currently take about 12 months in Germany on average, about 7 months in Britain, if not less. The authorities in

Newcastle had in fact promised to approve the new Siemens plant within 21 days - they met this self-imposed deadline with 2 days to spare ...

It would be quite wrong to assume that all this has been put on just to improve German-British relations. We are not talking philanthropy here. The simple fact is rather that competition for investment and labour markets is growing tougher within the European Union and, thanks to the rationalisation of its cost structure in the Thatcher years and other streamlining measures, Britain now leads many of its European competitors in both deadlines and conditions. This advantage is too obvious for German industry not to exploit it - together with other similarly attractive foreign investment locations. Even more so as the home market is increasingly plagued by the problems outlined above.

But even if this is merely an inevitable consequence of globalisation, of international economic interdependence, it can certainly do German-British relations no harm. For money and work are not abstract quantities. They can create new links between people and, in the long term, change traditional patterns of behaviour and attitudes between individual members of the European family. In the Midlands, the north-west of England or South Wales, where increased German economic activity has created new jobs, people may in fact begin to change their attitude towards "the Germans" and reject the shop-worn image presented by the popular media.

At first, there may be little sign of such change. Not surprisingly, the tank is still the most popular stereotype used to portray the advance of German capital on the British market. But in its tracks, so to speak, one hopes a new way of thinking will gradually emerge and transform such set images into a more light-hearted reminder of outmoded attitudes.

The most spectacular German take-overs in recent years (and comparable in financial terms with the Siemens investment) included the acquisition of Rover by BMW (£ 920 million), the take-over of the London Investment Bank Morgan Grenfell by the Deutsche Bank

(£950 million) and the acquisition of the pharmaceutical division of the Boots chain of chemists by BASF (£ 850 million).

In 1994, the Deutsche Bank even started transferring its entire investment banking and shares business to London, a development which had a strong influence on other German financial institutions. By acquiring Kleinwort Benson, the Dresdner Bank obtained their own London bank in order to concentrate their capital market transactions in a similar way to the "German Morgan Grenfell". Thornton Fund Management was then added by the Dresdner Bank for asset management. Plans by the Commerzbank to take over Smith New Court fell through, but in spring 1995 it was able to announce that it had purchased the reputable London investment company Jupiter Tyndall plc.

London and Frankfurt: two centres of an ellipse ...

Frankfurt may have won the competition for the seat of the future European Central Bank; its precursor, the European Monetary Institute (EMI), is already established there. But London's position as a banking metropolis and an international financial centre remains unshaken. The volume of global investment and financial transactions conducted in London has actually increased in recent years. Many US giants, such as Merrill Lynch, like doing business via the City. There are more than 500 foreign banks and banking houses located in London - compared to Frankfurt's 258, of which 188 are only small representations anyway.

At the end of 1994, there were 3,189 shares officially quoted on the London Stock Exchange; Frankfurt paled in comparison with only 875. And the gulf is widening. How so? Well, the cautious Germans have never been very fond of shares as a form of investment. That may change as German banks step up their investment activity in the City. Frankfurt can only compete with London in the field of fixed-interest securities, and it overtakes London in government bonds: 7,693 listed in Frankfurt, 6,414 in London (figures also for end of 1994).

... but where did all these private City bankers come from?

Many of Britain's commercial banks and private financial institutions are of German or German-Jewish origin. They date back to North German banking families who shifted their trading business to London when it was the centre of the British colonial Empire. Hambro, for example - the name arose from a misspelling of Hamburg in 1779 when a Copenhagen official had intended to issue the Hamburg merchant Calmer Levy with a trading licence in the name of his home town. A branch of the family later founded the "Bank Hambro" in London. Nor should one forget the Rothschild family. Nathan Mayer von Rothschild, one of five sons of the Frankfurt bank's original founder, Mayer Anselm Rothschild, went first to Manchester in 1798, before eventually establishing his business in London in 1803 at the age of 26. He supported Wellington in his campaigns against Napoleon and allegedly made an enormous killing on the London Stock Exchange as a result of his early knowledge of Napoleon's defeat at Waterloo. An interesting case of insider trading... Nathan's sons then continued the business under the name "N.M. Rothschild & Sons". Kleinwort also has its roots in Hamburg while the banking house of Schroder came from Quakenbrück. Finally, the famous name of Warburg, the great merchant dynasty from Hamburg (founded in the Westphalian town of Warburg). Siegmund Warburg and the still inexhaustible Henry Grunfeld fled to London from the Nazis and founded their merchant bank S.G. Warburg there in 1946. And then there is the now infamous name of Baring. The family, originally from Bremen, first transferred its banking business to Exeter and later, in the 19th century, to London - until a certain Nick Leeson in Singapore gambled with the fortunes of the merchant bank Barings - and drove it to bankruptcy.

Germany's regional banks did not want to be left behind. The Westdeutsche Landesbank (West-LB) in Düsseldorf was the first of them to enter the investment banking sector with its own London subsidiary, "West Merchant-Bank". It intends shortly to increase its staff from 350 to 600 employees to deal with its international share-trading and loan transactions.

With so much restructuring in the financial business sector going on , it is noticeable that the local British expert often, indeed usually, retains or is given authority over his German counterpart - even if the latter continues to operate from his base in Germany. The intention being to remain or become British, although German money is involved. London as a financial centre has a global appeal and that is precisely what the German banks are after in the tough battle for investment markets.

As with all transitions, this causes endemic problems, of which three stand out. First, the cut-throat practice of poaching staff. This annoys many of the competitors whose personnel resources are "tapped" in this manner. Second, disappointed faces among some of the company's own experienced German staff who see their independence in Frankfurt undermined by London-based superiors. No doubt they are all nice guys, but much younger and with the drive and ambition of high-fliers, motivated perhaps by the earlier specialisation offered by British banks, in contrast to the German all-purpose banks. Last but not least, the question of how to reconcile these different trading practices, culled as they are from American, British and German business traditions, under the roof of a single investment house.

So the transitional phase encountered teething trouble. No matter. Now is the time to expand in a promising market and make up for lost time. London, with its venturesome financial culture, is transforming the more security-minded Germans or at least steering them in a new direction. Everyone is trying to get into the fast lane, mobilising German investments. And none too soon, either. For what will happen to the millions of Deutschmarks soon to be inherited by the sons and daughters of Germany's first post-war generation? Who will take care of their investment needs? Nota bene, following the collapse of Barings, all investment houses have promised their customers new security nets in the delicate dealings with capital markets, shares, loans and derivatives.

The list of German business activities in Britain ranges from the elite level to the no less significant small and medium-sized companies. Among the large players in the field, Bosch of Stuttgart first put its faith in the improved prospects for the British car market in the late 80s and made a major investment in South Wales, its biggest so far outside Germany. They built a production plant in Miskin/Cardiff for engine components, specifically for a newly developed high-performance alternator. A Bosch-designed fuel pump is also assembled here, all according to the latest principles of "lean management". For South Wales, a region hard hit by recession, Bosch brings a similar boost of hope as Siemens does with its planned chip plant for Newcastle.

Vorsprung durch Technik (II): British design helps Schumacher to victory - BA helps the Germans to cheaper flights.

Now that Michael Schumacher, twice Formula I world racing champion, has switched to the Ferrari stables, the British can be released from their obligation to make understatements: without the Benetton technology centre in Enstone, Chipping Norton (Oxfordshire), without its 190 marketing experts, co-ordinators and technicians, the German racing champion from Kerpen near Cologne would not have achieved his world titles.

Hidden away deep in the English countryside, on the edge of the idyllic Cotswolds, lie the headquarters of Benetton Formula Ltd, production site of the 1994 and 1995 winning model "Mild Seven Benetton Renault B195 Formula I". The Whiteways Technical Centre occupies an area measuring 17 acres, high-tech with a high-efficiency look, everything logically arranged and perfectly integrated. The plant was built in 1993 to work on an engine supplied by Renault. The rest is British workmanship, skill in designing and styling racing cars and experience in their manufacture. An engineering feat you would expect more in the realms of aerospace. Nowadays, Grand Prix cars are built to specifications which push technology to the very limit.

British workmanship makes Michael Schumacher King of the Road

But Benetton Formula Ltd is a European joint venture: Italian enterprise, French engine technology, British engineering expertise - and for two years a German driver who steered the team to victory.

If one could measure the quality of German-British relations by the number of flights offered daily by the two national airlines British Airways (BA) and Lufthansa between the two countries and their major destinations, one would have to award top marks. No other European countries can compare.

But partnership is only one side of the coin - the other is competition. In 1994, Lufthansa acquired a 38.4% share in Business Air, the airline which hit the headlines in 1993 with its first "Bank Shuttle" between London's City Airport and Frankfurt/Main. Through Business Air, Lufthansa has also acquired a new regional *centre in Manchester with connecting routes to Scotland and Wales.*

For its part, British Airways took over Delta Air in 1992 and founded Deutsche BA, a new independent airline in which the parent company holds a 49.5% share. Deutsche BA now "shadows" Lufthansa on almost all German domestic routes. And how. In summer 1996, the Federal Government gave Deutsche BA the lucrative contract to carry civil servants on the Bonn-Berlin shuttle. In view of the forthcoming transfer of government business to the new capital Berlin, this contract will be worth a penny or two.

With its new flights on foreign routes Deutsche BA has also introduced more price competition - to the benefit of customers who can now fly to Moscow, for example, on Deutsche BA for about one third less than before, as long as one is not deterred by the stopover in Berlin.

Incidentally, with its maiden flight to Leipzig in March 1992, British Airways was the first foreign carrier to open up a route between England and Saxony.

Four further examples from a long list may serve to illustrate the diversity of German investments in Britain:

- **Environment** - The Birmingham subsidiary of the Düsseldorf Lindemann group has become the largest British manufacturer of special machines for recycling industrial and household waste.

- **Telecommunications** - The VEBA group has taken a 10% shareholding in Cable & Wireless, with the intention of further options, in order to improve its position on Europe's future deregulated telecommunications market. (By the same token, British Telecom has recently concluded a deal with the German VIAG to help it compete with Deutsche Telekom in Germany.)

- **Food** - Through its Shropshire subsidiary, the milk products chain of Alois Müller now controls 25% of the British yoghurt market.
- **Utility vehicles** - In 1989, the German fork-lift truck manufacturers Linde merged with the English firm Lansing-Bagnall to create what is now the world's leading company in this sector, "Lansing Linde". An investment of £ 45 million was immediately injected into the manufacturing plant at Basingstoke in Hampshire. Five years later, the German firm Jungheinrich followed Linde's example by acquiring Britain's second largest fork-lift truck manufacturers, Lancer Boss.

What is the secret of the entrepreneurial synergy between the two countries? In an interview with the Financial Times in 1995, the former President of the Confederation of British Industries (CBI), Sir Bryan Nicholson, spoke of *"the complementary factor"* and said that the different business cultures of the British and the Germans mutually enhance and reinforce one other. *"You get the best deal if you combine the best of both"*, is how John Towers, chief executive of the BMW-owned Rover works, put it in the same interview with the *Financial Times*.

Long-term German investment strategies, with their emphasis on training, on employee co-determination, on *"assertion, precision in detail and work discipline"* (John Towers). These are the German strengths. Conversely, the Germans themselves benefit from the lower production costs in Britain, greater British expertise in some high-tech areas such as telecommunications and above all from greater flexibility at the work place and in the production process itself. Sir Bryan draws an optimistic conclusion:

"German companies' emphasis on employee consultation has helped speed change towards more constructive UK labour relations".

But there is another factor, perhaps the most important one: German management generally endeavours to maintain the independence of its British acquisition, whilst both sides attempt to learn as much as possible from each other.

Bernd Pischetsrieder, chairman of the executive board of BMW, stressed this particular point during the first joint management meeting of Rover and BMW at the British Motor Industry Heritage Centre in Gaydon on 18 April 1994, shortly after Rover was taken over by the Bavarian company. In so doing, Pischetsrieder made a careful distinction between BMW Rolls Royce, which merged into a single company for aircraft engines in 1992, and Rover BMW respectively:

"Unlike BMW Rolls Royce, BMW and Rover will not move forward along a single path, but on two parallel ones leading to a common goal. Our brands and our companies are to remain independent. On the market and in the eyes of the public, the two partners will each demonstrate their own strength."

This was welcome news at the time for Rover and some wary observers in Birmingham and the rest of Britain. BMW has kept its promise: the British company, home of such famous makes as Austin, Morris and MG, Trident, Landrover, Riley and Rover, enjoy even greater independence under the aegis of BMW capital than under its former owners, Honda and British Aerospace. To quote John Towers again:

"I cannot think of a scenario made in Britain that would have resulted in the investment we have today. We have a greater chance of prospering and being successful under BMW than under any other circumstances that were being deliberated."

The University of Birmingham obviously saw it the same way. In July 1996, they awarded Bernd Pischetsrieder an honorary doctorate in recognition of his achievements.

spotlight 35

"Jaeger" and "Doc Martens":
Even the clothes we wear speak of the German-British symbiosis.

"How do you do?" the British ask, expecting nothing more in response than "How do you do?" But in Germany, a similar question about your well-being may be answered with a comprehensive report on your current state of health. For health is a favourite topic of the Germans and provides the background for two of the most astonishing stories in German-British trading relations.

Questions of health fascinated the ailing naturalist and physiologist Professor Gustav Jäger from Stuttgart. Observing soldiers who returned sick from the Franco-Prussian War of 1870/1, he noted that they had brought some of their problems on themselves by wearing the wrong clothing - cotton underwear and other plant fibre material on top. Animals, Jäger argued, fared much better because of their natural covering of wool or hair. For Jäger the conclusion was obvious: humans should also wear woollen clothing! Wool insulates the body against extremes of temperature and, even when wet, it causes virtually no chills or rheumatic ailments. He propounded his ideas vehemently in the paper "Normalkeidung als Gesundheitsschutz" ("Normal clothing as health protection" - 1880).

One immediate convert was a certain Mr. Tomalin, a London grocer, who translated the book and made it into a bestseller under the title "Health Culture". But Tomalin went even further. He purchased from the Professor the right to use the name "Jaeger" and started manufacturing clothing according to the "Jäger principle" in 1884. He gave his company the rather unwieldy name "Dr. Jaeger's Sanitary Woollen System Company Ltd." A world-wide success story with a German name and British business acumen in the making. Soon Jaeger woollen clothing appeared everywhere: Stanley was wearing it when he went in search of the missing Dr. Livingstone in the Congo, Scott and others wore it against the Arctic cold, Oscar Wilde and G.B. Shaw while they were working - as Michael Jenner has discovered.

Nowadays, Jaeger as a company is no longer quite so strict about the original objection to synthetic fibres ... but wool, mohair, cashmere and camel hair still characterise the brand, now with stylish fashionable designs.

The next story also has a health angle. The time: early in the Second World War.

The place: Seehaupt on the Starnbergersee. "Summer surprised us, coming over Starnbergersee / With a shower of rain...", T.S. Eliot wrote in "The Wasteland" (1922). But this time it was winter and one Dr. Klaus Maertens was in Seehaupt convalescing from a skiing accident. The pain in his foot was so persistent that Maertens and his colleague Dr. Funck designed a comfortable walking shoe with a kind of air-cushioned sole - made out of old car tyres. This brought such rapid relief that the two inventors decided to patent the idea and exploit it commercially. With great success. Initially conceived as a comfortable shoe for elderly ladies with foot trouble, the air-cushioned shoes were soon selling widely throughout Europe to both sexes.

In the late 1950s, Maertens and Funck resolved to expand the business from a base in Great Britain. As their partners they chose Wollaston Vulcanising (now part of the Griggs group), which received the world-wide distribution licence for the soles in 1960. Wollaston anglicised the name into "Dr Martens" and began production on 1.4.1960 (the model "1460" which is still popular today was named after the first day of production). What no one could have predicted then: in the late 60s, young people chose these "bovver boots" as their protest symbol. None of the "beautiful people" and no punk would be seen without their Doc Martens, their "DMs". Nancy Sinatra allegedly had them in mind when she wrote the hit song "These boots are made for walking"... They are still worn by fashion models and pop stars - but unfortunately also by skinheads as a macho symbol.

At any rate, the shoes with the outstanding sole have written a chapter of German-British symbiosis which itself can only be described as outstanding.

Safe in the knowledge that it could retain its own individual profile and entrepreneurial independence, backed by the financial reserves of BMW (which is forgoing dividends on its British acquisition for the time being) and last but not least, with the exchange rate advantages of the Pound over the strong Deutschmark, Rover was able to make an important long-term investment in 1995: £2 million will be set aside for new product development over the next five years. That is a 60% increase in investment over the previous five-year period and improves the company's competitiveness on the British and international markets at a stroke.

Siemens has successfully adopted similar, internationally proven principles with its British subsidiaries: wherever possible, local management takes important decisions itself. The advantages for everyone concerned are obvious.

Does anyone still have any questions about German-British stereotypes? Certainly not members of the business community on both sides of the Channel! German capital in Britain has steered an important economic as well as cultural and sociological development. Strange "Huns" indeed, who turn their Anglophilia into long-term business decisions of mutual advantage. And that in a country presumed to be dominated by tea-breaks, layabouts and strikes...

How the British first enforced the "Made in Germany" label
- and shot themselves in the foot.

The story of the "Made in Germany" label is a perfect illustration of how rivalry can boomerang on the most eager competitor. This episode in German-British trade relations may seem funny in retrospect - but the British were certainly not amused at the time.

In the closing decades of the 19th century, the economic might of the newly founded German Reich was beginning to make its presence felt on the world scene and was also infiltrating the British market to an unprecedented degree. British industry suspected treachery - German manufacturers of finished household goods were denounced as pirates of English branded articles! It was claimed that they were producing items disturbingly similar to the English design - especially tableware, cutlery, kitchen utensils of silver, brass or steel - thus confusing the honest consumer who erroneously believed that he was buying British.

Court actions were passionately fought - especially in Sheffield and Manchester - and won: in 1887, the House of Commons passed the "Merchandise Marks Act", the law making it compulsory for German goods to display their place of origin. The intention was to stigmatise and discriminate against these German articles with the compulsory label "Made in Germany".

None of the MPs could have expected this measure, which was designed to protect British industry, to backfire on them. "Made in Germany", a label originally intended as a mark of Cain on the brow of Britain's main foreign competitor, soon became - what irony of history - a recommendation for its superior quality. German industry, in its drive to conquer new markets, could not have thought up a better advertising wheeze.

This is what happened: customers were much less interested than Westminster MPs had originally hoped in distinguishing between the original and the alleged copy. Or rather, they were - but for a different reason. Now that they were constantly confronted with these newly labelled products, they quickly learned to distinguish between good and less good items - all too often to the detriment of the British product! Discrimination was indeed the consequence - but not in the intended direction. Thus began the career of the quality hallmark "Made in Germany".

The British also damaged their position on overseas markets, particularly within the Empire. This piece of "freebee advertising" (David Head) made it easier for local industries to identify products of German origin and to make direct contact with the German manufacturers if they wanted to order further deliveries or other products from their range.

In short: demand for products "Made in Germany" soared and could no longer be checked even by a later amendment to the Act of Parliament stipulating that all imported goods had to bear labels identifying their country of origin.

"Vorsprung durch Advertising" - with a little help from one's rival!

2. British involvement in the new Länder and Berlin: "Vorsprung durch diversity"

When it comes to effort and involvement, the British can certainly hold their own. Their latest sphere of operations in Germany is the new *Länder*. "Holding their own" does not refer here to the volume of investment; it would be nonsense simply to compare investment figures since Great Britain has the developed market of a highly industrialised nation to offer whilst the new *Länder* are a region still coping with the legacy of socialist mismanagement. Effort must be measured here in terms of diversity, the sheer variety of British commitment. And in terms of the entrepreneurial courage to venture into completely unknown territory - even if supported occasionally by British subsidiaries already established on the (old) West German market.

The German Government's Trust Fund Agency *"Treuhand"* sold 125 companies in the new *Länder* to British firms - placing Britain at the top of the European league table. Construction, consultant engineering, energy, environmental protection, infrastructure, development projects - the range is impressive. DM 2.5 billion have so far been committed, saving around 15,000 jobs.

Be prepared for some outstanding examples and also some surprises, such as in the environmental sector. British companies have meanwhile built up their own experience in cleaning up the environment - water, polluted soil (e.g. military sites) etc. The following list, while far from complete, may give an indication of the diversity of the overall involvement of British capital in the new *Länder*:

ReadyMix...

... is investing DM 500 million in an environmentally friendly plant for the newly acquired ReadyMix cement factory in Rüdersdorf.

Carbon Link (Wigan)...

... has bought the *Aktivkohle und Umweltschutz Technik GmbH (AUG)* in Doberitz, a new production site for active carbon for water purification, flue-gas cleansing and other fields of application in the environmental protection sector.

spotlight 37

A straight answer please: What is Great Britain really doing for the environment?

We have all inherited a rich legacy - of prejudices. While Britain is still haunted by the ghosts of the militaristic, monocled, regimented German, older Germans, who have not grown up with the Beatles, think they know all about the island which has little music, a lot of business - and even more fog. But London's "pea-soupers" are a thing of the past. One is more likely nowadays to get fog warnings in the region surrounding Munich's new airport. Furthermore, Britain's fog was never a natural phenomenon but a man-made problem on a massive scale. Vigorous measures were taken as early as in the 1956 Clean Air Act to combat pollution from fossil fuel, above all in the conurbations of southern England. The outlook soon brightened: in winter, the British now see 70% more sun than they did 40 years ago.

Next on the list came the river Thames - heavily polluted with sewage and chemicals. Here too the record has improved significantly: the first trout was sighted near Westminster Bridge in the early 1980s... A report issued by the UN environmental organisation UNEP in 1985 confirmed that the Thames was less permanently polluted than the Rhine or the Seine. Incidentally, one of the early campaigners for a pollution-free Thames in the 1970s was a certain Richard Adams, then a civil servant in the environment office of the Greater London Council (GLC). Adams is now better known as the author of such modern children's classics as "Watership Down" and "Shardik" - which enabled him to exchange his desk job for the independent life of a writer.

And then came the EC ... Brussels clearly accelerated ecological thinking in Britain. The EC (now the EU) is not necessarily an institution to which most Government departments in London would point as evidence of their success. But the contrary is true at the Environment Ministry, which happily quotes EC Directives because they are a yardstick which makes Britain's environmental policy look increasingly effective. In the period 1983-1995, only two actions were brought against Britain before the European Court of Justice on charges of infringing EC environmental legislation. After Denmark, Britain has the second-best record of *"ecological misdemeanours" of all Member States.*

The British Environmental Protection Act of 1990 and the "national strategy for ecologically sustainable development" of January 1994 are beginning to bear fruit. In the period 1985-1993, mercury, cadmium and lead discharges into coastal waters fell by over 50%, mercury levels alone by over 69%. 86 wetland biotopes and 102 bird sanctuaries were placed under the protection of the international Ramsar Convention. The recycling sector also took a leap forward. Every community now has easily accessible bottle banks and other waste recycling facilities.

At the Rio Summit, the British Government announced to the participating States that Britain will not only reduce its emission of carbon dioxide and other greenhouse gases to 1990 levels by the year 2000 as promised but may even undercut this figure by 6-14 million tonnes.

The picture is less rosy when one looks at waste incineration plants and the dioxin they release. In February 1995, the Environment Ministry had to concede that 19 of the country's 21 major waste incineration plants were far exceeding the maximum permissible levels for dioxin. Although industrial sulphur dioxide emissions have been reduced by 50% since 1970, they still represent the greatest environmental danger to people's health. The increase in asthma cases is causing great concern. A commission of experts has now recommended setting a new SO2 "indicative limiting value" for Great Britain.

On 6 February 1995, Environment Minister John Gummer launched the "Going for Green" campaign to heighten public awareness of environmental protection and ecological thinking in Britain. One element of the advertising campaign was a cartoon commercial on TV. It portrayed a family of dinosaurs constantly arguing about environmental matters: father Ron is the indolent reactionary, the Alf Garnet of nature conservation, mother Brenda is a rather helpless figure caught in the middle, whilst son Billy represents the ecologically-minded younger generation.

As if to confirm Britain's record, The European Environment Agency appointed Derek Osborn from the British Environment Ministry as its new chairman in 1995. Derek must be one of Billy's brothers - a dinosaur with a future.

British Gas...

... is involved inter alia in gas supplies in Halle, Saxony-Anhalt, the "Verbundnetzgas" in Leipzig and the "Gasversorgung Leipzig GmbH". Once again it is *Vorsprung durch Technik* at work: British Gas has concluded contracts in Leipzig, Berlin, Halle, Magdeburg, Dresden and Chemnitz thanks to the expertise which it can bring to joint projects with local companies. In the eastern part of Berlin, for example, modern polyethylene pipelines were laid inside rusting steel pipes, thus obviating the need to remove them.

BMW Rolls-Royce...

... was created in 1992 and is now constructing a new assembly plant in Dahlewitz, just outside Berlin, for the jointly developed aero-engines of the new 700 series - a successor to the world famous Rolls Royce Tay engine. The new Gulfstream V corporate jet will be equipped with BMW Rolls Royce BR 710 engines for non-stop flights from New York to Tokyo or London to Singapore.

GKN...

... a leading British manufacturer of car components has acquired the VEB Sachsenring Automobilwerke Zwickau Mosel - now GKN Gelenkwellenwerk Mosel (GWM) - and made it into a major supplier of homokinetic drive shafts which are now exported to both Eastern and Western Europe.

Seymour Powell...

... is in the process of giving the former GDR bicycle manufacturer MuZ a complete facelift, namely with the "Skorpion", a British-designed bike for young people which was given an enthusiastic reception at the Birmingham Bike Show in 1994. The revolutionary feature of this bike is that it is glued not welded and has an ideal weight/acceleration ratio.

BICC Cables...

... one of Europe's leading cable manufacturers has acquired Kabelwerke Oberspree (KWO) with 2,200 employees. There are extensive plans for investment. This acquisition will make BICC one of the major cable suppliers for the whole of Germany and Eastern Europe.

Agricultural science

British companies, many of which were already working with new agricultural co-operatives in eastern Germany, have pooled their resources to sponsor students of agricultural science at Berlin's Humboldt University to attend a business management training programme at Sparsholt near Winchester (Hampshire), a leading agricultural college in Britain.

The collapse of the Wall, triggered by a political revolution, has carried a cultural revolution of immeasurable proportions in its wake. Half an entire continent, which had been denied the chance to shape its own history, has turned its attention westward. There is a lot of ground to make up and this has generated an almost insatiable demand. The answer cannot be simply a "commercial" one, however urgent the need for economic recovery may be. Man cannot live on balance-sheets alone.

How Tim Evans, a farmer from Sevenoaks in Kent, became a "Brossi".

Back in the summer of 1992, Tim Evans was on the point of giving up. In search of farm and grazing land in eastern Germany at a good price, he almost fell foul of his inadequate German, stubborn bureaucrats and tight-fisted bankers. But then, on one of his last evenings, he met a West German at a dinner party whose brother-in-law was in the process of reclaiming his family's farm in Saxony-Anhalt. He immediately drove to the farm, Gut Wittenmoor, and spent six hours touring the 2,500-hectare property. Then he travelled straight to Bonn, where the prospective partner lived, quickly worked through the figures on a lap-top computer and the deal was clinched.

"As far as I know, I'm the only British farmer, probably the only one mad enough to come here. But since 1992 the thing has just snowballed" he told a local TV team. Tim Evans, a British livestock farmer among "Ossis" in the new Länder - which makes him the sole representative of a new species - a genuine "Brossi".

Once again, many of the new expectations focussed on questions of life styles, on the Western way of life. Anglo-Saxon culture, beginning with the English language, is high up on the wish-list of those who have regained their freedom. At this interface, "business" overlaps with "culture", financial transactions with communications, economics with the search for individual happiness.

The BBC, the British Council and the Central Bureau for Educational Visits and Exchanges have their work cut out for them as they tackle this challenge and make corresponding investments in the new *Länder* and Berlin. Since 1990, 350 teachers of English from the new *Länder* have worked as language assistants at British schools. In the other direction, 150 British teachers came to schools in eastern Germany. Specialist scholarships exist for students of economics, law, management, international relations and the environment. There is also an extensive youth exchange programme (cf. also chapter II,7).

The status which Germany enjoys can be seen from the fact that a quarter of all public funds for youth exchange in Britain is spent on exchange programmes with Germany alone. That may not appear very exciting in absolute figures, but the ratio speaks for itself.

In September 1994, a former British military school in Berlin-Charlottenburg was reopened as Berlin's first private school offering a British curriculum and aimed principally at the city's expanding international business and future diplomatic communities. Everyone is getting into position, their toes on the starting blocks.

That applies particularly to the media. Editors from broadcasting corporations and their regional offices in Potsdam, Chemnitz, Dresden and Leipzig are conducting exchanges with their counterparts at the German-language service of the BBC at Bush House in London. In addition, the BBC has equipped "Antenne Brandenburg" in Potsdam and "Sachsen Radio Dresden" with satellite receivers so that they can broadcast BBC news and other programmes via their own frequencies. "Sachsen Radio Leipzig" also transmits BBC programmes received via satellite. "Auntie" BBC, who has been putting out German-language programmes since 1938, seems to have found a new vocation. If all goes to plan, it should be possible to receive "BBC World" TV throughout Germany by 1997.

In the overall pattern of Anglo-German relations, individuals count just as much as large organisations. But when the two meet, individual energy and institutional backing, one can expect to see remarkable results. As is the case with Penelope Willard, a 44-year-old German scholar from Sussex. As Secretary of the time-honoured "Frankesche Stiftungen" in the eastern German town of Halle, Ms Willard's intention is to add a cultural profile to the foundation by building a centre for historical and philosophical research. She is pursuing this objective with tireless energy, supported by the international renown of the new director of the "Stiftungen", Paul Raabe. When the "Interdisciplinary Centre for European Enlightenment and Research into Pietism" is up and running, the people of Halle will have this Englishwoman to thank for the town's additional academic attraction.

Nowhere are the close links between Germany and Britain more visible than in architecture and nowhere can one find better examples than in Berlin. Nicholas Grimshaw is responsible for the  design of the new Chamber of Industry and Commerce (IHK); the late Sir James Stirling left his mark with the *Wissenschaftszentrum* (he also built the extended Staatsgalerie in Stuttgart); John Thompson, a friend of HRH Prince Charles, will convert the prefabricated housing estate in Berlin-Hellersdorf (formerly in East Berlin) to give it a more humane character.

Nicholas Grimshaw: architect of Berlin's new Chamber of Industry and Commerce

In historical terms, the architectural link between Berlin and Britain naturally bears the name of Friedrich Schinkel, the great Prussian architect of the 19th century. Schinkel, who studied British industrial architecture on a trip through Britain in 1826, was greatly inspired by the ionic columns of Sir Robert Smirke's British Museum for his own design for the Altes Museum in Berlin's Lustgarten.

In turn, it is a British architect, Sir Norman Foster, who personifies this unique link between the two countries and it is again in Berlin where architectural history is being made. Foster won the prestigious competition to convert the Reichstag. *"It was inconceivable that someone could seriously consider giving the responsibility for a new German parliament to British architects"*, Sir Norman admitted in a newspaper interview. Foster's design is based on the concept of transparency for both light and the viewer's eye; the principle of open access for everyone at this centre of the parliamentary system. No one can fail to be touched by the symbolism of the fact that, having made such an essential contribution towards rebuilding German democracy after the Second World War, Britain should now provide the architect who is renovating the future seat of German democracy.

Industry and human resources, economics and design - they interface to an extraordinary degree. Assets abound. We benefit from material and intellectual products, receive salaries and signals, fees and surprises, we consume and communicate, there is growth in business and comprehension. German-British relations could soon leave the injuries of this century behind them; they have become a piece of modern life in a Europe based on peaceful competition.

The irritations and uproar over Mad Cow Disease and the single European currency will not change that - hopefully.

More light for the Reichstag: Norman Foster's contribution to German democracy

Britain's role in building German democracy

Official and unofficial co-operation

I. *At the gates of Hell*

In the summer of 1945, the writer Stephen Spender (1909-1995) travelled around war-worn Germany on behalf of the Allied Control Commission, of which he was a member, to reconnoitre possibilities for democratic reconstruction and the restoration of cultural institutions in the defeated country. Spender had caused quite a stir with an essay on "Hölderlin, Goethe and Germany" published in the magazine "Horizon" in October 1943 in which he had resolutely defended Germany's cultural tradition against the barbarities of National Socialism.

The author knew Germany well from extensive visits since 1929. Like his contemporaries Christopher Isherwood and W.H.Auden, he felt a great affinity with German culture and was therefore able to speak out with authority and conviction on behalf of "the better Germany" at a time when the country's international reputation was at its lowest ebb.

The book he wrote about his experiences in the spiritually and materially bankrupt country ("European Witness", 1946; "Deutschland in Ruinen", 1995) aroused considerable interest. Along with the descriptions George Orwell penned for the Observer on journeys through Germany that same summer, this was one of the most important eye-witness accounts of German history's "Zero Hour". Its keen observations and insight make it an enthralling read even fifty years later.

Spender knew the audience he was writing for; or rather, what feelings to expect from British readers. An immediate post-war opinion poll showed that 54% of the British population admitted "hating" the Germans. This was more deeply-rooted than the anti-German hysteria of the First World War. There was nothing to gloss over, hide or mitigate: Germany's shame was there for all the world to see. In England, memories of the "Battle of Britain", the traumatic fear of invasion in 1940, were still all too present. The British soldiers who liberated Bergen-Belsen concentration camp in April 1945 and, to their horror, discovered mountains of corpses were seized by the feeling of standing at the gates of Hell.

But Spender was determined not to let himself be overwhelmed by the shock of the moment and to sink into pessimism or recrimination. It was not easy for him. Everywhere he went, Spender, like many of his compatriots, encountered the terrible destruction Germany had suffered from aerial bombardment. Here were the apocalyptic depths of misery into which civilisation itself might descend. This thought struck him as he clambered out of the ruins of the Reichskanzlei in Berlin. His record of those reflections is still poignantly accurate today:

" *As we went away, I was thinking that the psychological clue to Nazism itself and to the hold which it had over its followers may well lie in the fact that Hitler before, as it were, he became Hitler, was the student of architecture who failed to pass the examinations which would have enabled him to study architecture at the University of Vienna; and that Goebbels before, as it were, he became Goebbels, was the student at the University of Heidelberg who wrote a bad verse drama on the life of Christ. The architect who failed to build had turned the foundations of every city in Germany to sand. The prophet who could not understand God had become the Satanic agent in a society where so far Satanism had ruled only in some pages of Baudelaire and of Dostoyevsky. These were not just tyrants who appeared for a time and then disappeared leaving a great deal of material destruction and physical destruction behind them (...) What they destroyed, once and for all, is the modern middle-class idea that man, as a social being, does not have to choose between good and evil. They involved almost the whole of the German middle classes - and a great section of the middle classes of Europe and the rest of the world - in physical and moral damnation by forcing them to be really wicked and to be involved in wholly sinful actions..."*

Spender added to this analysis a general comment on the end of the naively bourgeois belief in progress which, as he wrote, had always relied on the fact that open competition and the urge for individual self-fulfilment would automatically lead to happiness and an enrichment of humanity. Amid Germany's ruined landscape, the author roundly rejected this crude optimism and formulated what was to become the creed of the best British minds involved in reconstructing the vanquished country:

"(...) there could not be the least doubt that the only answer to this past and this present is a conscious, deliberate and wholly responsible determination to make our society walk in paths of light."

Stephen Spender, 1945: experienced at first hand the devastation in Germany

From rivalry to hatred - and disillusionment:
A century of German-British crises.

No book on Anglo-German relations would be complete without examining the historical escalation of rivalry between Britain and Germany - a rivalry that was to degenerate into blind hatred. I do not propose a full inventory - a few selected examples ought to provide sufficient background (cf. also SPOTLIGHT texts 2, 5, 22, 34, 40).

This rivalry took on sharper contours from about the middle of the 19th century and reached its first climax around 1900 when it became clear that the industrial output of the German Reich had overtaken that of Great Britain. The German Government further fuelled the conflict by intensifying its fleet-building policy - a classic case of ill-judged brinkmanship by a world power.

Bismarck must have turned in his grave. The first German Reichskanzler believed that England should be kept out of the affairs of Continental Europe - he regarded the British as "unreliable in the foreign policy sector" (Wolfgang Mommsen). He felt that England's interest in the Continent was "extremely superficial", an impression he had gained on his first visit to England in 1862, shortly before his appointment as Prime Minister of Prussia. He was never to change this opinion, formed after talking to leading British politicians of the day such as Lord Russell, Palmerston and Disraeli.

On the other hand, Bismarck took great pains not to offend any of the precariously balanced European powers unnecessarily. He pursued a policy of "friendly indifference" (Lothar Gall) towards London. Even in 1884, when Germany unsettled the British by securing colonies in South West Africa, Togo, Cameroon, East Africa and the Pacific Islands, the Reichskanzler appealed for a cautious approach. Addressing the Reichstag on 28.6.1884, he said:

"On no account do I want to act rashly towards a Government and a country with which we have such close and friendly ties and risk prompting a conflict with the English ... at the expense of a valued friendship."

But public opinion in Britain had already become distinctly less friendly during the Franco-German war when there was a sudden volte-face in the latent pro-German feeling. The date can be pin-pointed to December 1870 when the German army turned its guns on Paris...

"I hear they have begun to bombard Paris!" Queen Victoria sorrowfully reflected in a letter to her daughter Vicky in Berlin on 28.12.1870. *"If only it would soon end. To my despair, the feeling is becoming more and more bitter here against the Prussians."*

Vicky shared her mother's concerns. Although married to the Prussian Crown Prince Frederick in Berlin, she was labelled "the Englishwoman" and cold-shouldered by Bismarck and his circle for her liberal views and candid criticism of conditions in Prussia. In spring 1871, she wrote:

"One thing I own torments me much; it is the feeling of animosity between our two countries: it is so dangerous and productive of much harm (...) I live in continual dread that the bonds which united our two countries for their mutual good may be in time quite severed."

Her mother's reply was prompt:

"How difficult my path is! - distrusted and suspected on account of my relationship and feelings. To see the enmity growing up between the two nations - which I am bound to say began first in Prussia, and was most unjust and was quite fomented and encouraged by Bismarck - is a great sorrow and anxiety to me, and I cannot separate myself or allow myself to be separated from my own people..."

The future Emperor did much to widen the gap between the British and the Germans. Because of his British blood ties, William II, Vicky's eldest son, felt torn throughout his life between feelings of admiration and rejection for England. This was finally to intensify rivalry between the two countries to a fatal extent. As a child, he once exclaimed: *"I want to lose every last drop of English blood from my veins."* Yet he later confessed to the American President Theodore Roosevelt in 1911: *"I simply love England!"* His interview with the Daily Telegraph on 18.10.1908 became infamous. In his swaggering manner, he condescendingly portrayed himself as a would-be backer of Britain (*"I am a friend of England, but I stand alone in Germany with this opinion!"*), thus unleashing a storm of criticism, also in his own country.

On the subject of Germany's fleet-building programme, the Emperor's favourite project, the American historian Robert M. Massie comments wryly in his book "Dreadnought. Britain, Germany and the Coming of the Great War" (1993):

"The Kaiser was really only motivated by a desire to build such ships himself and by the plan to possess a fleet as beautiful as the English."

That was William's way of trying to gain England's respect... At any rate, he did not want to compete with his British relations for the "place in the sun" which he claimed for Germany as a world power. His uncle, King Edward VII ("Bertie"), could not stand him. Yet the two of them lovingly comforted the dying Queen Victoria during her last moments at Osborne Castle on the Isle of Wight on 22 January 1901.

John Mander neatly sums up the tension which built up prior to the First World War: "Until the advent of Bismarck the Hohenzollerns were indeed the 'good boys' of Europe, with William I the paragon of modesty. However, the advent of Bismarck, and Industrialisation: these were the factors that were to bring into being the parvenu, over-reaching empire of which William II was so disastrous and appropriate an exemplar."

One powerful source of competition between the two sides was their mutual claims to cultural superiority. With its pragmatic, philosophical tradition and the freedom rooted in its parliamentary system, Britain regarded itself as the more advanced society compared with the German "dreamers" and "autocrats". Germany, in turn, felt philosophically and culturally superior to the allegedly superficial empiricism of the British Enlightenment, to the British "shopkeeper mentality" and British materialism - despite the fact that the so-called "Gründerjahre" of the first German Empire could easily have matched any other in terms of commercial greed (which Friedrich Nietzsche was soon to attack in his "Untimely Meditations").

Even Friedrich Schlegel, one of the leading figures of the German Romantic movement, called the British "a nation divided between mercantilism and mathematics". Richard Wagner took this idea further and accused the English of seeing only the material benefit in things whilst the Germans tended to do "something for its own sake". Even such a self-confessed Anglophile as Theodor Fontane considered excessive materialism as the basic ill of British society in the mid-19th century. During his second visit to England in 1852, he wrote the following about the traces of "mammonism" (which he, like Nietzsche, was to encounter again later in the era of Emperor William II):

"England is dying of materialism. (...) Speculation, running and chasing after money - the whole cult of the Golden Calf is the great sickness of the English people."

But the criticism was mutual. When the "Edinburgh Review" wrote about the first edition of Madame de Staël's "De l'Allemagne" in 1813, it could not understand what the French author found so fascinating about the speculative talents of the Germans. On the contrary, the reviewer was repelled by the concept:

"German philosophy is founded in a repugnance to every system which has experience for its basis, or happiness for its end."

... an idea for which Thomas Macauly later coined the timeless bonmot: "An acre in Middlesex is better than a Principality in Utopia."

However, it is precisely this attitude which Friedrich Nietzsche branded the classic cultural handicap of the British. "They are no philosophical race - these English", he snorted in "Beyond Good and Evil" and continued with a scathing indictment:

"There is no real depth of spiritual view (...) Kant rose and revolted against Hume. (...)Hegel and Schopenauer were agreed in the battle against the English mechanistic reduction of the world. (...) Hobbes, Hume and Locke have humiliated and devalued the term "philosophy" for more than a century."

Strong stuff indeed. In 1914 all this was finally unleashed in the madness of war, with the clichés and stereotypes on both sides serving to fuel passions still further. Werner Sombart again denounced "the dirty tide of commercialism" in England; his book "Händler und Helden" (1916) ("Traders and Heroes") speaks volumes about the spirit behind this controversy. The philosopher Max Scheler set "German heroism" against "English petty-mindedness". Perfidious Albion! Gerhart Hauptmann wanted to rescue Shakespeare from its clutches. Even Thomas Mann virtually conceded a traditional enmity between Germans and Anglo-Saxons by drawing a dividing line between "German culture" and "Western civilisation" in his "Observations of an Unpolitical Man".

Hysteria turned to hatred and German-British relations were condemned to die on the fields of Flanders or be smothered under a mass of propaganda, as Peter Edgerly Firchow wrote in his pioneering study "The Death of the German Cousin" (1986). The most notorious example on the German side was the 51-line "Hymn of hate to England" by the hack Ernst Lissauer, which ends as follows:

> " Sign up the peoples of the Earth
> Build protective walls of gold ingots
> Cover the seas with ships bow to stern
> That would be shrewd, but not shrewd enough.
> What do we care about the Russians and the French
> Shot against shot and blow for blow
> We fight the fight with bronze and steel
> And make peace again at some later stage.
> But we shall hate with a lengthy hatred
> Hatred on the seas and hatred on the land,
> Hatred of the head and hatred of the hand
> Hatred of the hammers and hatred of the crowns,
> The choking hatred of seventy million
> Who love together and hate together
> Who all have but one enemy
> England."

More sophisticated in terms of poetic structure but no less forceful is Rudyard Kipling's treatment of the subject of hatred in his poem "The Beginnings":

> " It was not part of their blood,
> It came to them very late
> With long arrears to make good,
> When the English began to hate.
>
> They were not easily moved,
> They were icy willing to wait
> Till every count should be proved
> Ere the English began to hate.
> (...)
> It was not suddenly bred,
> It will not swiftly abate,
> Through the chill years ahead,
> When time shall count from the date
> That the English began to hate."

In view of such excesses, it is all the more amazing how quickly both the English and the German side put these tirades behind them after the exhaustion of the Great War. Admittedly, that could not prevent the humiliating conditions imposed on Germany in the Treaty of Versailles. The Cambridge economist John Maynard Keynes was among the first British voices to warn against the repercussions of this vengeful peace settlement. Keynes, head of the British Treasury delegation at the Versailles Peace Conference, displayed prophetic talents in a famous essay entitled

"The Economic Consequences of the Peace" (1919):

"Moved by insane delusion and reckless self-regard, the German people overturned the foundations on which we all lived and built. But the spokesmen of the French and British peoples have run the risk of completing the ruin, which Germany began, by a Peace which (...) must impair yet further (...) the delicate, complicated organisation (...) through which alone the European peoples can employ themselves and live."

There was a widespread belief among the British elite of the 1920s and 30s that the terms of the Versailles Treaty had been unjust on the Germans. It combined with a general wave of post-war pacifism and eventually led to the policy of appeasement towards Hitler which Winston Churchill later strongly denounced. During a lecture trip through Germany in autumn 1994, the historian Michael Howard summed up this extremely illuminating phase in German-British relations as follows:

"What is much more remarkable is the speed with which the British themselves came to regret (the settlement) and to feel over the Versailles Treaty a degree of guilt far greater than the Germans were ever to feel about the war. Because that sense of what we might term 'Peace-Guilt' was to give birth almost at once to the policy known as 'Appeasement', and because a new generation was to make that in its turn the basis for a new charge of 'War Guilt' against the statesmen who practised it, the whole topic has now been for the best part of half a century the subject of innumerable revisionist, counter-revisionist and re-revisionist studies (...) But if the hostility that developed between the two nations played a major role in causing the First World War, the British attempt to appease that hostility and restore friendly relations with Germany played, ironically, at least a comparable role in bringing about the Second."

John Mander also made an original contribution towards explaining the pacifist about-turn in Great Britain after the First World War:

"Perhaps it is that the English are not good haters. Perhaps its true roots are to be found in a profound revulsion from the realities of modern land warfare, of which Anglo-Saxons had known so little before 1914."

Indeed, the reports which George Orwell published in the Observer and the Tribune about his travels through France and Germany in 1945 reveal - like Stephen Spender's book of the following year - something of this British lack of talent for hatred. Perhaps the British sense of fair play has a disqualifying effect... On 3.3.1945, the author wrote from Paris:

"What immediately strikes a new arrival is that almost every Frenchman takes a tougher stance on Germany than almost every Englishman. (...) The French find it difficult to believe that the Germans belong to the same human race as them."

And on 28.4.1945 from Germany:

"Some DPs (displaced persons) and French seem to feel a grim sense of satisfaction at the sight of the devastation caused by the bombs. I personally could not feel anything of the sort."

On 9.11.1945, in an article written for the Tribune under the headline "Revenge is sour" (later included in Orwell's "Collected Essays"), we come across this observation:

"The Nazi torturer of our imagination, this monstrous figure (...) Who would not have jumped for joy in 1940 at the thought of seeing SS officers kicked and humiliated? But when that actually becomes possible, it is simply pitiful and disgusting. The entire concept of revenge and punishment is just a childish daydream."

2. Re-education - persuading people to accept democracy

The answer, Stephen Spender had concluded in the ruins of the Reichskanzlei, could only lie in the responsible determination *"to make our society walk in paths of light"*.

But how? And in particular, how could this be achieved with the vanquished enemy, the Germans?

Even during the war, this had been hotly debated in both Houses of Parliament as well as in Cabinet and at the Foreign Office. But at no time was there a generally approved policy for the British occupation zone or occupied Germany as a whole. After all, the final conquest of Nazi Germany still lay ahead, in line with Churchill's motto: "No policy beyond unconditional surrender."

But initial ideas had formed around the concept "mobilisation of the sense of guilt" - the German people were to be made aware of the scale of their failure to pursue democracy. Great Britain was also to be "projected" as a model of free democratic structures. The British Cabinet agreed from an early stage that a democratic Germany would be the best safeguard against a revival of German aggression. As David Welch described in his essay "British Political Re-education and its Impact on German Political Culture" (1992) the debate wavered *"between historical interpretations of German national character traits, and on the other hand, pragmatic short-term improvisations to changing political circumstances."*

"Re-education", which was not an official term of British occupation policy, nevertheless soon attained the status for many (particularly among the Germans) of an official designation for the British campaign of democratisation in their part of post-war Germany. "Re-education" became as much a by-word as the infamous "questionnaire" employed during the denazification campaign. The word was first used by Viscount Cecil of Chelwood during a debate in the House of Lords on 10 May 1943. Chelwood posed the rhetorical question as to what would happen after Nazism had been crushed and Germany disarmed - and then answered the question himself: *"Germany should be given the opportunity of 're-educating herself'"*.

At around the same time, the Chairman of a sub-committee on Germany at the "Political Warfare Executive (PWE)", Con O'Neill, presented a confidential paper which not only predicted the outlines of Britain's actual post-war policy towards Germany, but also looked almost prophetically into the distant future. O'Neill began his study with the following sentence:

"Our long-term aim is presumably to integrate Germany into a peaceful and prosperous European order."

Then he identified the following three themes for the British approach:

" *1. To convince the German people that we mean business in Germany.*

2. To convince them that we would uphold in all our dealings the ideal of the Rechtsstaat.

3. Thereby to persuade the German people that its way of life and destiny are bound up with those of the Western Powers."

Despite the high moral tone of these good intentions, dealing with German affairs proved extremely difficult at first. This was also due to the ban on "fraternisation" imposed in March 1945 by General Montgomery, Commander-in-Chief of the British forces and comrade-in-arms of US-General Eisenhower in conquering the German army in the West. Montgomery's seven-paragraph letter ended with the sentence: *"In short: you must on no account fraternise with the Germans."*

Obviously, this could not last long. How were people supposed to "re-educate" the Germans and put the country on the road to democracy whilst maintaining such distance between the "educators" and their "pupils"? That would be neglecting the essential ingredient of democracy: humanity. As a result, the ban on fraternisation was duly lifted in September 1945.

Humanity: the watchword of the hour - then and ever since.

It was everyday life itself, everyday life in the defeated and ailing Germany, which thwarted all attempts at regulating relations between the occupiers and the occupied. It was the rank-and-file servicemen who first experienced this at first hand. Hardly was the battle to liberate Europe from the Nazi yoke over, the enemy conquered, than the problems began. Germany was totally devastated, its structures destroyed and its people destitute. Who was there when help was urgently needed? The occupiers! More than anything else, it was these feelings of needing and being needed which were responsible for bringing people closer together.

A Welsh war veteran, ex-corporal Dai Evans from the 53rd Welsh Division, recalled this period in an interview with the "Hamburger Abendblatt" on 2 May 1995. A few days after Hamburg had surrendered to Brigadier Spurling, commanding officer of the 131st Infantry Brigade, on 3 May 1945, Evans was ordered by his superior to drive a heavily pregnant German woman quickly to hospital in a requisitioned Mercedes. After the woman had given birth to a healthy child and expressed her thanks for the assistance, a nun working in the delivery room added: "Please also thank your officer for his humanity."

Now whenever Evans heard the word humanity, he had to think of this nun. At the time his lieutenant had reacted by saying: "What a strange world! We spent years trying to finish these bastards off, and now we are killing ourselves to save them."

Many of the British soldiers ("Tommies", as they were known in Germany in those days) developed a feeling of solidarity with the former enemy - a hand reaching out across all the trenches and graves to clasp another. The various associations of war veterans which developed friendships on both sides soon after the war ended were just one of the many signs of reconciliation evolving between the British and the Germans.

spotlight 40

There were quite a number of officials within the British occupation administration who had little time for the slightly pejorative term "re-education". Robert Birley, for example, the "Educational Adviser" in the British zone. *"The idea of re-education was anathema to him"*, recalls Michael Thomas (*"Deutschland, England über alles"*, 1984), *"he never used the term. He was interested in reviving the German traditions which had been smothered by the Nazi regime and in breathing a bit of English spirit into them."*

Of the three main attitudes which - as David Welch writes - could be identified in the British occupation machinery (*"high idealism, arrogant colonialism and pragmatic improvisation"*), Birley and most of those involved with the tough day-to-day work applied a mixture of the first and the third. As for the second category, the distinguished historian Lord Annan, at the time a young staff officer with the senior military command, gave this description in a BBC interview in 1987:

"Military Government officials resembled civilised and agreeable officers in a rather forward-looking Bedouin country - tending to treat Germans in the beginning very much as intelligent natives."

A "manual" issued by the Allied Senior Command contained general instructions on how to deal with the vanquished population. Like many documents of its kind, the underlying theories proved more or less inadequate for coping with practical realities. But one important principle turned out to be of lasting value: the principle of "indirect rule" - the attempt to use as many viable and unimpaired German institutions as possible to prevent a "breakdown" of allied rule.

One has to bear in mind a few basic facts of these trying times: there were 23 million people living in the British occupation zone (Hamburg, Schleswig-Holstein, Lower Saxony, Bremen and North Rhine-Westphalia, which was established in 1946). That was the equivalent of nearly half the population of Britain. To cope with these numbers, the British Control Commission employed some 20,000 people in Germany. Against the background of a hopelessly over-extended British economy at the end of the war and the strain on supplies to the British people that this situation created (food rationing continued until 1951!), it was hardly surprising the United Kingdom was compared to an *"undersized giant snake which was virtually suffocating on its oversized prey, Germany"*. Indeed London had *"neither the financial nor the personnel resources"* (Jochen Thies) for the task of occupation.

Taxes had to be collected in 1945 too!
And the Germans were as diligent as ever. How come?

Just what "indirect rule" meant in concrete terms can be demonstrated with the example of Emsland in north-western Germany. What was the first German administrative office to resume its activities in Meppen, at the heart of the Ems region, on 1.5.1945, even before capitulation? The Inland Revenue Office. All taxes were collected as before, including the advance payment on turnover tax due on 10 April... (Joachim Kuropka: "British Occupation Policy and the New Beginning of Public Life", in: "Neubeginn 1945", Vechta 1988)

For many of the observers who reconnoitred and evaluated the situation for the occupation authorities at that time, the main impression they came away with from their various trips through the ravaged country was that of the German people's unbroken will to work. This was also the impression gained by Sir Ivone Kirkpatrick, First Secretary at the British Embassy in Berlin from 1933-1938, a member of the political office of the Allied High Command in 1944/45 and British High Commissioner for Germany from 1950-53. In a letter to the Foreign Secretary Anthony Eden, dated 26 June 1945, Kirkpatrick wrote that his "first and most striking impression from post-war Germany" had been the "diligence of the people".

spotlight 41

This had struck him particularly when compared to France. The Germans also seemed less pessimistic and possessed of greater self-confidence than the French.

The reasons for this astonishing strength were eloquently summarised in a report compiled by the "Political Intelligence Department" of the British occupation forces and dated 23.8.1945. The line of argument went roughly like this:

"Relieved at having escaped the catastrophe, most Germans do not think much about the past, and feelings of guilt are not uppermost in their minds. The idea that each people is responsible for its leader is very difficult to convey to the Germans. That could be due to the burden of dealing with the current problems of survival which pushes everything else to the back of their minds. But there seems to be a typically German reaction involved here too, a feeling of having been powerless to prevent National Socialism, leading to a certain self-pity as expressed in the much-repeated lament: "We have been lied to and deceived." (Joachim Kuropka)

The implication of this analysis is quite clear: As Germans mustered a renewed willingness to work and reconstruct their country, one obviously could not expect them at the same time to face up to their grisly crimes. Indeed, only when the Germans felt reasonably secure again did they wake up to the reality of their past.

Nevertheless, there were tasks which had to be performed and ideas about how best to tackle them very soon focused on involving the Germans themselves - at least those who had not been corrupted - in the administrative and reconstruction work. The principle of "indirect rule" was thus equally motivated by both philanthropic and economic reasons: offer help so they can help themselves, but also accept help in order to help *yourself*.

Nor was there any doubt that the way forward had to be "from the bottom up"; the structures themselves had to be built with the participation of the people, at the grass-roots. *"Projecting Great Britain"* was taken as the slogan: the cure called for a model to which the "patient" could aspire. And what could be more attractive than Britain's democratic institutions?

At no point in its history has Britain come closer to the American concept of "manifest destiny" than in those years when an attempt was made "to make Germany safe for British-style democracy". A confidential Foreign Office directive of September 1945 spelled this out in proud and clear terms: *"Our democracy (is) the strongest in the world. (...) We export it and, carefully tended, it blossoms and blooms in different lands."*

The British idealism of those early years of German reconstruction, the "naiveté" which it allegedly shared with the Americans, has often been held up to ridicule - just as the underlying premise of cultural superiority has often been criticised, even by the British themselves. Con O'Neill, for example, warned against succumbing to the temptation *"to run the conqueror's culture down the conquered's throat"* - an impression which was unavoidable in view of the principle of "projecting Great Britain". Some Germans did in fact moan about "re-education" being a presumptuous policy of Anglo-American "Commissars".

Occasionally, this complaint appeared quite justified, but mostly on the grounds of certain acts of sovereignty by the Military Government which often wielded power like a colonial governor.

Anyone with good contacts in high places among the occupying power could make his mark in the local community - sometimes by means which were not entirely above board, as Joachim Kuropka recounts. A joke circulating at the time drew unpalatable comparisons:

"O Lord, hear our prayer!
Give us the Fifth Reich,
Because the Fourth is just like the Third."

Underlying this moroseness was Germany's complex psychological situation as a vanquished country struggling to find a new sense of self-worth and trying to win some breathing space by going on the defensive. Yet the overwhelming majority of Germans were well aware that their self-esteem was closely connected with the reconstruction of a democratic Germany. "Democracy" eventually developed its own head of steam and became as irresistible as school meals were to children in the British zone...

Along with democracy came western literature and popular music, including jazz, which had been sorely missed since the "Golden Twenties". In short, the more relaxed Anglo-American "way of life" began to establish itself in post-war Germany.

Enlightenment was the great motto of the day. "The human face of democracy" was the title of a 1947 publication by the "Civic Education Office of the Land Government of North Rhine-Westphalia", part of a new "Series of Publications with a political and cultural content". According to the editors, the purpose of the series was to: *"bring the country's major political events and the philosophical foundations of the new democratic order to the attention of the widest possible readership in a lively and popular style. Its intention is to win people over for the idea of democracy."*

Trust in common sense! Mistrust power!

In the summer of 1950, John Macmurray was invited by the Hanover-Münden branch of the "Deutsch-Englische Gesellschaft e.V." (cf. also Chapter IV, 4, p. 140) to conduct a lecture tour. The respected Scottish philosopher (whose communitarian ideas were later to have a great influence on Tony Blair...) chose to explain British thinking to his audiences.

The title of the booklet containing Macmurray's speech text was "England - Wegbereiter der kommenden Weltkultur?" ("England - the pioneer of future world culture?") - a deliberately provocative formulation (the original title had been more modest: "The Philosophical Pattern of Our Time") designed to prompt "German authors, essayists, artists and philosophers ... to produce counter-theses", for which prizes would be awarded, as the wrapper around the slim volume promised.

This attempt to generate a debate was assisted by the aspects Macmurray highlighted in his lecture. They shed a typical light on the transport of culture across the Channel to Germany, which has since served as a basis for German understanding of the British character. Trying to explain the Anglo-Saxon mentality, the Scottish philosopher stressed two aspects in particular: empiricism and common sense coupled with a sceptical view of power.

"The British have developed a tradition and a history where the tendency to think and act in personal categories and to regard human values as personal values is paramount. They resist the pressure of 'analogous ideas' in the human sphere which attempt to get the better of society with mechanistic designs or biological purposes ('survival of the fittest'). That is the source of their empiricism and their common sense. The British cope with the technical problems of modern civilisation by separating theory and practice. 'That is quite correct in theory', they say, 'but it does not work in practice.'"

This was Macmurray's second central idea:

"Modern history has been about the accumulation of power in order to gain dominance over nature. (...) But power can never really be a goal in itself since it is merely a general word for means or instrument. (...) The true purpose of gaining

power is freedom. The use of power requires self-knowledge and self-control."
One might assume that, by the summer of 1950, Germany was fertile ground for
Macmurray's ideas and arguments. After its terrible awakening, the country was
virtually reborn with the idea of vigilance against the temptations of power. An early
example of this can be found in the speech made by Reinhold Schneider at a
memorial ceremony in 1947 for the victims of the assassination attempt on Hitler on
20 July 1944: "We must learn to carefully scrutinise those who strive for power. Each
one of us must recognise our joint responsibility for the just administration of power.
(...) We Germans have been too much in love with introspection..."

"Winning people over for the idea of democracy" was now the German watchword par excellence. It echoed the "projecting Britain" motto of British planners and their hope that Westminster-style democracy would "blossom" when exported to foreign countries. The secret of its success in Germany was the fact that democracy was not a completely alien concept to Germans. German Liberals had always looked to the British parliamentary system as a model, an aspiration left unfulfilled under the conditions of Prussian autocracy. Only now, after the failed democratic interlude of the Weimar Republic, was it possible to assert itself with the assistance of its highly esteemed role-model.

Exactly 44 years after the historic turning point in 1945, Europe experienced a second turning point and, to a certain extent, a return to the situation at the end of the Second World War. Eastern Europe was finally able to cast off the yoke of Communism and reach out for the democratic institutions which had been in sight in 1945 - before Stalin brought down the Iron Curtain separating hope from fulfilment. It's true, there were no "Allied Commissars" watching over the Eastern Europeans when they abandoned the ruins of a Communist legacy and set out on the path to democratic renewal.

But that may have spared them the irritations of occupation which Germany went through 50 years earlier. Indeed, Eastern Europe was very much left to fend for itself, without the spiritual and material assistance that had helped the work-driven Germans get back on their feet so quickly.

This is eventually what shaped the psychology of relations between the British and the Germans, not their initial roles as occupiers and occupied. In any case, under the impact of the Cold War, the "occupiers" rapidly developed into "protectors" and then into "friends". What had begun as constructive involvement in Germany after 1945 became a unique pas de deux of history despite the fact that, only a short while before, the two countries had fought a life-and-death duel and Allied bombers had reduced Germany's cities to rubble.

Historic breakthroughs obviously owe as much to "patient drilling away at thick planks" (to quote Max Weber) as to the almost surrealist element of surprise. Such turning points often follow periods of utter exhaustion - exhaustion in the wake of war and devastation in 1945 as well as the exhaustion of a crumbling ideology in 1989/90.

3. *The British hand in reconstruction: specific examples*

On 19 October 1945, the united British military commanders of Vechta and Oldenburg celebrated a memorable day: the opening of the first *Kreistag* (district assembly) of the British Occupation Zone in Vechta. The proclamation to mark this occasion said it all:

" The district of Vechta will become known as the birthplace of democratic government in Germany. It is the first district in Germany where people can see that Germany's successful reconstruction depends on self-government by the

people. No foreign government is being imposed on you. You yourselves will vote for the government you want. But before the elections it would be good to learn the correct form of democracy. It is like learning to walk - you should not try to run before you can walk. (...) It is the same thing with self-government."

Self-government, democracy "from the bottom up" - that had a good German ring to it: subsidiarity. "The inadequacies of personnel in all areas of the British administration" (Angelika Volle) were gradually overcome as the occupying authorities increasingly delegated management tasks to German civilians, beginning with the lowest administrative groups at local and district level. To help establish such groups, it became important to found political parties, democratic magnetic fields to attract and harness the political forces. Britain was the first of the allied occupying powers officially to permit political parties in its zone in February 1946.

That same month, the British Government also created the "Zonal Advisory Council", consisting of representatives of the political parties, trade unions, industrial associations and the regional governments. Restrictions on this senior German advisory body were, however, very tight indeed; every item on the agenda had to be approved by the British liaison staff before it could be discussed.

A review of British influences on the institutional fabric developing in post-war German structures produces a mixed picture. Evidence of a British "hand" most certainly cannot be denied - but neither can the shortcomings, which the occupiers either could not overcome or which they preferred to leave alone. Here are a few examples:

Local government reform

The German tradition of concentrating power in the hands of local mayors was a thorn in the side for planners in London. They feared (rightly, if one looked at the period of National Socialism) that this could again produce an unwelcome *"Führer"* figure. It was consequently decided to adopt the British system of having two leading officials - a mayor, in an honorary capacity and a town clerk, as head of the administration. The municipal council was to be the sole decision-making body and the mayor merely *"primus inter pares"*.

By contrast, attempts to introduce another facet of the British system, the non-political senior civil servant, were less successful. Germany's party political tradition proved stronger in this particular sphere.

Trade unions

Because Britain had sprouted hundreds of individual trade unions, the concept of an umbrella organisation was one which had always eluded the British on their home ground. They were all the more determined to establish it in Germany as part of their administrative responsibilities there. Consequently, in October 1949, the German Federation of Trade Unions (DGB) was constituted from 16 separate industrial unions throughout the occupation zones. Eventually, this developed its own momentum far in excess of what British planners had envisaged, leading all the way to *"Mitbestimmung"*, employee co-determination in employer decision-making.

Media policy: the press

Licences for new magazines and newspapers in the western zones of Germany were among the most highly coveted prizes the occupiers had to award.

That said, the British deserve a special compliment in that some of the most powerful and influential German national papers emerged under their post-war authority. This shows how carefully they selected licence-holders. The list of those awarded licences in Hamburg between 1946 and 1948 makes impressive reading: the radio listings magazine *Hörzu*, the weekly newspaper *Die ZEIT*, the news magazine *Der SPIEGEL*, the illustrated magazine *Stern* and the daily paper *Die Welt* - all of them household names today.

An independent press "made in Britain" - a model for post-war German journalism

School of journalism (I):
The daily newspaper "Die Welt" under Scottish management.

Die Welt played a special role in the media policy of the British occupation zone. Unlike the other newly established national papers which were given free licences, this paper remained expressly in British hands until 1953 as an "All-party newspaper for the British Zone" as its subtitle proclaimed until 1949. It was designed to be a flagship of British media tradition for factual, objective and fair reporting. In fact, it fulfilled this task more accurately than its owners would probably have liked. This was due entirely to its intractable editor-in-chief, the Scot, Steele McRichie. In his memoirs, Michael Thomas, a German Jewish Émigré in Britain who returned to Germany as an English officer during the occupation, made the following comment about McRichie:

"Under McRichie's leadership the paper resisted all attempts at interference by head office and granted its English and German employees the freedom to create an excellent newspaper whose reports on Germany provided a better model of objective journalism than even their British equivalents."

Not surprisingly, Die Welt advanced to become the most widely-read national daily newspaper in Germany during that period. In its heyday, circulation figures topped the million mark. It was sold to the publisher Axel Springer in 1953.

Media policy: radio

One of the most important projects in the British occupation zone was the establishment of an independent radio station. Little headway was made until the Director General of the BBC, Sir William Hayley, decided to send one of his best men, the director of the BBC's German language service, Hugh Carleton Greene, to Germany in 1946. Hugh Greene, brother of the novelist Graham Greene, knew the country from pre-war days. He had worked as the *Daily Telegraph* correspondent in Berlin from 1934-1939. Then in 1940, at the tender age of 30, he was put in charge of the BBC German language service, established in 1939 as a weapon against Nazi Germany and lovingly known as "Londoner Rundfunk" by those who worked for it.

During the first few years under Greene's brilliant leadership, the phrase "Hier spricht London!" was a signal of hope for many Germans living under oppression. They secretly tuned in despite the threat of draconian punishment ("enemy radio!"). Hugh Greene was posted to Hamburg in 1946 and it was not long before his organisational talents and inventiveness had turned the "flea circus", which was having problems getting off the ground, into the new *Nordwestdeutscher Rundfunk* (NWDR) - and promptly became its first director. (He finally rose to become Director General of the BBC in 1960, a position he held for eight years).

Hugh Greene fervently believed that news was the fundamental element of BBC-style radio journalism; he broadcast without bothering too much about the views of London head office. This produced one particularly delightful episode. When Cardinal Frings of Cologne publicly declared during the severe fuel shortage in the freezing winter of 1946/47 that the Seventh Commandment "Thou shalt not steal" did not apply to pilfering coal (the verb in the vernacular for this practice soon became "fringsen"), Greene went one step further by having the routes and arrival times of the coal trains announced over the air...

School of journalism (II): The German language service of the BBC.

spotlight 44

Looking back, it is hard to appreciate just how important the German programme of the BBC's External Services was for those who worked on it during the war and post-war years. Initially it gave Émigrés like Erich Fried, the poet, Martin Esslin, the renowned Brecht expert or Richard Friedenthal, author of popular historical biographies, the opportunity to influence German journalism from London.

Subsequently, one important factor in the reconstruction of media freedom in post-war Germany was the large number of cross-Channel "commuters" who had all spent part of their career with the BBC and brought principles like objectivity, impartiality and fairness to German journalism. To mention just a few of them: Franz Schnabel, who became Director of the "Norddeutscher Rundfunk" after his time with the BBC (in the mid-1950s the NWDR was split up into the "Norddeutscher Rundfunk" in Hamburg and the "Westdeutscher Rundfunk" in Cologne); Franz Woerdemann, later editor-in-chief of WDR; Werner Baecker, who went on to make a name for himself as the New York correspondent for German television (ARD); the late Carl Brinitzer (who wrote one of the best books about the "German BBC" in 1969: "Hier spricht London"); and Hans Joachim "Hajo" Friedrichs, sadly also no longer with us, who became a household name in many spheres of broadcasting.

What made the German language service of the BBC the "best school for journalists in the world"? This question was once posed by another of its "graduates", Rudolf Walter Leonhardt, for many years feature section editor of Die ZEIT. The answer: invaluable learning experience, which Leonhardt summed up as follows:

"That sound knowledge of one's craft is important; that it is not sufficient to be a specialist; that there is no piece of information which cannot be formulated in a comprehensible way; (...) that there is nothing which reasonable people cannot discuss reasonably with one another; that it is quite easy to be brilliant and quite difficult to be fair; (...) that even the (...) enemy has to be taken seriously before one can combat him; that a sports reporter often produces something more important than a leader writer; that there is no good irony without self-irony; (...) that parliamentary democracy is the most humane of all contestable forms of exerting power..." (Die ZEIT, 9.5.1975)

Leonhardt's litany is reminiscent of what the much-criticised "re-education" process had really wanted to provide: an opportunity to practise democratic modes of behaviour and to assimilate them until they became second nature. Nowhere was this practice more necessary than in the central area of communications - the media. Those with British "schooling" felt up to the tasks of their profession. Candidly and not without a certain pride - typical for this post-war generation - Leonhardt, author of an early standard work on Britain ("77mal England") admits his debt of gratitude:

"We have filled our tanks with so much British fuel that it will last us till the end of our life's journey. We are prepared and even well-equipped to criticise the British; but at the bottom of our hearts we are probably incurably Anglophile."

However, the Director was less successful in his efforts to equip the newly founded NWDR with an independent board of control like the BBC's Board of Governors, which is run by leading public figures, but contains no party politicians. Greene could not prevent the emergence of proportional party representation and jockeying for position. Worse still, "party allegiance" started to become important for journalistic careers in German State broadcasting corporations.

Hugh Carleton Greene: established the Nordwestdeutscher Rundfunk (NWDR)

Education system

To the great regret of many who would have preferred to see things turn out differently, the British zonal administration capitulated in the face of the federal sovereignty of the German Länder on the subject of the education system. Robert Birley, the Military Governor's "Educational Adviser", paid regular visits to the Education Ministers of all the occupation zones in an attempt "to bring them out of their petty-minded federalism and onto a uniform course" (Michael Thomas). To no avail.

While the decentralisation of power structures in Germany was one of the constitutional principles favoured by Britain's policy towards Germany, a passionate educationalist like Birley was quick to recognise the dangers fragmentation could pose for the education system.

Faced with an intractable situation, the British control authority had no choice but to hold back on reform of the German higher education system. It opted instead to exert its influence through the establishment of adult education institutions. It is too painful to contemplate what a great opportunity the German university system missed by the British reluctance to impose their own successful college model, which offers the possibility of an interim graduate qualification through the Bachelor Degree to those who do not want to pursue a wider academic career. In this way, the British could have shown their gratitude for what the German education system had brought their universities 120 years before.

Sadly, it did not happen. Instead, post-war Germany reverted to its old practices and today largely follows the traditional structure of what is euphemistically called "academic freedom". This often results in a seemingly endless period of studies, when in fact earlier graduation, i.e. earlier contact with practical work experience, could be crucial not only for the maturing of young adults but also for survival in an age of increasing global competition.

Parliamentarianism

When it came to the fundamental area of democratic activity, parliament, the Germans needed little encouragement from the occupying authorities. As explained above, the liberal elite had long been keen to adopt British parliamentary traditions. The Westminster system of parliamentary committees, for example, was copied right away - a system enabling the legislative assembly to acquire an equivalent level of knowledge to that of Cabinet Departments.

However, it proved impossible to introduce more of the House of Commons style of spontaneous dialogue into everyday parliamentary business. There seems to be an inherent inhibition here, which may be due to the fact that, unlike in Britain, the German education system offers little training, if any, in the art of debating. As a result, in situations where trained wit and presence of mind are required, people are reluctant to show they might lack these skills - especially in front of TV cameras. That is why speeches and statements in the Bundestag are generally read out from prepared texts.

Heine praises the debates in the House of Commons -
Goethe wavers in his support for German federalism.

Heinrich Heine, the wit who really could not forgive "perfidious Albion" for capturing his beloved Napoleon and banishing him to St. Helena, was nevertheless entranced by the impressions he gained during his trip to England in 1827. Among his reports from that time is a wonderful description of the debating style in the House of Commons which Heine particularly enjoyed because it matched his own sense of humour so closely:

"The more important a subject, the funnier it must be treated... The English know this, which is why their Parliament offers such a merry spectacle of unself-conscious wit and witty unself-consciousness; in major debates, where the lives of thousands and the fate of entire nations are at stake, no one would think of grimacing like a stiff German or making an emotional speech like a Frenchman.

Jokes, self-irony, sarcasm, sentimentality and wisdom, malice and benevolence, logic and poetry all spill forth in the most colourful fashion so that the annals of Parliament provide us with witty entertainment even years later. What a difference to the dry, stuffy and tedious speeches by our southern German parliaments whose dullness overtaxes even the most patient newspaper reader."

("English Fragments", 1828)

In the same year Heine published his tribute to the extemporised speeches in the House of Commons, Goethe declared his affection for German federalism in a conversation with Eckermann (23.10.1828) which must have echoed in the ears of the allied founding fathers of the Federal Republic:

"How did Germany become great if not through an admirable popular culture which has spread to all parts of the Empire. (...) Imagine if for centuries we had only had the two capitals, Vienna and Berlin, or even just one of them, I should like to see what state German culture would be in now? And the state of our general prosperity, which goes hand in hand with culture!"

But beware of citing Goethe as a principal witness in support of Anglo-Saxon attempts to decentralise Germany after the Second World War! Goethe said a lot about a lot of things - and often it was the opposite of what he had said before. Federalism is a case in point. It always depended on the angle from which he approached the issue. As far as culture was concerned, or at least exchanges among the best minds, Goethe could also perceive decentralisation as a great handicap: the scattering of individual artists to different regions of the country and their resulting isolation. That, incidentally, is just as true of Germany today as it was 170 years ago. Even Fax and Internet cannot alter that fact (but perhaps it will be different with Berlin as the capital, like back in the 1920s?). At any rate, Goethe was moved to complain to Eckermann on 3.5.1827:

"Basically, we all lead an isolated, miserable sort of life! (...) All our talents and our great minds are scattered throughout Germany. One is in Vienna, another in Berlin, another in Königsberg, another in Bonn or Düsseldorf, all (...) separated from each other so that personal contact and personal exchange of thought have become a rarity."

4. The official and unofficial fora for promoting understanding

Robert - later Sir Robert - Birley, whose name is so inseparably linked with Germany's democratic rebirth, operated out of a spacious villa in Bad Rothenfelde in the Teutoburg forest, where he brought prominent German and British figures together at his "weekend parties" to discuss the future - not only of Germany's reconstruction but also of German-British relations. To him, it was a matter of overcoming mistrust between the defeated population and the occupiers but also even greater mistrust on the British side of the Germans and their supposedly uncanny nature.

One day Birley was visited by a Dutch woman who had worked in the resistance against the Nazis and was now spending all her time helping out in the German Protestant Church. They talked about international relations and the rebuilding of trust between the previously warring nations: *"You see, the last war"*, the Dutch woman said, *"was not the kind of war that was won by winning the war. Winning it had to come after it was over."*

A paradox full of profound truth. It explained better than a thousand books the scale of the tasks facing the architects of European rebirth after 1945, of which German-British understanding formed just a part. Occupation policy regulated, stimulated, got things moving, helped lay the foundations of structures for a peaceful world in the future. But democracy is not about ordinances and dead letters. Democracy begins with the lively exchange of ideas, of opinion and dissent, as John Milton once wrote: *"Where there is much desire to learn, there of necessity will be much arguing, much writing, many opinions; for opinion in good men is but knowledge in the making."*

After 1945, it was therefore important to satisfy this "desire to learn" as comprehensively as possible - not just with theories from books and pamphlets, but with opportunities for dialogue, conversation and discussion. This is where the British feel their strength lies and this is where the planners saw a unique opportunity to breathe life into democracy in the post-war period.

An important chapter in the rebuilding of German-British relations after the Second World War was therefore the establishment of a rich variety of fora, discussion groups and organisations which promoted "knowledge" through an exchange of "opinions". Emphasis was placed on discussion not the textbook, on practising the Socratic democratic culture of debate rather than simply imparting the wisdom contained in learned tomes. Getting to know one another through personal contact, not by ingesting abstract truths - this was considered the true path to democracy and a way of shaping Germany's future elite.

Many of these institutions founded after 1945 still exist today. Others have transformed themselves to meet new tasks and challenges. All have played and continue to play a role as guarantors of a high culture of relations and sustained understanding between the British and the Germans.

Wilton Park

Wilton Park near Beaconsfield in Buckinghamshire is one of those British country houses set in apparently endless grounds where one could easily forget the outside world existed. "POW Camp 300", a camp for German prisoners of war, was established here in 1944. And this is where the German émigré Dr. Heinz Koeppler, an Oxford historian, was given a chance to test the idea he had proposed in a memorandum for the Foreign Office on future developments in Germany: an educational centre for POWs as part of the effort to prepare German citizens for assuming new responsibilities back in their own country - and thus to give Germany itself an opportunity to rehabilitate itself in the eyes of the world.

The Berlin-born lecturer on mediaeval history was just as averse to the term "re-education" as Robert Birley, the head of the "Education Branch" of the British occupation authority in Germany. *"Re-education"*, Koeppler used to say, *"is a horse born of ignorance, out of arrogance, and with such a pedigree will never win a race."* (Dexter M. Keezer, "The Story of Wilton Park", 1973). The news that "POW Camp 300" was to form the nucleus of his work must have come as quite a surprise. Little did he realise then that he would stay on as Warden of Wilton Park for thirty years. His was a unique career in the service of international understanding.

Participants in the seminars and discussion groups comprised POWs not only from Wilton Park but also from other camps inside and outside Britain. The tutors spoke fluent German and the emphasis was on discussion of the course material, among participants and in direct contact with the tutor. The "Nissen" huts scattered around the grounds of Wilton Park gave it somehow the atmosphere of a "POW college". In the first three years alone, from

1946 to 1948, no less than 4,500 German soldiers "graduated" from Wilton.

As early as 1947, the British authorities opened the courses to German civilians who were considered potential leading figures in the reconstruction of their country. Volunteers from the other allied occupation zones were also permitted to apply. Wilton Park and its culture of debate, this central feature of an "open society", became a testing ground for a new post-war German elite. Among them were Rainer Barzel, Ralf Dahrendorf and Hildegard Hamm-Brücher. On the occasion of its 25th anniversary in 1971, Helmut Schmidt, then Federal Minister of Defence, had this to say in the official "Bulletin" of the German Government:

"The image of Britain for almost an entire generation of German politicians was given clear contours at Wilton Park. At a time when German-British relations stood under a less favourable star than they do today, Wilton Park was one of the bridges which could be relied upon to take the load."

In 1950, the venue was moved from Buckinghamshire to Sussex, to another country house with a similar name, Wiston House, near Brighton. The courses, now extended to cover international relations, also take overseas participants (principally from America) and Wiston House itself has become an international conference centre. But the "Wilton Park Conferences" continue to exist as a British-German institution. Each year they bring established and emerging personalities together to ensure that the chain of bilateral and multilateral relations remains unbroken.

Die Brücke

They were originally intended as meeting places - information centres, newspaper reading rooms, libraries and lecture halls all in one: 34 addresses in the British zone permitted to use the name *Die Brücke*. On the square outside the main building of Münster's *Westfälische Wilhelms-Universität*, for example, *Die Brücke* was housed in a Nissen hut not unlike those used as POW accommodation in "Camp 300" at Wilton Park. But that did not matter. In those days the Germans - especially aspiring academics - had only one interest: to still their hunger for the intellectual fruits of which they had been deprived for so long. Consequently, wherever a town had *Die Brücke* to offer, it became a centre of reading, listening, discussion, learning - in short, part of the post-war democratic fitness programme. On average, 500,000 people per month (!) took advantage of the various services provided by these centres.

Die Brücke, like Wilton Park, came under the auspices of the Foreign Office, which held overall responsibility for cultural matters involving Germany. In 1958 this responsibility was devolved to the British Council, which combines the areas of interest pursued on Germany's behalf by the Goethe-Institut and the Deutscher Akademischer Austauschdienst. The last of the *"Brücke"* centres closed in the early 1960s, much to the regret of the German public. Most of the books were passed on to German universities and schools offering adult evening classes. The Council set up its German headquarters in the former premises of *"Die Brücke"* in Cologne, from which to manage its network of centres in Berlin, Munich, Hamburg and (from 1992) Leipzig.

The Deutsch-Englische Gesellschaft / Königswinter Conference

Among the many German-British organisations founded in the post-war years, one stands out in particular. It owes its existence less to the occupying authorities than to the single-minded initiative and tenacity of one German woman, Lilo Milchsack, the wife of a Rhine shipping entrepreneur from Wittlaer. The *Deutsch-Englische Gesellschaft* (DEG), founded in Düsseldorf on 18 March 1949, can boast an impressive *curriculum vitae*. In the shape of the Königswinter Conferences, which have been held annually since they were established by the DEG in 1950, it also possesses a forum for continued influence on the elite of the two countries.

Lilo Milchsack and her husband had survived National Socialism without politically compromising themselves. They kept their distance from the ruling ideology, concentrating instead on their Rhine shipping business - also to the benefit of the Dutch. It was this "Dutch connection" which helped the owner of the company to receive a "non-enemy alien" certificate from them after 1945 - the only German to do so, as Ralf Uhlig recounts in his book *"Die Deutsch-Englische Gesellschaft 1949-1983 - Der Beitrag ihrer Königswinter Konferenzen zur britisch-deutschen Verständigung"* (The Deutsch-Englische Gesellschaft 1949-1983 - The contribution of its Königswinter Conferences to British-German understanding").

Königswinter conference: relaxed atmosphere, historic encounters

Lilo Milchsack was a committed humanist who worked for the German Red Cross after the War and personally helped many "displaced persons" - foreign forced labour, penniless and often stateless, hoping somehow for repatriation - who were in a desperate plight at the time. Her activities came to the attention of Robert Birley, who was to become Lilo and Hans Milchsack's most important interlocutor and sponsor for their project of a German-British society.

Lilo Milchsack was no less concerned about the British than she was about the Germans - perhaps even more so?

For our tour d'horizon it is important to remember that Lilo Milchsack's idea to establish a forum to promote German-British understanding did not originate from the standard train of thought - i.e. helping to return Germany to the sphere of Western culture. Her motivation came from a different experience.

She had visited England in early 1948 at the invitation of the Foreign Office and the British Council as a member of a group of German women who were permitted to conduct talks in Norwich and Cambridge - "permitted" being the operative word. The trip was remarkable in that, as a rule, Germans living under occupation were not allowed to travel abroad in those days, as Ralph Uhlig recalls. The exception made for this group of women thus took on the character of high diplomacy. And that is exactly how Frau Milchsack and her group felt they were being treated throughout their trip.

The women were received in the kindest and most affable manner imaginable - which greatly troubled Lilo Milchsack. Her generation had experienced how the appeasement mentality in England during the 1930s had encouraged and even emboldened Hitler to pursue his aggressive policies. On her return to Germany, she confided in Robert Birley, the "Education Minister" of the British zone: might this expansive generosity of the British not perhaps one day lead them to miscalculate German policy once again or simply to look the other way if dark clouds re-appeared?

For Lilo Milchsack the idea of founding a Deutsch-Englische Gesellschaft, and the Königswinter Conferences to which this idea naturally led, was the recognition of a need on both sides. Practising the art of getting to know one another was intended to ensure that each side had a clear idea of the other and would never again base its policies on misunderstandings or misplaced sentiment.

Lilo Milchsack made no bones about what she thought, which earned her the rather disparaging nickname "red Lilo" in some quarters of the young Federal Republic. But it did not seem to bother her (Birley also had to live with some people calling him "Red Robert"...) She was sure of what she was doing and the success of the Königswinter Conferences confirmed that she had indeed discovered an important hinge for international relations: an institutionalised forum for the elite of the two countries to learn how to broaden and deepen their professionalism by exchanging experiences in talks and encounters between people and their counterparts.

What was the saying made famous by August Comte, the French 19th century Positivist?

"Savoir pour prévoir, prévoir pour prévenir".

That was the stuff Lilo Milchsack was made of.

The DEG now has twenty branches (*"Landesgruppen"* and *"Arbeitskreise"*) throughout Germany, each offering a rich programme of encounters, guest lectures and social events stretching into all regional areas of Germany - a further aspect which helps to maintain the high personal and professional quality of German-British relations. The DEG working groups also provided a welcome opportunity for British people working in Germany, for example the soldiers of the British Rhine Army (BAOR), to meet members of their host country with whom they and their families might otherwise not have made contact so easily.

This depth of German-British understanding is all the more remarkable if one considers that the DEG was established with private funds at a time when nothing seemed possible without official backing. So it came as no surprise when Lilo Milchsack was singled out for a special honour by the Queen, who appointed her an Honorary Dame Commander of the Order of St. Michael and St. George (DCMG) in 1972 - a unique privilege for a German woman. Dame Lilo lived to a grand old age and was thus able to witness not only the success of her original idea but also its blossoming growth. She died, aged 87, on 8 August 1992.

Königswinter, located just south-east of Bonn on the Rhine, was chosen as the venue for the Conferences because Bonn was the seat of the new Federal Government; geographical proximity to the centre of political power was regarded as particularly important for contact between German parliamentarians and their British counterparts - above all in the margins of the meetings proper. The Conferences have always been held at the Adam-Stegerwald-Haus, a former conference centre of the Christian trade unions, which was later taken over by the social affairs committees of the CDU.

Prior to 1970, Königswinter Conferences were convened only twice in Great Britain - once in Oxford (1964) and once in Cambridge (1970). It was not until 1974 that the Conferences acquired their now characteristic form of alternating venues between Königswinter and Great Britain on uneven and even years respectively. The British venue varied initially - Edinburgh in 1974, Oxford in 1976 and 1978. Then in 1980, the British side also decided on a permanent venue: St. Catharine's College, Cambridge.

("Königswinter", by the way, has only been cancelled once - in March 1966, due to the general elections in Britain at that time. But it was touch and go another time, namely during the Falklands crisis, when MPs and Government Ministers had to neglect their lecturing and debating "duties" in Cambridge to attend a rare Saturday session of the House of Commons in London. However, they returned to the Conference in the evening, with history in their briefcases... The German side twice recommended a departure from the usual routine - in 1991, Dresden to mark the year after unification, and Berlin in 1997. Two "steering committees" are responsible for the forward planning of each conference.)

Various countries have attempted to imitate the "Königswinter principle" in their bilateral relations. But not very successfully, it must be said. By its very nature, this British-German forum is unique: the unique free exchange between leading figures from industry, science, politics and publishing; the unique prestige which has developed over the years and the special statement which each of the 120 invitees (participation by invitation only) has to contribute, especially if he or she has been given particular tasks to perform during the sessions; and, despite all the conference rules, the uniquely informal atmosphere which turns "the margins" into an ideal meeting place for exchanging ideas and making contacts. That is something which is particularly appreciated by all those who occasionally need to escape the flood of their day-to-day paperwork. Away from Parliaments and Cabinets the ground is sometimes more fertile for new ideas...

This is also true within the respective delegations themselves. It was during the 1981 Königswinter Conference, for example, that the leaders of the Liberal Party and the Social Democratic Party (SDP), a breakaway party from Labour, decided to merge to form the "Alliance". The paper which David Steele negotiated with Shirley Williams made history as the "Königswinter Declaration". Königswinter Conferences have often been at the cutting edge of such events in contemporary history, lending them a higher profile and preparing the way for change. The forum itself is the product of a singular moment in history - a turning-point for the better in European and German-British relations.

The Anglo-German Association

Founded in London in 1951, the Anglo-German Association (AGA) is not unlike the *Deutsch-Englische Gesellschaft*, but it has less ambitious "philosophical" goals and no generally visible forum to compare with the Königswinter Conference. Initially, its tasks were quite different from those of the DEG, since the Association was more concerned with disseminating knowledge about Germany against the background of a traditionally British "benign neglect" of things European and with trying to overcome traumatic memories of two World Wars. The bilateral element grew as interest in Germany itself increased, awakened by the corresponding AGA events.

The idea to found the AGA was born in 1949, the year of bicentenary celebrations to mark the 200th anniversary of Goethe's birth. One of the speakers at the festivities in London, also attended by Thomas Mann incidentally, was Adolf Grimme, then Minister for Culture in Lower Saxony (and Hugh Greene's successor as Director of NWDR in 1946). By attending, Grimme was repaying a similar visit by the German scholar George Catlin to Heidelberg that same year. It was Catlin who had seized on Goethe's birthday as a great opportunity to improve Germany's image in Britain. He gathered a group of like-minded people at his house, including Sir Harold Nicholson, Lady Bonham Carter and the publisher (and Jewish émigré) Victor Gollancz, to discuss the idea of an Anglo-German Association.

The project probably came too soon, recalls George Turner in "Total War to Total Trust" (1976). Turner was among those on the British side who regarded Germany's reintegration into the West after the Second World War as one of their generation's principal tasks. He was, among other things, head of the information section of the British occupation authorities for 15 years, from 1948 to 1963, and Berlin paid a particular tribute to him for his achievements during the blockade (1948/49).

Two years later, however, the AGA's time had finally come and it was duly "christened" at a meeting of the group of friends at the House of Commons on 15 November 1951. The general public learned about the event from a letter to the *Times*, dated 15 December and signed by the AGA's 24 "godparents", one of whom - naturally - was Robert Birley, meanwhile head of Eton public school. The new forum, the signatories wrote, intended to place itself alongside other existing associations which cultivated bilateral relations with foreign partners in a similar manner. (The Anglo-French Association was already very active at that time.)

The purpose was *"to help spread knowledge about Germany, its way of life and way of thinking."*

The *Times* honoured the event the same day with a leader article, whose author, by adopting a grand historical perspective, gave a masterly treatment of the German-British issue:

"This new association will be most successful if it remains modest in its aims, strictly avoiding all intervention in politics and fully recognizing the limitations of all such bodies. The sad truth is that personal friendship and international policies have very little connection. Some of the most valuable and lasting alliances have been between nations whose peoples cordially dislike each other, while it is not necessary to look far to find a nation whose people almost every Englishman finds charming and attractive but whose foreign policy is detestable. Germany has never lacked friends and admirers in this country; it is her Governments that have been at fault.

Fortunately the prospect of a new and sounder relationship is better than ever before."

This assessment was to prove quite accurate. Consequently, the AGA increasingly assumed the role of architect of reconciliation. Among its achievements is an annual conference of young executives from both sides of the Channel who, like the participants of "Wilton Park", also met initially at Wiston House in Sussex.

It had such a strong influence on the Deutsch-Englische Gesellschaft that the latter also established its own "Young Königswinter" conferences, which have been held annually since 1967. Synergy and competition - the stimulating pattern of today's German-British exchange.

At the end of 1995, the AGA changed its name to BGA - British-German Association. This was primarily to comply with the wishes of the Scottish members and followed the example of the "Anglo-French Association", which now calls itself the "Franco-British Association".

The Anglo-German Foundation for the Study of Industrial Society

So is the term "Anglo-" finally out? Not quite. It lives on in many combinations. "Anglo-German relations" still trips off the tongue more easily than "British-German relations". But when a powerful voice from the British regions calls for an end to such "Anglicisation"... Nevertheless, there is one further important bilateral organisation which has retained the "Anglo-" in its name: the "Anglo-German Foundation for the Study of Industrial Society".

The intention to establish a foundation with a title as precise as it is cumbersome was announced in 1972, on the occasion of the State visit to Britain by Federal President Gustav Heinemann. This was the second visit of its kind, following Theodor Heuss in 1958. In the intervening years, British-German relations had matured into a close partnership; the two countries now no longer merely watched each other cautiously but looked together into a common future where they faced similar problems: the economy, the environment, the labour market, social welfare, industrial policy versus the free market, productivity, worker co-determination, technology, classical versus modern culture, etc.

To research these issues, exchange experience and tackle the future together was the agenda which the Foundation had set itself. Gustav Heinemann succinctly expressed these goals in his speech at the London Guildhall on 27 October 1972:

"Europe has set out to reorganise its political and economic life. Our two nations can render an essential contribution towards the solution of the tasks of the future which will confront modern industrial society. I should welcome it if these considerations were also to guide the work of the Anglo-German Foundation for the Study of Industrial Society, on whose early establishment our two Governments have agreed."

The Agreement governing the Foundation was signed by Prime Minister Edward Heath and Federal Chancellor Willy Brandt on 2

March 1973 and the Foundation itself was established by royal charter on 5 December of the same year.

By citing Europe, Heinemann looked to the future - yet Europe was also a topical issue for Great Britain at that time. In January 1972, Britain had signed the Treaty of Accession to the European Community which came into force on 1 January 1973. The British had become Europeans - at least with their minds. Their hearts were and still are searching for the meaning of this accession. The London-based Foundation was just the right forum to air this question and tackle its implications in a series of major conferences.

"The aims of the Foundation", it states in Article 2 of the Agreement, *"shall be to promote the study and to deepen the understanding of the problems of modern industrial society in the two States and the ways in which such problems may be resolved"*. In conjunction with the Königswinter Conference, the Foundation awards an annual media prize for outstanding achievements in the promotion of understanding between the Germans and the British. It is financed from German and British public funds in a ratio of two to one.

Since its inception over twenty years ago, this organisation has raised German-British contacts to a new level of professionalism.

The German-British Parliamentary Group

President Heinemann's State visit to Britain came at a time of improving relations between the two countries. With General de Gaulle's death, the obstacle to Britain's accession to the EC was finally removed; and in Willy Brandt, Germany had a Chancellor who knew exactly how to handle his British partners and who was held in great esteem in London on account of his political career.

A further "quiet factor" played an important role in improving the political climate: the German-British Parliamentary Group. This all-party association of back-benchers with a particular interest in German issues had been constituted at Westminster back in 1958. They were also united by a common concern: at the time, bilateral relations were in poor shape and had become noticeably cooler. The personal chemistry between Konrad Adenauer and Harold Macmillan was not very good; Britain and the Continent seemed to be drifting apart.

The idea of forming an association of Parliamentarians interested in Germany is a further initiative for which the Königswinter Conference can take the credit. Nowhere else did Westminster MPs have the opportunity to exchange information - also amongst themselves - about German issues in a faster and more comprehensive way than at Königswinter. After the annual conferences in Germany, it was easier to establish where people stood on issues back home in Britain.

The same was also true on the German side. Inspired by the British model, a similar group of Bundestag Deputies was established in 1960 to promote German-British contact among Parliamentarians. It was soon agreed to hold regular meetings in London and Bonn, scheduled to fall between the Königswinter Conferences.

One cannot overemphasise the incalculable benefits which such close contact brings in terms of education for the individuals concerned and for the overall political culture. In the year after the Wall came down, for example, it was obvious that a large majority of MPs in the House of Commons approached the German question with knowledge gained through intensive contact with their German colleagues. As a result, the debate was conducted in a much less emotional way at this level than at the top of the political executive.

At that time, there was a fear among Conservatives that Britain might fail to grasp the new realities of Europe - or that they might pass Britain by. However complex the new situation was, these MPs at least did not want to be guided by the retrospective sentiment of 1940, the sentiment of Britain's "finest hour" in the battle against

Hitler. Too many of them reacted to the tectonic shifts around them in a different manner to the Prime Minister. They called for political action to be motivated by something other than memories of past glories and fears. In Westminster, nostalgia and concern for the future were on a collision course, which finally claimed Margaret Thatcher as its most prominent victim.

"The New Germans" (1995), by the Labour MP Giles Radice, is the fruit of intensive research and evidence of what such efforts at parliamentary bridge-building can mean for the understanding of contemporary politics. Since 1989, Radice had taken detailed notes on trips by the joint German-British Parliamentary Group, enriched by historical anecdotes and other relevant material, to produce an overall portrait of the "new Germans". Some sceptics about Germany among the book reviewers were annoyed that the conclusions drawn by Radice were, on balance, rather positive.

John Major and Helmut Kohl: friends who may fall into the friendship trap ...

But it remains a remarkable fact that a British MP, despite the everyday pressures of his professional life, took the trouble to study and evaluate the complexities of his neighbours from across the Channel. When will the first Bundestag Deputy take the time to conduct a similar study of the British today?

German-British summits: the hour of the executive

Where the legislative advances, the executive cannot be left behind... So it was that on 7 February 1967 the then Prime Minister, James Callaghan, and his German opposite number, Chancellor Helmut Schmidt, agreed at a bilateral summit at Chequers that these top-level meetings should be held on a regular basis twice a year, the venue alternating between Britain and Germany, along the lines of the Franco-German summit talks.

This involved not only the Heads of Government themselves but also Cabinet departments, soon creating a dense network of continuous communications and - perhaps most importantly - personal friendships. When people speak of "close relations" today, they should not forget this underlying element of professional contact between decision-makers at all levels. Meetings where people no longer talk at but to each other.

On the other hand, so much bilateralism can occasionally suffer from attacks of "bilateralitis", an irritating complaint which provokes much head-scratching. It is brought on by the negative consequences of false expectations and the symptoms have been particularly evident at recent high-level German-British summit meetings. The pattern is always the same: the media are on the look-out for signs of a fresh crisis, whilst officials speak correctly of the personal friendship between Helmut Kohl and John Major. But woe betide if this friendship does not work miracles every time - before you know it, the press is reporting the imminent demise of German-British relations.

But it must be said that the individuals themselves are not completely blameless here. All good personal chemistry between political "protagonists" has to be constantly protected from the over-expectations it automatically generates if one is to avoid repeated disappointment. Indeed, if one takes a closer look, even exchanges at the highest level are not immune to such disappointments. There is a danger here of falling into one's own "friendship trap", so to speak.

Which is precisely what happened to John Major in May 1996 when Brussels renewed the world-wide export ban on British beef and beef byproducts it had imposed two months earlier. It was an angry Prime Minister who told the House of Commons that he had relied on some (unspecified) partners who had given their word that they would advocate a relaxation of the export ban.

The British press pointed the finger at what they considered the precise cause of Major's anger. *"PM's fury at Kohl role in beef ban"*, exclaimed the front-page banner headline of the *Financial Times* on 23 May. The FT is not a paper normally associated with the crisis-mongering cultivated by some sections of the British media. Yet its report insisted that Major felt particularly let down by Helmut Kohl. At the bilateral summit in London in late April, Kohl had allegedly promised to support a relaxation of the export ban - under certain conditions. This promise was in fact honoured, but not before the general public had been deluged with disappointing news about German-British bilateral relations.

The important thing is to keep matters in perspective and learn to distinguish between the objective state of bilateral relations and such misguided public perceptions. Otherwise, these relations would be permanently held hostage to the kinds of domestic crises which every country experiences from time to time. Take the debate on Europe, for instance. It shows the extent to which disagreements about topical issues can overshadow assessments of the long-term quality of a partnership. (cf. Chapter VI)

In its day-to-day business, the German-British partnership continues undeterred. Occasionally, this is also of direct benefit to their European neighbours. One recent example from the summer of 1996: the British Government, at Bonn's instigation, is now collaborating with the French in the newly established "procurement agency" (MRAV), aimed at the joint planning of future armaments production and military equipment. This is just one example of the outcome of close top-level consultations now so commonplace in Europe. Incidentally, such agreements are reached irrespective of any political dissension there may be between the governments concerned. One case in point is the Western European Union (WEU). The German side would like to see closer links between the WEU and the EU, a concept which Whitehall so far rejects.

Professional exchange and reciprocal interaction are now attaining unprecedented levels of co-operation. On 2 June 1996, Britain and Germany opened a joint Mission in the Icelandic capital

Reykjavik. Diplomatic "joint ventures" are entering uncharted territory. A similar arrangement already exists for the Kazakh capital Almaty, where German, British and here also French diplomats share Embassy premises. These are just the first of many such co-location projects in the pipeline. Similarly, it is now common practice for officials to spend several months on secondment to the corresponding Ministry in their partner country. The popularity of these European "further education" schemes speaks for their great success.

En passant: understanding as realpolitik

We have not yet finished with the *Times* leader article of 15 December 1951 and what it had to say about the founding of the Anglo-German Association. After the catastrophes of two World Wars within a single generation, the author had every reason to conclude *"that personal friendships and international politics have little to do with one another"*. He was probably thinking of Talleyrand's maxim that nations do not have friends, only interests. Let us take an objective look at the facts. What use did the British and the Germans make of the blood ties between their two monarchies when it would have been of overriding importance to erect bulwarks against the advent of war? What use did they make of friendships in the higher echelons of British and German society, of friendships which had developed in the course of history? It all proved pointless. A clash of national interests meant war.

But if one agreed that what the *Times* leader writer said about the past also applied to the future, then this would be condemning modern societies to commit the same old mistakes in each new generation and to subscribe blindly to a form of politics which took no account of the state of relations within the "family of man", for example within the European family. The traditional interpretation of "national interests" would continue to apply: a principle for which one is ready even to sacrifice one's own people, to say nothing of the enemy's.

Europeans joined ranks after the Second World War precisely to prevent this ever happening again. Destruction on the Continent had reached such proportions that people feared Europe would not survive a repetition of confrontation and war.

This left politicians with the task of excluding the possibility of such catastrophes recurring once and for all. Vital to this endeavour was the construction of new alliances (including the treaty-based commitment of the USA to Europe's future destiny) and all forms of alliance management. An equally invaluable part was played by the many official and unofficial fora for promoting understanding, which also provided an anchor for German-British relations.

The underlying principle, however, did not stem from some blue-eyed philanthropic concept. It was something much more concrete - a reversal of Europe's traditional course. Arguably, co-operation and peaceful competition were not entirely unknown in the Old World - the Greek philosopher Aristotle had been one of the first to struggle with the concept of just peace settlements. But it had never been entirely possible to prevent national interests from occasionally straying off the path of co-operation and peaceful competition. It was like the missing link in a chain of logical arguments: the realisation that national ambitions are best served by striving to maintain peace.

So 1945 did not stand for a "farewell to *realpolitik*". It was more a matter of finding "new contents for realpolitik", new identifications and new definitions. Talleyrand's maxim is defused if "friendship" and "interests" are no longer contradictory and countries finally recognise that peace offers the best opportunity for the furtherance of their national interests. *That* is the real turning point which 1945 marks in European history, *"an end of social conflict and the beginning of mutual social understanding"*, as Hartmut Kaelble wrote with regard to Franco-German rapprochement.

The politicians who took Europe's destiny in their hands in those days came to embody this new quality of history. To mention just one of these illustrious figures: Jean Monnet (1888-1979) was the first President of the newly established "European Coal and Steel Community", the precursor of our current European Union, from 1952 to 1955. In a recently published biography, his long-time friend and colleague François Duchêne calls him *"the first statesman of interdependence"* - a neologism which neatly sums up what I have attempted to explain in this brief interlude.

Town-twinning

Good relations enhance security. But this is something which concerns people at all levels of society, not just the politicians. After the war, personal contacts between citizens of different countries were an important element in the network of "understanding" which the Europeans built to feel safer - also with respect to one other.

We, the people: town-twinning between Chemnitz and Manchester

Once again it was the British and the Germans who played a pioneering role in an area which was to become the most popular form of cultivating contact in post-war Europe: town-twinning. These twinning links now exist between all Western European countries at local, district and regional level. But the Germans and the British were the first, with links between Oxford and Bonn, Düsseldorf and Reading as well as Hanover and Bristol forged as early as 1947.

How two mining towns found one another.

The following story is typical of the way town-twinning arrangements grew up between the two former wartime enemies:

In 1944, a certain Leslie Suggit met a certain Ernst Schwarzenberger in a camp for German prisoners of war. Met? Actually, it was Suggit's job to guard Schwarzenberger & Co. But they took a liking to each other and decided to stay in contact by letter after the war. In 1961, Mr. Suggit - meanwhile mayor of the mining town of Swinton & Pendlebury in Lancashire - recounted the tale of his friendship with a former German POW at a meeting of English mine-workers. Ernst Schwarzenberger also lived in a mining community, in the Westphalian town of Lünen near the Ruhr. The English mine-workers asked Suggit to send their greetings to their colleagues in Lünen via Herr Schwarzenberger.

This is when things took off: initial exchanges of letters developed into a regular correspondence, leading in 1963 to a three-day visit to Lünen by the first English delegation, headed by Mr. Leslie Suggit. The friendship snowballed: a delegation from Lünen, led by its mayor Heinrich Czerwinski, paid a return visit to Lancashire the following year and the partnership between the two towns was sealed in an official ceremony at the town hall of Swinton & Pendlebury in 1966.

Diplomacy without the instruction manual. Do-it-yourself friendship. War and barbed-wire just a memory.

The Hanover/Bristol link is a particularly illuminating example of the early phase of this friendship movement (cf. the documentation "Twinning - Partnerschaft" published by the German Embassy in London in 1974). In the starvation year of 1947, parcels containing food and clothing were the gift offered by the British town to its German "twin"; in return, Hanover sent a youth choir to Bristol to sing their gratitude in English schools and concert halls. Had there not been a "personal union" with England before? This time, it went deeper, to the level of personal friendships. The 1947 exchange was called "Music for Old Clothes" ... *Honi soit qui mal y pense*.

There are now about 400 local twinning arrangements with Great Britain. But their significance far exceeds the sum total of their individual programmes over the years. They form the humus on which international relations thrive - a fact which the numerous summit conferences between Heads of State sometimes make us forget...

Town-twinning exchanges now cover a multitude of activities: from official town council delegations to local bowling clubs or sports associations. As usual in such cases, there are more requests (above all for sports competitions) than funds available to finance them. In this context, twinning arrangements between schools are also central to the planning on both sides of the Channel. There are already over 800 school links which enable more than 10,000 British and about 20,000 German schoolchildren to visit their partner country each year (cf. also Chapter II, 7).

Foreshadowing our modern concept of the "Europe of the Regions", the conclusion of partnerships at the highest level - between German *Länder* and the comparable geographical areas in Great Britain - had been another salient feature of the twinning experience. For example, Bavaria and Scotland have forged formal links, as have Baden-Württemberg and Wales. Within these regional partnerships, there are particularly close relations between the respective capital cities - Stuttgart and Cardiff, Edinburgh and Munich. The particularly active investment policy pursued by the Stuttgart company Bosch in South Wales (as detailed in Chapter III, 1) reflects this close regional partnership. People in Wales and Scotland now regard these bridges as their own paths to Europe, independent of national government policies.

After the Wall came down, East German communities were finally able to copy the pattern in West Germany and also set up twinning arrangements with British counterparts. Only Weimar and Dresden had previously enjoyed such links, with Stratford and Coventry respectively. Now there was a flood of new partnerships: Halle/Nottingham, Leipzig/Birmingham, Chemnitz/Manchester, Magdeburg/Bath, Potsdam/Oxford and Erfurt/Leeds.

From Bert Trautmann to Jürgen Klinsmann:
a sporting test of British-German relations

The road to the revival of friendly ties between the British and the Germans is strewn with many human episodes. If one adds the element of sport, with its high emotional content, there is a great chance of relations being elevated to a new qualitative level - or plunging to new lows. But the football hooliganism of the past few years cannot eclipse the wealth of memorable events in sporting history between the two countries in recent decades.

German hero in goal for Manchester City, 1956: Bert Trautmann makes a diving save

One has to start with Bert Trautmann, the legendary German-born goalkeeper who was a member of Manchester City's cup-winning team in 1956. But it was not so much that *he won which made Trautmann a legendary figure as* how *- namely by insisting on playing out the last 15 minutes of the game despite a cracked vertebra in his neck. As a result, Trautmann was declared a hero by the sporting press who named the former German paratrooper and ex-POW England's "Footballer of the Year".*

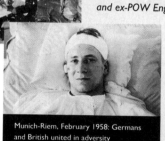

Munich-Riem, February 1958: Germans and British united in adversity

Two years later, in February 1958, the world was shaken by a tragic event. Manchester United had been playing a European Cup game in Munich but on the return flight the plane carrying the English team crashed shortly after take-off from Munich-Riem airport. Many of the players were killed and several seriously injured, some of whom received life-saving emergency operations in the Munich hospital "Krankenhaus rechts der Isar". The doctor in charge, Professor Maurer, was appointed Commander of the British Empire by Queen Elizabeth in May 1958 in recognition of his efforts. In his memoirs "Von Adenauer zu Brandt" (1990), the German Ambassador to London at the time, Hans von Herwarth recalls how, after the award ceremony in London, he accompanied Professor Maurer and his wife to Manchester to watch a game at Manchester United: "When Maurer entered his box at the ground, the entire crowd rose to its feet in his honour, to the tune of the German national anthem."

For German football fans, 1966 will always be a year of mixed memories. Was that third goal really in or not? No, of course not, the German fans protested at the time - and that remains their standpoint to this day. The third goal. There was a lot at stake - after all, it was the final of the World Cup in London's Wembley Stadium on 18 August. The score after normal time in the match between England and the Federal Republic of Germany was 2:2. Then came Geoff Hurst in the first half of extra-time and his famous shot cracked against the underside of the cross-bar. The ball rebounded down **onto** the line

1966: a goal or not a goal, that is the question. The dispute continues

(as the Germans claimed) or **behind** the line, as the linesman saw it and a goal was awarded. It was followed shortly afterwards by a fourth, giving a final score of 4:2, but the German fans were still grief-stricken over the third - which pains them to this day. Especially as a computer simulation of the controversial scene conducted in Britain has since concluded that the ball was indeed not over the line ...

The tormented German soul was slightly assuaged in the mid/late 80s when Boris Becker and Steffi Graf wrote Wimbledon history, making German tennis world-famous overnight. Germany had seen nothing like it since the pre-war days of the tennis gentleman Gottfried von Cramm. In 1985, Boris Becker was the youngest Wimbledon champion of all time (not even 18 years old); Steffi Graf won the women's title in 1988. But that was just the beginning for these two German tennis stars who came to fame on England's grass courts.

Wimbledon champion at the age of 17: Boris Becker

One English export item by the name of Kevin Keegan won the hearts of Hamburg spectators in the 1980s because "Mighty Mouse" Keegan was such a powerful attacking forward for the soccer club Hamburger Sportverein. But that was nothing compared with Jürgen Klinsmann, who in 1994 delighted not only the fans of Tottenham Hotspur with his spectacular goal-scoring but also England's sports journalists who voted him Footballer of the Year - only the second German to receive the title after Bert Trautmann. It is a pity that Klinsmann, who also had a good sense of humour (which the British do not usually associate with Germans), left London after just one year, accepting an offer he could not refuse from Bayern Munich. It would have been good to see him playing in England as Germany's ambassador of football a while longer...

For a brief moment in June 1996, during the EURO '96 football championships in England, this dream actually came true. But this time Klinsmann was a member of the German national team and, as fate would have it, the semi-final produced a remake of the classic encounter between England and Germany at Wembley. This time the Germans had the stronger nerves - they beat England in a penalty shoot-out, thereby exorcising the ghosts of 30 years ago and qualifying for the final, which they subsequently won.

Victorious smile: Jürgen Klinsmann captains the winning team at the 1996 European Football Championship

Sometimes it can take all of 30 years to overcome bad memories. Sometimes just a matter of days. At least, that is what happened to the Daily Mirror, which on the Monday before the England-Germany semi-final had allowed itself a widely unappreciated joke by addressing the guest team with the front-page headline "Achtung! Surrender". Just two days later, it had the opportunity to eat its words.

Fairplay off the field: the German Football Association thanks the hosts of EURO 96

The link between the cities of Dresden and Coventry had always been particularly significant. No other two names stand more distinctly for the disaster of the last War than the names of these two cities: one the early victim of aerial warfare, the other selected as a target for retaliation. No other two names more powerfully embody the tragedy of German-British enmity this century, something which the Duke of Kent clearly expressed when he represented the Queen at commemorations to mark the 50th anniversary of the bombing of Dresden. During this visit, the Duke also handed over the framed drawing of the cross which the British Government is donating to the reconstruction of the *Frauenkirche* and which will adorn the top of its dome. This is more than just a symbolic gesture: it is a commitment to friendship and reconciliation - the response to war and death.

For the gross aberrations of Nazi Germany still haunt people's memories. It remains a mystery why the Germans and the British, representative of all Europeans, took so many wrong turnings before they reached the point they have today. Prince Charles expressed similar thoughts when he addressed his German audience in Hamburg on 3 May 1995 at the celebrations to mark the 50th anniversary of the liberation of the city by British troops (cf. also Chapter IV, 2 - SPOTLIGHT 40). But he left his audience in no doubt about what the path since 1945 means in his mind:

"It is a tragic part of our history that during this century Britain and Germany should have drifted apart and should have come to the extreme of fighting each other. This will never happen again. (...) Since 1945 we have come a long way; and we have travelled further because we have travelled together."

At a memorial banquet in London's Guildhall three days later, the Queen took up this theme and gave it a European dimension:

"Today we are re-establishing a European family of nations. It must have one purpose above all other - true and lasting peace in Europe."

Harmony on the 50th anniversary of the end of the war: Queen Elizabeth, Prince Philip and Helmut Kohl (with interpreter, Dorothee Kaltenbach)

The Rebirth of Europe; and the Atlantic Community

London helps to integrate West Germany into the western Alliance - Bonn helps Britain on her path to the European Community

After two World Wars, Europe was drained of energy and resources. The fight against Hitler had left few reserves for the post-war reconstruction effort. The role of restoring order to Europe thus fell to the USA whose economic and military intervention was required in order to stabilise the old world and strengthen it against the new threat from Moscow. The Europeans had exhausted themselves in two fratricidal wars; the American era was now dawning.

This also affected bilateral relations between Germany and Britain. America increasingly became Germany's main point of focus whilst Britain, as the USA's "junior partner", had to content itself with the role of political backer for Germany's integration into the western community of States. This was extremely important for developments in Europe, although it now became part and parcel of the new global East-West conflict: the Cold War.

When the European Community later gave shape and purpose to the new Europe, London and Bonn saw their roles reversed for a while: the Federal Republic became the political backer, the trailblazer of close links between Britain and the Continent. Today, a generation later, it is clear that such German ministrations are no longer unanimously appreciated in London since the British keep their own counsel on matters regarding the future integration of European institutions.

The irritations this causes may make people forget just how much progress Europe has made since 1945; how strongly the British and the Germans have been affected by this common experience; and how indispensable they have become to one another in this period. The following chapter will therefore examine the development of this community of shared interests, to which there was no alternative after the destruction of two World Wars, and the policies which helped anchor this community of interests in a European and global context.

1. *The United States take a load off London's shoulders*

Britain emerged from the Second World War with enormous debts - victorious, but economically strained to breaking point and politically overstretched. The world's previously biggest lender was now its biggest debtor and Britain's position as a Great Power seemed consigned to history. Sterling devaluations, capital outflow and a debt of $14 billion to the USA alone were facts which spoke for themselves.

Responsibility for Britain's occupation zone in Germany represented an additional major burden. The costs were disturbingly high: £238 million in the period 1946-1948. £60 million of an American loan earmarked for the purchase of supplies for the British people were spent on food for the starving Germans in the occupation zone. In addition, 112,000 tonnes of American wheat and 50,000 tonnes of potatoes from Britain's own food supplies were given to the German people in November and December 1945 alone (Angelika Volle).

"This is the most quixotic act in history!", the MP H.F.C. Crookshank angrily exclaimed during a debate in the House of Commons in 1947. *"We defeat a country and then call on our own taxpayers to grant 80 to 100 million Pounds a year to put them back on their feet again."* But Mr. Crookshank's frustration may also have been directed at his own colleagues in the House. As Hans-Peter Schwarz reminds us in his book *"Vom Reich zur Bundesrepublik"* (1966), *"in no Parliament of any of the victorious powers was the fate of the German people discussed so frequently and with such generosity and sympathy as in the House of Commons."*

The situation in Europe was confused and full of contradictions. On the one hand, the Attlee Government first considered continuing the wartime friendship with Stalin: *"We must at all costs avoid trying to seek a cure by building up Germany or by forming blocs aimed at Russia..."*, the Prime Minister told a close colleague in August 1945. As a result, London initially supported the dismantling measures which the wartime allies had agreed.

On the other hand, it rapidly became apparent that the cost of maintaining an economically weakened Germany over a long period would also further weaken Britain itself. It was therefore in Britain's own interest to help German industry back on its feet again. Ernest Bevin, Foreign Secretary under Attlee, was the first to call for Germany's economic reconstruction. Stalin's confrontational policies then lent extra urgency to British deliberations.

When the British Government merged the northern section of the Prussian Rhineland province with the province of Westphalia to create the Federal Land "North Rhine-Westphalia" on 18 July 1946, its hand was already guided by increasing concern about Moscow's intentions. The new *Land* was to be put beyond the range of Soviet calls for further dismantling and secured as a key industrial centre. Speaking in Stuttgart on 6 September 1946, US Secretary of State James E. Byrnes finally made it clear that the Americans also officially favoured a policy of German economic recovery. Any thought of "a ruralised Germany" (the infamous "Morgenthau Plan") was thus swept aside.

Incidentally, George Orwell had warned against such plans in his reports on Germany for the *Observer* the previous year. *"It would not be a good idea to turn Germany into a kind of rural slum"*, was Orwell's classic understatement in a piece which appeared on 8 April 1945. This echoed John Maynard Keynes (1883-1946) and his famous essay "The Economic Consequences of the Peace" with which the Cambridge economist had shaken his contemporaries after the First World War and warned them against taking economic revenge on Germany. (cf. also p. 121)

Keynes' text of 1919 was no less prophetic after 1945. On the contrary:

"(These millions of Germans), if deprived of the means of life, remain a hardly less danger to European order. (...) Around Germany as a central support the rest of the European economic system grouped itself, and on the prosperity and enterprise of Germany the prosperity of the rest of the continent mainly depended. (...) In our own case we sent more exports to Germany than to any other country in the world except India, and we bought more from her than from any other country in the world except the United States. (...) If the European Civil War is to end (with the Western countries) abusing their momentary victorious power to destroy Germany (...), they invite their own destruction also..."

In this essay, Keynes had already called expressis verbis for American reconstruction aid for war-drained Europe - but it was not until after 1945 that his prophecy came true: America's "European Recovery Programme" (ERP), better known as the Marshall Plan, was announced in 1947. Washington's role was vital after 1945 and the "special relationship", to which Britain had made such urgent appeals during the war, virtually turned into a form of emergency "first aid".

This became immediately apparent with regard to British responsibilities in occupied Germany. In January 1947, the British and American occupation zones were merged to form the so-called "bizone", which considerably reduced costs for the British Government, although it did not remove them altogether. In return, Attlee had to drop the nationalisation plans he had envisaged for the British zone in 1948.

Very fortunate for him - but even more fortunate for Western Germany.

2. *Western integration takes shape. Churchill's role. The Berlin blockade and its aftermath*

At this historical juncture, a high-profile role was played by the man who was voted out of office in the 1945 general election: Winston Churchill. While in Opposition, the great war-time Prime Minister continued to exert influence, this time through a series of lectures and books. Two of his speeches in 1946 received considerable attention throughout the world and influenced future political developments: his speech on the university campus of Fulton, Missouri on 5 March and later in Zurich on 19 September (cf. chapter V, 4).

"From Stettin on the Baltic to Trieste on the Adriatic, an "Iron Curtain" has descended across the Continent", Churchill said in Fulton. *"Behind that line lie all the capitals of the ancient cities of Central and Eastern Europe - Warsaw, Berlin, Prague, Vienna, Budapest, Belgrade, Bucharest and Sofia. All these famous cities and the populations around them lie in the Soviet sphere, and all are subject in one form or another not only to Soviet influence but to a very high and increasing measure of control from Moscow."* For Churchill, there was only one possible response: Western Europe had to be firmly consolidated.

The speech also had repercussions back in Great Britain. Attlee finally abandoned his efforts to achieve a uniform policy on Germany among the former war-time allies and shifted from a pro-Soviet policy of co-operation to a more adversarial stance towards the Kremlin. As Günther Heydemann writes: *"The British were thus the first to accept a possible division of Germany."* Security policy considerations, as well as economic and financial reasons, were equally decisive in determining this change to more realpolitik.

This time, Churchill's thought-provoking ideas did not brand him a lone maverick as they had done back in the 1930s. His position reflected the foreign and security policy consensus in Britain at that time, as the Labour Government under Clement Attlee soon demonstrated. In quick succession, it advocated major steps towards the integration of Western Europe, including the Brussels Treaty of 17.3.1948, the so-called "Western Union" between Great Britain, France and the Benelux States (precursor to NATO, which was founded a year later) and the establishment of the "Organisation for European Economic Co-operation" (OEEC) on 16 April 1948, the umbrella organisation for Marshall Plan aid (which later became the OECD). At the London Six-Power Conference in spring 1948, it was also decided that a Soviet veto should not be allowed to prevent the creation of an independent state in western Germany based on free democratic principles and a federal structure.

But there was an ulterior motive behind all this. The aim was to "entice" the USA (Ernest Bevin) to provide Europe with more than just Marshall Plan financial assistance. The urgent requirement was for US *military* commitment to Europe, with two initial tasks: to safeguard peace in western Europe (containment of Germany) and to guarantee security against Stalinist aggression (containment of the Soviet Union). Admittedly, as the Soviet threat grew, West Germany became increasingly important as a friend and ally and so was soon able to cast off its role as the Cinderella of world politics.

The true extent of this new threat to peace became abundantly clear on 24 June 1948 when the Russians blocked the access routes to

Berlin's three western sectors overnight - the Berlin blockade had begun. Just two days later, the western allies established an airlift to Berlin, maintaining supplies of food and clothing for the people and ensuring that Berlin's industry could remain in production. 2.3 million tonnes of goods were airlifted into the besieged city between June 1948 and May 1949 - a total of 277,000 flights. The airlift also cost the lives of 29 British helpers from among 70 fatal allied casualties due to accidents such as crashes etc.

The Berlin blockade changed relations between the Germans and the occupying forces more than any other post-war event. There was great respect in western capitals for the determination of the people of Berlin to resist Soviet intimidation. The mood in Britain, which until then had remained very critical of Germany, now also changed. Bevin made it clear that abandoning these resolute Berliners would undermine the credibility of Germany's new democratic order in which so much time and effort had been invested.

Berlin airlift: the occupiers become saviours and friends

Bevin's line of argument proved a key factor. It is no exaggeration to say that the perseverance of the people of Berlin during the blockade not only encouraged the western powers to make their own historic achievement, the airlift, thus saving the western part of the city. Something of even greater importance asserted itself: the feeling among the victorious powers that the reconstruction of German democracy had begun to pay off. The Germans had shown that they were well on the way to joining the community of free nations.

This "credibility test" also worked the other way around: the occupying powers had proved themselves both as protecting powers and as friends.

3. *Anthony Eden designs the rescue plan: Germany joins NATO*

Following the Berlin blockade, security policy finally became a central consideration of the western allies, and with it the realisation that Germany would also have to make its contribution. Churchill even spoke of the "necessity" for German rearmament. Ernest Bevin countered with arguments which were to become fashionable again in Germany forty years later during the Gulf War under the heading "cheque-book diplomacy": no German troops please, but a financial contribution from the Federal Republic towards western defence costs, so that German industry would not gain an unfair competitive advantage.

The problem was resolved when a fresh chapter in the Cold War suddenly flared up: the Korean War (1950). This became a catalyst for numerous developments: the Americans began in earnest to plan the stationing of US forces in western Europe and at the same time increased pressure on the Attlee government to agree to German rearmament - otherwise America would refuse further aid for British armaments programmes. This was a clear message to the British government whose defence spending in 1950 was proportionally even higher than that of the USA ... The Empire east of Suez had not yet been "wound up".

This to-and-fro on the issue of German rearmament was also kindled by the question of what to do with the "little tin soldiers", as they were called in a popular German song of the time. To what organisation should they belong? The USA said NATO. Attlee's idea was a European army. The French tended towards Whitehall's concept but with no great enthusiasm. And so the Pleven Plan of 1950, the idea for a "European Defence Community" (EDC), was born and the corresponding treaty signed in Paris on 27 May 1952.

This was a major step for the fledgling German democracy. Frank Roberts, head of the German Department at the Foreign Office (and later British Ambassador to Bonn) expressed a widely held view when he referred to Germany a year later as: *"rearmed, but once again a healthy member of the Western family."*

But people had reckoned without the French hosts ... who foiled plans for the EDC on 30 August 1954 when the National Assembly in Paris decided by a majority of 319 : 264 votes not even to debate the treaty. The French had been plagued by last-minute doubts about whether it was advisable to put their beloved army under supra-national European command.

The British were not particularly unhappy about the collapse of the EDC. They had always been slightly ambivalent and had only half-heartedly agreed to the new organisation without displaying much willingness to actually participate. Actually, the *"non"* from Paris saved the British Government from an embarrassing ratification debate of its own in the House of Commons.

But the Germans were inconsolable. Non-ratification of the EDC Treaty meant that the Convention on Relations between the Three Powers and the Federal Republic of Germany, which had also been initialled in May 1952 and held out the prospect of sovereign rights for the young West German Republic, was also stalled - its fate was linked to successful ratification of the EDC Treaty.

This was to prove the hour of British diplomacy, the hour of Foreign Secretary Anthony Eden, later to cut such an unfortunate figure in the Suez crisis (the Tories had been elected back to power in 1951). Just one month after France rejected the EDC, Eden convened the London Nine-Power Conference at which he announced a pioneering proposal - the so-called Eden Plan. This provided for the following:

- the expansion of the Brussels Pact of 1948 to include Italy and the Federal Republic of Germany to form the Western European Union (WEU);

- the admission of the Federal Republic of Germany to NATO;

- the deployment of four British divisions and a tactical airforce on West German territory to establish a new 55,000-strong British Army of the Rhine (BAOR).

Even France could not resist this offer which contained a calculated and not inconsiderable security guarantee - for Germany but also against Germany. A counter-weight to German rearmament designed to soothe French nerves. As Gottfried Niedhardt put it, Germany was *"strengthened - yet at the same time under greater control."*

Approval for these proposals came quickly - the respective "Paris Treaties" were signed on 23 October 1954. Where the EDC had suffered a woeful end, Eden's plan produced an immediate new beginning. No time had been lost. West Germany's NATO membership was sealed, the German right to reunification reaffirmed and the occupation statute repealed on 5 May 1955. For the first time in its history, the Federal Republic of Germany was a sovereign nation - with the exception of the rights of the four victorious powers "in respect of Germany as a whole" which remained in place until German unity was restored in 1990.

What was the quintessential feature of German-British relations in the 1950s? History books tend to make a great deal of Konrad Adenauer's mistrust of Britain's policy towards the East, his concern that the British Government might be prepared to sacrifice German interests for a settlement with Moscow. This idea preoccupied the German Chancellor throughout his time in office (until 1963). It was mirrored during the period of détente in the post-Adenauer era by a British concern that Bonn might be moving ahead too quickly, thereby damaging western positions.

No love match (I): Adenauer and the British.

Konrad Adenauer and the Anglo-Saxons - a difficult alliance, sometimes almost a misalliance. It began soon after the war ended. The Americans had captured Cologne in April 1945 and immediately reinstated the 69-year-old Adenauer in his former post as city mayor from which he had been removed by the Nazis.

But the US military found Adenauer an awkward and obstinate person to deal with. So when the British started to establish themselves in their occupation zone they were virtually told to oust the unwanted politician as quickly as possible - the Americans claiming that they had not had time to do it themselves.

It finally fell to the British Governor of the Rhine province, Brigadier Barraclough, to take this step. Adenauer was duly sacked on 9 October 1945. Barraclough gave him a 15-minute dressing-down, during which - to make matters worse - he was forced to stand. The main reasons for his dismissal were allegedly his inefficiency in getting rubble cleared from the streets of Cologne and a "lack of sufficient energy and initiative", especially in connection with the building of shelters for the coming winter months. Adenauer was also forbidden to participate in any form of political activity and banned from setting foot in Cologne.

When Michael Thomas, liaison officer to General Templer, the commander-in-chief of the British occupation zone, later approached Barraclough to discover the background to this summary dismissal (Templer to Thomas: "Barraclough has obviously made a mistake, but I have to back him"), it all poured out of the Brigadier, as Thomas recounts in his memoirs:

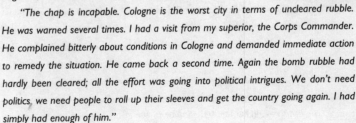
Cologne in ruins, 1945

"The chap is incapable. Cologne is the worst city in terms of uncleared rubble. He was warned several times. I had a visit from my superior, the Corps Commander. He complained bitterly about conditions in Cologne and demanded immediate action to remedy the situation. He came back a second time. Again the bomb rubble had hardly been cleared; all the effort was going into political intrigues. We don't need politics, we need people to roll up their sleeves and get the country going again. I had simply had enough of him."

When Thomas asked why Adenauer was no longer permitted to set foot in the city, the answer was: "So that he has no opportunity to get involved in political activities there."

Just two months later, Templer lifted all the restrictions - the ban on political activity, on entering and living in Cologne. It was again Barraclough who had the job of informing Adenauer in a second personal encounter on 14 December 1945.

Federal Germany's first Chancellor later said with a smile that he really owed his post-war political career to the British. By removing him from office, they had freed him for his political work which began with the organisation of the CDU in the Rhineland. He became its leader in February 1946. That was the month in which the British permitted the foundation of political parties in their zone.

What were Adenauer's relations with the British like later? Well, he developed a good rapport with Winston Churchill (they were about the same age: Churchill was born in 1874, Adenauer in 1876). But his relations with Harold Macmillan were cool by comparison. And indeed most British found Adenauer difficult to handle. His mistrust towards them (above all over London's policy vis-à-vis Moscow) often rubbed them up the wrong way.

Has there ever been a "personal" relationship between a German Chancellor and his British counterpart anything like as cordial as relations between many ordinary citizens in the two countries or even between the political leaders of Germany and France? The answer probably has to be no. Edward Heath and Willy Brandt were politically close because of their common ground on Europe. Helmut Kohl and John Major call each other "my friend", but the true test of that friendship is yet to come, when the difficulties over "Maastricht II" have to be resolved without losing sight of the common path.

Hans von Herwarth, Germany's first post-war Ambassador to London in 1955, makes an illuminating comment in his memoirs as to why Adenauer never warmed to the British:

"It is difficult to explain why England was not so much his "cup of tea" as France. The British mentality was less familiar to him than the French. In my opinion, he was irritated by the inherent self-confidence of the English political class. Such likes and dislikes certainly influence politics."

Mirror images - sometimes with shadow-boxing. But these fade as the years pass and nobody now remembers the constant squabbling between Bonn and London about the costs of "off-setting" the stationing of BAOR. What remains, by contrast, is the memory of this milestone political decision by the British in 1954 to go beyond the commitment to rebuilding German democracy. By establishing a military presence on German soil, Britain became more directly integrated into the security structures of the European Continent than it had ever done before.

The fact that this step was probably also motivated by traditional British "balance of power" thinking in no way detracts from its significance.

This integration within Germany in 1954 also placed Britain in a better position to promote German integration. Forty years on, this idea is a familiar aspect of German policy, this time not in the context of NATO but of the European Union. Since German reunification, the Kohl Government has been arguing that only greater European integration can ensure that Germany is firmly and permanently anchored in Europe so its neighbours no longer have cause for fear.

History always lives in the shadow of memories. These cannot be eradicated from a nation's psychology by willpower alone. People expect more nowadays and only feel relatively secure if inter-dependence is enshrined in treaty language.

4. *London gives top priority to Franco-German reconciliation*

Reconciliation between the two arch rivals France and Germany after 1945 required more than just the endeavours of the two countries concerned. Because there is so much talk nowadays of the dichotomy between Paris/Bonn on the one hand and London on the other, people often forget that Britain made early and determined efforts to promote Franco-German reconciliation as the pre-requisite for European recovery. This is where Churchill's second great speech of 1946, in Zurich on 19 September, was of such pioneering importance.

The former Prime Minister focused his comments on three intersecting circles, three principles of British foreign policy: relations with the USA, with the Commonwealth/Empire and finally with Europe. London wanted to maintain "special relations" with all three of these, but Churchill attributed particular importance to a future process of European unification:

"If Europe were once united in the sharing of its common inheritance there would be no limit to the happiness, prosperity and glory which its 300 million or 400 million people would enjoy. (...) We must build a kind of United States of Europe."

Admittedly, Churchill himself left no one in any doubt that Britain did not intend to join this union. As an independent major power with global commitments it was best to remain outside such a European system. For Churchill, the real European emphasis lay elsewhere, as he stated with great rhetorical aplomb:

"I am now going to say something that will astonish you. The first step in the re-creation of the European family must be a partnership between France and Germany. In this way only can France recover the moral and cultural leadership of Europe. There can be no revival of Europe without a spiritually great France and a spiritually great Germany."

The idea of a partnership between Germany and France as the core of this future western European order (with London as the friendly travelling companion, a sort of "godfather" figure) fitted well into established British thinking, where concern about the stability of France played an important role alongside concern about a possible resurgence of German aggression. While still war-time Prime Minister, Churchill had insisted on granting France the status of a major power with a right to its own zone of occupation in post-war Germany as well as a permanent seat on the UN Security Council. By proposing a close partnership between France and Germany, Churchill hoped to remove two of London's main headaches at the same time.

The French angle continued to influence British policy into the early years of the Fifth Republic. Adenauer was initially very reserved towards General de Gaulle, the new French President on whom the National Assembly had conferred the task of forming a Government in 1958. What could one expect from this backward-looking General? It was Harold Macmillan of all people who persuaded Adenauer to drop his scepticism. *"You must go and visit him!"*, he implored Adenauer. *"Don't forget: the crucial thing is to reach an understanding with France. Nor must you forget that Germany lost the war. That is why you have to take the first step."*

Winston Churchill: a vision for Europe - with a British accent

Hans von Herwarth, who chronicled these comments in his memoirs, has this to add:

"Years later when de Gaulle and Adenauer had developed a close partnership, which was beginning to have unfavourable repercussions for England, Macmillan said to Adenauer with a smile: 'I regret, Mr. Chancellor, that you followed my advice at the time rather too closely.'

The British Government would not be quite so sanguine today. There is a belief in Whitehall that Franco-German bilateralism and plans for a future "core Europe" are looking worryingly like a new "Carolingian Europe", from which Britain would automatically feel excluded. Indeed, such a plan would not tally with Britain's self-perception as an undoubtedly European nation despite its overseas history. Nor does London regard it as a viable basis for future European enlargement.

Yet the British Government quite understands the "French antenna" of German foreign policy - and not only because Britain was itself once a fervent advocate of Franco-German rapprochement. Nor has it escaped the notice of Whitehall observers that potential disagreements between Paris and Bonn - such as over the future role of the European Parliament, where the French are more reticent than the Germans - seem to be of little consequence compared to similar differences between Bonn and London.

Such disagreements are habitually played down by the political elite in Germany and France because Franco-German relations are regarded as indispensable and therefore inviolate. Bilateral relations between Germany and Britain have never enjoyed such a sacrosanct status. The designation "Quiet Alliance" was just a makeshift alias. But the quietness has long since been shattered by the loud collision of differences over Europe (cf. Chapter VI). By contrast, London and Paris are now moving closer together in the field of military and security policy. The circles overlap and intersect.

5. *Great Britain's path to Europe: Germany's contribution*

Looking at Britain's post-war policy on Europe, one cannot help thinking that London somehow wanted to have its cake and eat it - to maintain a military presence on the Continent and yet remain aloof from European affairs and European unification. Was the British Army of the Rhine (BAOR) perhaps no more than a variation of the old balance-of-power politics with a transatlantic ingredient thrown in this time? This was the conclusion many people reached as Britain abstained from further European integration until Macmillan made Britain's first application to join the European Community (EC) in 1961.

No one was more unhappy about this than the Germans. They too had a problem of balance: namely with Britain and France. Germany needed France because there was no real alternative to reconciliation and close co-operation with Paris; but Germany needed Britain as well, because a Europe without Britain was equally inconceivable - a view shared incidentally by important figures in Britain itself. Even Robert Vansittart, Under-Secretary at the Foreign Office and once regarded as ultra-germanophobic, changed his tone remarkably after the war and pointed his country towards Europe, as this extract from his memoirs "Events and Shadows" (1947) clearly shows:

"It would be unthinkable that Britain should stand outside Europe (...) and bless a federation headed by France and Germany in partnership. (...) The integration of the West should be the first step forward toward an ideal which is not yet a project. (...) It is my hope that a western integration will at some later stage turn, without need of magic, into a Western Federation. (...) It has ever been the destiny of the West to set examples, and we must continue to be true to that destiny."

Vansittart thus went further even than Churchill had done in his Zurich speech the previous year when he had prophesied, if not actually postulated, a turning point in European history - albeit without British institutional participation. This ambivalent attitude was to prevail for many years after 1945. London remained in favour of Europe - but not 100% committed. Britain played hard to get, whilst Germany admonished and enticed. The following dialogue between Adenauer and Churchill at a meeting in London in December 1951 was typical. *"You may rest assured"*, the Prime Minister said at a certain point in their conversation, *"Great Britain will always stand by Europe's side."* To which Adenauer replied: *"Prime Minister, you disappoint me somewhat, England is a part of Europe."*

That was the standard German line. Preference for the British "cousins" was far too ingrained, awareness of their presence in European history too unbroken and admiration for their diplomatic skills too great for Germany even to contemplate European unification without the British. And under no circumstances did Germany want to be left alone with the French.

Adenauer's ideas on this matter are well-documented. Since he was convinced, after the catastrophe of 1945, that Europe could only re-establish itself in world politics through supra-national institutions (an idea which was to form the basis of future German policy), he assumed that the British would also seek salvation in a return to such a Europe. He regarded Britain's post-war policy, tethered as it still was to its global responsibilities, as unrealistic for a country whose means were over-stretched and over-strained. In a letter dated 5 November 1946, he wrote:

"The English are pursuing a policy against their own interests. They can only maintain their global position as leaders of an economically united and politically balanced Western Europe."

Adenauer knew exactly what the British represented - to him they were an essential factor in building the future Europe. Britain's inherent stability and liberal tradition *"which stand in clear contrast to Continental Europe"* were indispensable for the unification of the

Continent, he wrote in a letter dated 12 December of the same year. Consequently, it was of paramount interest to all Britain's partners to ensure that she considered herself a European power.

There was a lot of wishful thinking here. German politics, restricted to a relatively small portion of the world after 1945, had virtually no understanding of London's foreign policy with its network of overseas commitments. In post-war British politics, relations with the Federal Republic of Germany were always secondary if not totally subordinate to these global ties. Adenauer at least felt this. So it was inevitable that the hopes he placed in England were repeatedly disappointed. In a letter dated 12 June 1949 he bemoaned "England's short-sightedness" and concluded:

"European integration is not a very promising prospect because England, presumably with regard to its dominions, appears to be preventing any real integration."

At a meeting of the CDU party executive in early 1950 he varied this appraisal:

"Britain is obstructing all efforts for European integration. England regards itself more as a neighbour of Europe than as a European nation."

Soon afterwards, London rejected the Schuman Plan, the seed of the later European Community. The principle of supra-nationality was considered unacceptable, but Britain wanted to "co-operate with Europe" - on an inter-governmental basis.

Déjà vu? Yes, as one can see, the British have remained consistent in their basic attitude to Europe. Adenauer was pleased that London wanted to be at least a "half-partner" in the planned "European Defence Community" (EDC). At the height of the ratification procedure, before the French National Assembly had pronounced its *"non"*, the Chancellor again made his ideas plain to his party's federal executive in March 1953:

"I should very much welcome Britain having a certain influence in the future EDC so that we are not left alone with the more or less hysterical French."

But as things turned out, he had little choice ... For when the British Prime Minister Harold Macmillan finally submitted the United Kingdom's application for EC membership on 10 August 1961, President de Gaulle had long since decided to let the British stew in their own juice - outside Europe. De Gaulle vetoed the UK application on 14 January. An unfortunate coincidence: Adenauer and de Gaulle signed the Franco-German Treaty in Paris eight days later, "the crowning achievement of my life's work", as the German Chancellor repeatedly stressed.

However, German parliamentarians did not take this lying down. They had not bargained on this turn of events, which caused great consternation. On 6 April, Fritz Erler, leader of the SPD parliamentary party, challenged the Government with a sarcastic question in the Bundestag. Did one have to pay for the Franco-German friendship *"with the alienation of Great Britain"*? A majority emerged among Bundestag Deputies calling for a clarifying text on this subject to be added as a preface to the Treaty with France. De Gaulle was annoyed, Adenauer was greatly worried. Tough luck: he could not prevent the Preamble to the Franco-German Treaty of Friendship. The text approved on 16 May contained a passage stating that the unification of Europe had to be continued along the path now taken *"incorporating Great Britain and other states willing to accede."*

That was unambiguously clear. Germany's political élite were not prepared to be uncoupled from their highly valued links with Great Britain for the sake of reconciliation with France, however desirable that might be, nor to exclude Britain from political deliberations on the future of Europe. London can still draw on this capital today. German parliamentarians also feared that de Gaulle would force them into a choice between "Atlantics" and "Europeans", when in fact German politics wanted to be both - Atlantic *and* European - and required Britain at its side for these two aims.

Opinion polls conducted in the 1960s confirmed this view. In October/November 1967, 74% of Germans regarded the relationship between Britain and Germany as "very good". It scored even higher than Franco-German relations (65%). At the same time, the British regarded the Federal Republic as their best friend on the Continent. The Preamble to the Friendship Treaty with France was thus a correction to the francophile slant of Adenauer's foreign policy - it also signalled the end of the Adenauer era (Wolfgang Mommsen).

Since those memorable debates, Britain has been able to rely on Germany as an enthusiastic advocate of its path to Europe. However, the fact that the British did not always appreciate this enthusiasm, to put it mildly (sometimes there was a clear message of "no thanks!"...) inevitably led to repeated irritations between Bonn and London.

On his first official visit to England in 1966, Adenauer's successor Ludwig Erhard reaffirmed German support for British membership of the EEC; and Willy Brandt, who was highly regarded in London, emphasised this in his first Government Statement on 28.9.1969.

"The Community needs Great Britain as well as the other countries willing to join. In the concert of European voices the British voice must on no account be missing if Europe is to avoid damaging itself."

Addressing the British House of Commons in March 1970 (it was the first such invitation extended to a Federal German Chancellor), Brandt made an avowal which is just as valid today as it was then:

"I hope and, indeed, I take it that, in the years ahead, the United Kingdom will find its place in the enlarged European Community. That Community then will be directly enriched by British traditions, the historical experience of the Commonwealth, your continuing world-wide connections, your appreciation of foreign cultures, the practical talent, but also the resourcefulness, efficiency and modern outlook of your people."

The United Kingdom gained its membership, although it is still struggling to find its precise place - as are the newly united Germany and the other Member States of the still incomplete European Union.

The Future of the European Union

Harmony and discord between the British and the Germans

The 20th century experienced probably its greatest caesura in the period 1989-1991: the collapse of the Soviet Union, one of the world's last empires. But the failure of Leninist ideology and the victory of democratic principles by no means marked "the end of history", as the American political scientist Francis Fukuyama was quick to predict. On the contrary, history made a completely fresh start. A long-suppressed desire for self-determination in Central and Eastern Europe, Russia and many other parts of the world was unleashed, bringing new imponderables - and opportunities - to the formative process we call politics.

Nowhere was this more acutely felt than in the old Continent of Europe where, despite all efforts at détente, the flow of history had been dammed up for decades along the "classic" demarcation line between East and West. When the Berlin Wall was breached and the flood gates opened, the currents were particularly strong in Europe.

The people most immediately affected were the Germans. Their national objective, German unification, was suddenly within reach. But there was one important factor to be considered: it had long been assumed that overcoming the division of Germany was only conceivable within the framework of a new peace order in Europe. So from the very beginning, German politicians were anxious to place unification in the context of further European integration. Working to achieve the former also meant increasing your efforts for the latter. The linkage became apparent at the Strasbourg EC Summit in

December 1989. Nor was it just a German concept - it was accepted by all Member States as a priority for Europe. The result was the Maastricht Conference in December 1991 with its far-reaching decisions on future Economic and Monetary Union as well as further steps towards closer European integration.

Apart from all the political aspects, it was quite natural for the Germans to desire the integration of their country, reunited virtually overnight, into an ever more closely meshed Europe. There is complete consensus on this in German society. But British and French reservations about the speed of German unification had not gone unnoticed. Germany also read the signs which indicated continued worries about its powerful position at the centre of Europe. Germany accepted unification as a gift of history - but with the explicit self-imposed obligation to place even greater emphasis on the new and larger Germany's commitment to Europe. There should no longer be any doubt about the "German course": it lay in Europe and nowhere else. After the events of 1989, this long-held conviction became a national priority for German politicians and the population as a whole.

But as the deadline for implementing the Maastricht decisions approached, the debate about the actual design of European integration intensified. *"The Maastricht process polarised opinions in several Member States"*, the British Government stated in its White Paper on the Intergovernmental Conference (IGC) on 12 March 1996. *"That has exposed a level of public unease and alienation which must concern all those, like this Government, who want the EU to fulfil its potential."*

Britain and Germany have long held differing views on the European question, as testified by the struggle for greater British participation in the shaping of Europe since 1945. No one could be in any doubt that Britain as a European Member State would always oppose supra-national plans for further integration. It was equally well-known that British politicians would repeatedly invoke the pre-eminence of "national interests", also in the context of Europe.

Nevertheless, Britain managed to constantly annoy the other Member States with its own interpretations of Treaty regulations, especially when the Thatcher Government challenged Brussels with precise and unrelenting demands in the early 80s for a fairer distribution of EC contributions (Margaret "I want my money back!" Thatcher) - and got its way, much to the delight of the Germans who also benefited from the redistribution of resources.

No love match (II): Thatcher and the Germans.

The sudden events of autumn 1989 caught politicians in East and West completely unprepared. This created particular problems for two of Germany's allies: the French President, François Mitterrand and the British Prime Minister, Margaret Thatcher. Both feared the force emanating from a suddenly united and larger Germany if the appropriate European peace framework were not first created to provide the necessary stability.

In a conversation with Foreign Minister Hans-Dietrich Genscher on 30.11.1989, Mitterrand even resorted to an open threat, as Jacques Attali recounts in his diary of that time (Verbatim III):

"Either German unification is established after European unification or you will have a triple alliance (France, Great Britain, Russia) against you and the whole thing will end in war. If German unity comes after European unity, then we will help you." (Frankfurter Allgemeine Zeitung, 12.10.1995)

Events took a different course, as became evident by the spring of 1990 at the latest. In March of that year, Margaret Thatcher convened a confidential seminar of historians at Chequers to consider the German national character and the anticipated nature of the future Germany (cf. Chapter I, p. 10). Thatcher trusted neither and continued to maintain in her memoirs that "angst and aggressiveness" were the most prominent characteristics of the Germans.

Helmut Kohl was very sportsmanlike in the face of Thatcher's reservations, of which she made no secret. Speaking at the Königswinter Conference in Cambridge in late March 1990, he attempted to beat her at her own game:

"Anyone who wishes the united Germany to be firmly integrated into European structures must also logically be in favour of progress on the process of European unification."

The Chancellor enjoyed his side-swipe at the Prime Minister, whose dislike of Brussels was as great as her dislike of Germany.

The relationship between the two Heads of Government - never cordial, but always respectful - had reached its nadir. Fearing that it would be too risky to place the two politicians side by side at the banquet in Cambridge, the British chairman of the Königswinter Conference, Sir Oliver Wright, decided to seat himself between them. Karl-Günther von Hase, Oliver Wright's German counterpart at that time and a former Ambassador to London, was also present that evening. Mrs. Thatcher confided in him that it would "take at least another 40 years before the British could trust the Germans again".

As Alan Watson writes in a brilliant character study, Kohl and Thatcher "represented a very different sense of history. Margaret Thatcher's history was that of the island race. It was peopled by heroes and villains. It was specific. By contrast Helmut Kohl, a historian by academic training, loved the broad sweep of history. He believed the British Prime Minister in reality lacked any sense of history. He confided to his own Foreign Office that Margaret Thatcher was 'pre-Churchillian' while he was 'post-Churchillian'. What he meant by this was that, while Margaret Thatcher may have been an instinctive practitioner of the balance of power, she simply had not understood its actual operation in the 19th century nor its enormous potential for damage and conflict."

It was not until autumn 1995, at a symposium in Vail, Colorado, that Margaret Thatcher referred back to Helmut Kohl's speech in Cambridge five years earlier:

"Some people say one has to anchor Germany in Europe to prevent these characteristics (its superior strength) from reappearing. But Germany has not been anchored in Europe, rather Europe has been chained to a Germany which is once again predominant. That is why I call it a German Europe."

(Die ZEIT, 8.3.1996)

Long before this dispute blew up, a slow fuse had been burning between Mrs. Thatcher and German politicians in another explosive area: the modernisation of short-range nuclear missiles. Thatcher was decidedly in favour - Bonn equally decidedly and stubbornly against. Just how much bad blood flowed in German-British relations at that time is evident from an entry in Hans-Dietrich Genscher's memoirs "Erinnerungen" (1995):

"(At the EC Summit) in Venice in 1987 there was an exchange between President Mitterrand and Margaret Thatcher on the subject of short-range missiles. During an intensive discussion, Mrs. Thatcher asked the French President: 'Will you not use your short-range missiles if the Russians capture Cologne?' To which President Mitterrand unambiguously replied: 'Cologne is an allied city. We shall not do that'. François Mitterrand himself told me of this controversial exchange which I had not experienced at first hand..."

However, the perception of German-British divergence on Europe has grown since those years, almost as if responsibilities were being divided up for the possibility of fresh political conflicts. The British would strictly adhere to the gradualist pragmatic approach while the Germans, equally predictably, would go beyond such pragmatism, tirelessly issuing reminders about the vision of an ever closer political union.

Mirroring this development, several negative stereotypes have established themselves in one nation's perception of the other: in Germany, the idea of Britain dragging its feet over European unification; in Britain, the view that the Germans, blinded by their love of abstract concepts, have lost sight of the natural limits to the institutional integration of potentially 400 million Europeans.

As decisions loom in connection with what is popularly called "Maastricht II", the German-British dialogue has developed into a fundamental debate about diverging views. The two Governments have finally grasped this nettle in the form of an "honest disagreement", which is inevitable when friends are frank with one another. As evidence of this candour, neither side is now pulling its punches.

Without actually mentioning the British by name, Helmut Kohl made no bones about his position in a speech he delivered in the Belgian town of Louvain on 2 February 1996:

"The slowest ship must not be allowed to determine the speed of the convoy in the long term. If individual partners are not prepared or able to participate in certain steps towards integration, the others must not be denied the opportunity to move forward and develop increased co-operation in which all partners are welcome to take part."

No less a person than the Foreign Secretary Malcolm Rifkind immediately took this as a cue for a statement the following day in London:

"The other side of that coin is that the convoy ceases to exist if you do not accommodate all the ships within it, so you have to find a balance. You have to find a structure which all the countries concerned are comfortable with."

(The Observer, 4.2.1996)

There is a certain irony in the fact that Winston Churchill, in his famous Zurich speech of September 1946, had used a formulation which comes closer to the current German idea of a "core Europe" than Britain's divergent view. To quote Churchill:

"If at first all the States of Europe are not willing or able to join a union we must nevertheless proceed to assemble and combine those who will and who can."

Yet Churchill's "we" specifically did not include Britain - what double irony! Federal President Roman Herzog could not resist quoting this passage in a speech to the "Bertelsmann Forum" on 19 January 1996 and adding this comment: *"The wisdom of this idea cannot be denied."*

It would be misleading, however, only to identify differences of view between Britain and Germany as far as the European question is concerned. In fact, more often than not, it has been precisely the points of common interest between the two countries which have accelerated European progress. Would it have been possible, for example, to eliminate the "eurosclerosis" diagnosed in the early 80s without the concept of the "Single Market", without moving from the principle of unanimity to qualified majority voting on internal market affairs? This was precisely the idea contained in a confidential paper which the British Government presented to its German partners in 1985 and which Bonn - much to London's chagrin - then incorporated in a joint Franco-German initiative. Subsequently, it was a British EC Commissioner, Lord Cockfield, who successfully guided the plan through all the necessary stages.

As far as shared German-British views on the future shape of Europe are concerned, Foreign Minister Klaus Kinkel recently summed up during a speech in Oxford (19 January 1996) what former Parliamentary Under-Secretary of State Tony Baldry had said during a debate in the House of Commons on 24 May 1995. Parts of Kinkel's list are reminiscent of many of the joint projects the "Anglo-German Foundation for the Study of Industrial Society" (cf. Chapter IV, 4, p. 153ff) has embarked upon:

"Together we are committed to a liberal world trading system and opposed to protectionism in Europe and world-wide.

Together we are fighting for the structural renewal of our economies in order to solve our unemployment problems. We reject dirigisme in our industrial policies.

Together we are in favour of opening up the Euroatlantic institutions to the young democracies in Central and Eastern Europe soon.

Together we are changing the development of the vital bridge across the Atlantic. Peace and stability in Europe without America is inconceivable to us.

Together we have drawn up a successful peace settlement for Bosnia in the Contact Group. (...) Together our troops are now safeguarding peace there."

Tony Baldry had mentioned two additional important points. At London's insistence, the principle of subsidiarity - a concept so central to the Federal German experience of decentralisation - had been firmly secured in the Maastricht Treaty as a guideline for future European policy. Furthermore, both countries have signed up to deregulation and appropriate financial control of the Brussels bureaucracy.

It is the fate of such hallowed principles that they are immediately suspended when one of the European partners perceives a threat to its national interests. When the chips are down, all communality of purpose is insufficient to prevent collisions from occurring. That is what happened in spring 1996 when the British Government responded to the EU's world-wide export ban on British beef and beef byproducts in May by boycotting EU decisions. When interests clash in this manner, every "honest disagreement" becomes a recipe for an almighty row. Diplomatic finesse gives way to assertiveness.

The British Government always believed that the export ban *"was a disproportionate reaction, unjustified by science"*, as John Major wrote in a signed article in the *Frankfurter Allgemeine Zeitung* on 21 June, a week before the European Council meeting in Florence at the end of the Italian Presidency. The other European governments were equally insistent that the British measures to control BSE were inadequate and thus unconvincing.

This was an almost classic confrontation between two mutually exclusive positions. On the one hand, the governments for whom consumer confidence is the highest political priority requiring urgent action. On the other hand, the Prime Minister who responds by saying (as Major did in the afore-mentioned *FAZ* article) that, in his Government's view, consumer confidence *"is not a basis for banning trade"*, although he accepts *"that it is important"*. The British Government prefers to give the British public the following advice:

"Here are the facts, here is what the best independent scientists say. We have always acted on their advice. You are grown up. You can make a choice as intelligent consumers."

The Florence agreement to introduce a gradual easing of the export ban in return for Britain taking appropriate culling measures is only a truce in the tug-of-war between Britain and its EU partners. Beef is not the central issue of future European integration. Yet even this compromise was threatened when British scientists were forced to concede just one month later that sheep and calves born of BSE-infected cows might also carry the infectious agent. This raised fresh questions, not only about the agreed scale of culling programmes in Britain but also about the planned steps for lifting the EU embargo on British beef and beef byproducts.

But let us not lose our sense of proportion here. Beef is by no means the main cause of Britain's headaches over Europe. It has been a particularly high-profile issue recently, but it is not the most menacing in political terms. Much more serious is the long-term strain on relations caused by the currency debate - by which I do not just mean the rapidly approaching deadline (1 January 1999) for the introduction of the single currency, the "Euro". Speaking at a British-Bavarian symposium in Hohenkammer on 24 July 1996, the Minister at the British Embassy in Bonn, Robert Cooper, recounted the unfortunate tale of disagreements on this subject.

To be sure, the shock of "Black Wednesday" in late September 1992, when Sterling was forced to leave the Exchange Rate Mechanism (ERM), has scarred the British psyche. Did the Bundesbank deliberately abandon the Pound? But more important is the fact that Britain had joined the ERM two years earlier in an honest attempt to bring its economic policy in line with Maastricht, including the possibility of accession to Monetary Union at a later stage.

The parity rate for Sterling was undoubtedly set too high when it entered the ERM and this unrealistically high level may have condemned the entire experiment to failure from the very outset. Be that as it may: *"We had been trying to be Europeans; indeed we spent every penny of our reserves in the attempt, but no-one else seemed interested in sustaining this effort."* (R. Cooper). This is the bottom line from a British point of view.

Even more unfortunate is the fact that, following Sterling's enforced departure from the ERM and its subsequent devaluation, the British economy immediately began to pick up (some commentators now speak of "White Wednesday"...). This has tended to reinforce British prejudices against the ERM and feelings against the EU as a whole. One thing is certain: it has fuelled the debate about Economic and Monetary Union, a topic which has split the Major Government into different camps.

Just how divided the Government is on this issue became clear when the Tory MP, David Heathcoat-Amory, relinquished his post as Paymaster General at the Treasury on 22 July 1996. In his letter of resignation to John Major, he put his finger on the sore spot:

"At the Foreign Office and more recently at the Treasury I have dealt with the European Union at first hand. I have supported a policy of attempting to reform it and building a relationship which protects British interests and prevents unwarranted interference in our affairs. This policy is not working. (...) In particular, I am convinced that joining a single European currency would be disastrous, both politically and economically..."

Whether we take BSE or the "Euro", mad cows or complex monetary issues, it all comes down to the same thing: Britain's fundamental reservations about Europe. Deeply embedded within them lie equally fundamental differences of opinion with Germany which, due to its weight (and partly also to Chancellor Kohl's political weight), is rightly regarded as the real motor of European institutional integration. Paradoxical as it may sound, the European

Union, which was designed to strengthen ties between Member States, has actually placed a greater strain on German-British relations. So let us now take a closer look at the philosophical disputes underlying this German-British dichotomy.

Nationhood and national interests

In British politics, it is customary for the "national interest" to take a front-row seat. Speaking in the House of Commons debate on the Government White Paper on Europe, Malcolm Rifkind said: *"We want a partnership of nations working together to advance their national interests. (...) This country's national interest is the starting point for our approach as, for all free nations, the national interest can be defined as the collective expression of the democratic process."* The White Paper goes on to state that *"national Parliaments are the primary focus of democratic legitimacy in the Union."*

This sentence is crucial because it treats the question of national sovereignty not in terms of the balance of power or power politics, but as a fundamental concern of a modern state seeking "democratic legitimacy". It cleverly refers to the debate about the "democratic deficit" which is unfortunately not treated with the urgency it deserves - either in Brussels and/or in the national capitals.

British concerns on this point are impossible to ignore but difficult to dispel. Robert Cooper also broached this subject at the above-mentioned seminar when he spoke of the individual states of Europe as the *"fundamental political units"* forming the basis *"on which democracy is practised and liberty is preserved."* By contrast, the British view of Europe was not exactly reassuring:

"We fear that diluting the power of institutions which are well understood and legitimate and increasing the power of institutions which are neither well-known nor legitimate with most people is in the long run going to make difficulties."

But the British Government does not conclude from analyses like these that the European Parliament needs new powers. On the contrary. Strasbourg is rejected as the solution to this "democratic deficit". To quote the White Paper again:

"The Government believe that the European Union will succeed only if it respects the integrity of the independent democratic nation states that comprise its membership and if it is flexible enough to accommodate their political and cultural differences."

The gulf between that position and German thinking could not be wider. *"We have no desire to return to the nation state of old"*, Helmut

Kohl said in Louvain on 2 February 1996, summing up a belief which has become *de rigueur* in his country since the failure of German nationalism in the 20th century. National policies, pursued for their own sake, can only lead to *"Sonderwege"* (unilateralist aberrations), which in turn pose the danger of new conflicts if not war.

Europe advances from summit to summit

In the light of this renunciation of national policies, it is perhaps easier to understand why Chancellor Kohl felt he had to adopt a warning, if not prophetic tone when he said that *"European integration is in reality a question of war and peace in the 20th century"*. By contrast, it would be inconceivable for a modern German politician to comment on Europe in such a detached way as the following extract from the British White Paper: *"The European Union is not the only framework in which we pursue our political and commercial interests."* This differs sharply from a key sentence in Klaus Kinkel's Oxford speech: *"Our interest is Europe."*

None of that is particularly surprising. It is important to remember here that Europe does not exactly represent the most glorious phase in Britain's recent history - which is at least partly Britain's own fault. Germany, on the other hand, sees Europe as a kind of salvation. *"We neither suffer from the German historical nightmares, nor from the German fear of being alone"*, is the way Robert Cooper succinctly sums it up before going on to identify a *"vicious circle"*:

"The more the Eurosceptics portray Germany as aggressive, the more determined the Chancellor becomes to integrate Germany thoroughly into Europe and the more threatening this seems to people in Britain."

Cooper concludes his thoughts with a heartfelt sigh: *"I wish that the debate in Britain (on these issues) was more serious. And I wish that there was a bit more debate in Germany."*

Centralism / Federalism

In an introductory statement to the Government White Paper on the IGC, Malcolm Rifkind highlighted another central aspect of the differences between Britain and Germany:

"The Treaty on European Union - like the original Treaty of Rome - calls for an 'ever closer union among the peoples of Europe' - not, let it be noted, among the states of Europe or among their Governments. That aspiration for strengthened co-operation and friendship across the whole of Europe is a noble one, and is fully shared by the Government. However, it should not mean an ever closer political union in the sense of an inexorable drift of power towards supra-national institutions, the erosion of the powers of national Parliaments or the gradual development of a united states of Europe. The Government reject that conception of Europe's future."

The German Government would heartily endorse the second part of those comments. In all their speeches, Chancellor Kohl and Foreign Minister Kinkel also reject the idea of a European super-state or even what Churchill called "the United States of Europe". They also swear by subsidiarity as the fundamental principle of true federalism, namely the principle of leaving as many decisions as possible to the national governments and only referring the most pressing political business for decision at the highest European level.

And there's the rub. The idea of federalism, which sounds so convincing, has become a big stumbling block in the United Kingdom. So much so that federalism - the "F" word - is now anathema to the British. Politicians avoid the term like the plague. This is due to an astonishing confusion over the meaning of the word. When the British hear "federalism", they understand it to mean "centralism" - exactly the opposite of what is actually meant by the term subsidiarity.

To quote Malcom Rifkind once again, speaking in the House of Commons on 12 March 1996:

"The Government believe that the European Union will succeed only if it respects the integrity of the independent democratic nation states that comprise its membership and if it is flexible enough to accommodate their political and cultural differences. The Government are totally opposed to a monolithic, centralised, federal Europe."

"Monolithic, centralised, federal" all in one breath - a German audience would not understand what he was talking about! Surely, the one precludes the other, doesn't it? Yet the riddle is not difficult to solve because both sides are of course right in this debate. By "federal Europe", the Germans believe they want the same as Malcolm Rifkind, namely to preserve the individual identity of individual nations. For their part, the British regard the federal idea as the Trojan horse of increasing conformity.

According to British logic ("federal = centralist"), the European Union is facing decisions which will automatically lead to greater centralisation as European policies are "communitised" under the terms of the Maastricht Treaty.

"Unification" instruments are being sought to ensure that the EU does not drift apart. The single currency, for example, is one such instrument.

Historically, the American "Federalists" Alexander Hamilton, James Madison and John Jay put forward similar arguments in the constitutional debate of 1787 when they claimed that a strong dose of centralism was a *sine qua non* for the emerging Union of New England States. What is a single currency if not a means to centralise fiscal and monetary policy? As Josef Joffe wrote in the *Süddeutsche Zeitung* (21.6.1996):

> *"Monetary Union means: others determine my finance policy; I no longer have sole control of interest rates, money supply, exchange rates and with them the economic policies which may be crucial at the next election."*

Let's not beat about the bush here. No one can deny that if Europe is to deserve the title "Union", it will first have to go through a process of further harmonisation and standardisation. By definition, that must be the case. There is no avoiding this fact, no matter how persistent people claim to be acting with the best federal intentions. According to the *British* definition, European federalism already exists where democratic governments do business with one another independently, i.e. where the "intergovernmental" co-operation of sovereign states comes into play, except in those areas where they have subjected themselves to the majority ruling of the "Single Market". Changing this state of affairs by an "ever closer union" between governments and their policies requires a determined step towards greater centralisation of European political decision-making.

The present British Government is reluctant to take this step, whilst the Germans want to make it irreversible, as Helmut Kohl never tires of reaffirming.

That in simple terms is the central difference between the Germans and official Whitehall policy on the question of further European integration. Klaus Kinkel made the point absolutely plain in his Oxford speech:

> *"Europe must not regress into a community of convenience in pursuit of free trade and prosperity. 'Europe' has always been based on political ideas while economic integration has always been seen as a starting point for political union. We intend to retain this 'finalité politique.'"*

In their concern to avoid the differences becoming insurmountable, each side avidly seeks quotations by the other to substantiate its own position. In his Government White Paper, John Major quotes Helmut Kohl addressing the German Bundestag (27.5.94): *"We want unity in diversity. We do not want a centralised, European state that subsumes to regional, national and cultural traditions or dismisses historical experience."* Foreign Minister Kinkel in turn beguiled his British audience with a Gladstone quotation: *"We (British) are part of the community of Europe, and we must do our duty as such ."*

However, when one looks at the specifics of policy statements, the possibility of bridging the gap seems very remote again. The British White Paper on Europe states:

"We shall not accept harmonisation for its own sake, or further European integration which is driven by ideology rather than the prospect of practical benefit. Above all, we shall be guided by a cool assessment of the British interest."

German political statements on Europe contain none of this pronounced coolness. They are warmly enthusiastic, like this passage from Klaus Kinkel's Oxford speech:

"How much longer will we Foreign Ministers appear in front of the TV cameras separately after General Affairs Councils and explain what we have achieved for our own countries but not what we have achieved for Europe?"

Majority voting

The logic of the above makes it quite clear why Britain and Germany adopt very divergent positions on the issue of extending majority voting to the future Common Foreign and Security Policy (CFSP). This area has so far been exempt from collective majority voting procedures. *"We should therefore also break the taboo of majority voting on*

CFSP", Kinkel announced in Oxford. Helmut Kohl endorsed this view in Louvain (2.2.1996): *"We must not allow further progress to be blocked by inevitable difficulties over detail."*

When the Germans consider "breaking taboos", John Bull lowers his horns - or contemplates the next "opt-out"... *"The Government will therefore oppose further extension of qualified majority voting"*, John Major states quite unequivocally in his White Paper on Europe. *"If there is no collective will within the European Union to act, it is unwise to try to force action through artificial voting procedures."* Here are the old reservations emerging again. Britain will continue to hold empiricist views and mistrust concepts which it considers rigid and artificial.

So where do the United Kingdom and the newly united Germany stand on the Europe of the future? The two countries obviously have different starting points because of their different historical experience, and this makes it genuinely difficult to standardise policies for philosophical reasons alone. Furthermore, the British Government tends to measure its own loyalty to Europe in terms of tangible past success rather than vague commitments to the future. As far as the scrupulous observance of Common Market rules is concerned, for example, Britain claims to have the second best record after Denmark. In the period 1990-1994, the European Court of Justice in The Hague dealt with only six cases brought against the United Kingdom (compared with 4 against Denmark), whereas the average "penalty count" against all EU Member States in the same period was 30.

Such yardsticks appear insufficient to the German Government, which pursues greater visions and is horrified at what the consequences might be if the next steps towards closer European integration are not taken. Britain does not share this latent pessimism, this belief in the inevitability of a relapse into bloody conflicts between nation states if "Maastricht" does not go ahead as scheduled. Nor did the majority of British people share Margaret Thatcher's scepticism towards Germany in the year of German unification or thereafter. On the contrary, the country has long been regarded as firmly anchored in the international community. The disquiet felt nowadays has other origins.

"There is no sign that I can see that the state of Germany worries people any more than the state of Greenland or Guatemala," George Brock, European editor of the Times, quipped on a lecture tour through Germany in January 1996, making light of Britain's alleged fear of Germany. *"We are more interested in Germany, but interest in the sensational is not the same as fear of it."*

That is a slight understatement. London can also get annoyed - for example, at the effects of Bundesbank policies or when, after German unification, it remained unclear for a long time whether and to what extent the Bundeswehr would become involved in crisis management outside the NATO area. But issues of this kind never reach the degree of concern which would persuade the British Government to abandon the classic hallmarks of national sovereignty. Nor does Britain, despite all the internal wrangling, have a thoroughly negative attitude towards Europe. The negative comments are generally aimed at the alleged inevitability of European "centralisation".

A typical example of this is George Brock's account of a recent conversation with Geoff Mulgan, the young head of the respected London-based polling institute "Demos": *"I'm very pro-European,"* Mulgan confided. *"It's just the European Union I can't stand."* This view was endorsed by the former editor of the *Times*, William Rees-Mogg, who wrote on the conclusion of the British-German bilateral summit in London in spring 1996: *"We are too different to belong to the same Europe which Germany has decided to build."* (*Times*, 29 April 1996)

But these are merely two voices among many in the United Kingdom. The majority of British businessmen, for one, are clearly positive about further European integration, including Economic and Monetary Union (EMU). By contrast, one cannot draw any definite conclusion yet about where Labour stands on Europe from the statements by leading members of the party. Their rhetoric about European Union may sound a lot more upbeat than pronouncements by the Conservatives, who are extremely divided on the issue. (Although, let us remember, the situation was initially quite different when John Major visited Bonn as Britain's newly appointed Prime Minister and went on record as saying that his country wanted to be *"at the heart of Europe".*) Should Tony Blair and his party come to power, there is certainly one area where they would act differently to their predecessors. They would immediately withdraw Britain's opt-out from the European "Social Chapter" which John Major secured at the Maastricht Summit in December 1991.

But when it comes to the question of Monetary Union, the forthcoming test of loyalty to Maastricht, Labour is still very ambivalent. During his visit to Germany on 18 June 1996, Tony Blair sounded sceptical. He stated that Britain would only participate if a single currency was in its national interests. What does this tell us? It

Close encounter of the third kind: "Hello, I'm Anticlimax"

tells us that the Labour Party, in true British fashion, does not necessarily see any congruity between Britain's national interests and the European timetables of its Continental partners. Labour's motto on the "Euro" is: *"Wait and see".* The Party's foreign affairs spokesman, Robin Cook, struck an equally cautious note in a speech before the European Parliament in Brussels on 13 June 1996 when he contended that Monetary Union could actually cause more problems than it would solve if it were established prematurely. In his opinion, the general weakness of Europe's national economies and the massive unemployment problems were an inauspicious omen for the early introduction of a single currency. The picture, he said, had looked different back in late 1991 when the deadline for EMU was set at 1999.

The way things are going, it looks as if a recent cartoon in the *Daily Telegraph* (May 1996) could retain its validity for longer than many in the EU would like...

It portrays Astérix (Chirac), the ever-vigilant Gaul, presenting his friend Obélix (Kohl), who is sweating under the weight of the EURO currency, to John Major. With a wry smile, Major responds: *"Oh, I say, what a bit of luck! I'm Anticlimax. Let's shake hands old boy."* Who knows, perhaps Tony Blair will prove to be another Anticlimax when it comes to shaking hands on the single currency...

Does all this mean John Bull is on the verge of bidding farewell to the European Union? That is far too alarmist a question. All the latest opinion polls show that, despite continuing doubt about the process of closer European integration, the majority of people in Britain do not want to relinquish their EU membership. According to a Gallup poll conducted in May 1996, 57% want to remain in Europe.

John Major knows that too. Which is why he cautiously sidesteps the delicate issue of a referendum in Britain. But what is his own vision of Europe, which Europe does he have in mind? The Europe of which his young compatriot Geoff Mulgan has such a positive opinion? That would be too little for a country which, as a member of the European Union, cannot stand on the sidelines while the Union's future is being shaped. Which is exactly the point Malcolm Rifkind made before the House of Commons on 12 March 1996. Expanding on what John Major had said five years previously, namely that Britain wished to be *"at the heart of Europe"*, Rifkind stated with greater precision: *"Britain will be at the heart of the debate about the future of the European Union"*.

The man who told the German Chancellor that a convoy had to keep together otherwise it was no longer a convoy, suggested that the United Kingdom not only felt European in historical and cultural terms but also intended to participate in shaping and implementing European policies.

There can be no doubt that the debate has intensified and the various standpoints are now more sharply defined. Surely this kind of intellectual competition is just another feature of the cultural diversity we are all so keen to preserve. But are we ready for it in our day-to-day lives? Or will we revert to the old disparaging clichés at the first sign of dissent? Are we perhaps becoming captives of "Euro-political correctness"? That would be highly undesirable and would simply lead us in the wrong direction. Not for nothing have Europeans renounced all forms of discrimination in their political dealings with each other since 1945 and developed a modus operandi which both cushions these differences of opinion and may even be able to exploit them creatively.

There is, however, little sign of that yet in the current dispute over the future shape of Europe. So for the time being, one can only hope that German-British relations are sufficiently robust to withstand such differences of opinion. The core of what has been achieved since 1945, the irreversibility of friendship between the two countries, should remain untouched by such problems.

Queen Elizabeth II referred to these aspects in her speech at the London Guildhall banquet to commemorate the 50th anniversary of the end of the Second World War in Europe:

"We are thankful for the half-century of peace in Europe. We are thankful for the fruits of peace between nations and peoples, and we are thankful for the benefits which the wartime generation won for their sons and daughters and, through them, for the youth of today."

The fact that peace and peaceful co-operation have become the raison d'être of European policy is part of our present strategic security; earlier generations would gladly have known a little more of such security for themselves. *We* nowadays turn "disagreement" into a culture of "agreeing to disagree", whereas they may have gone to war over it.

Not long ago, in September 1994, the historian Michael Howard summed up this epoch-making metamorphosis on a lecture tour of Germany in the following way:

"Our societies have become peaceful, prosperous, bourgeois and materialistic. In fact, the worst nightmares of the pre-1914 ruling classes in both countries have come true: Britain has lost her Empire, and the Germans, turning their backs on their suicidal Sonderweg, have lost the will to acquire one. (...) Our differences and rivalries will continue, and we would only be deceiving ourselves by pretending that they will not."

It is always fascinating, though, to see how we appraise these differences and how we allow certain images to influence our view of each other. British (and French) fears about the reunited Germany after 1989/90, for example, were more about past experience of dealings with Germany than about any serious evaluation of current problems. But countries can also suffer damage through mistaken beliefs they hold of themselves. Did the Germans not erroneously cling to the conviction back in 1990 that they could easily afford the cost of unification - pay it out of "petty cash", so to speak? What an illusion that proved to be and how it prevented Germany from switching in good time to a more realistic policy!

A recent article by David Marsh aptly described this phenomenon:

"Sidetracked by unification, Germany has fallen behind in the game of adapting to a world in which China and the Czech Republic are now competitors to the 'Mittelstand' factories of Cochem, Chemnitz and Castrop-

Rauxel. In 1945, Britain's great triumph obstructed subsequent adjustment to the weakness that represented the cost of victory, exacerbating Britain's post-war decline. In similar fashion, Germany's reunification triumph in 1990 has made the task of tackling its own internal weaknesses all the more difficult - and may herald a period in which, contrary to all the overblown fears, German frailty will stand out more than German vigour." (New Statesman, 21.6.1996)

Is this not the point at which realpolitik should step in and address such issues instead of us wasting our energy in hurling fruitless accusations back and forth across the Channel? Europe's colourful diversity is also a reflection of the colourful diversity of its individual national problems, stemming partly from the various national idiosyncrasies. The path to European integration can only be one half of the answer to these problems - sovereign control over one's own domestic issues is the other. The true art of European policy-making lies in steering a middle course between what countries can sensibly do together and what each individual country must do for itself.

Last but not least
Crossroads and roundabouts

How different they are after all, the two cousins...

The images we have of one another go back a very long way. In earlier times, as European nations sought contact with their closest neighbours, there was a formative period in which opinions about each other were consolidated; that in turn sharpened people's view of themselves and their own societies. This constant interplay between esteem and disparagement, between competition, misunderstandings and honest endeavour, produced fixed images which were by no means solely derived from stereotypes. It was not all pure caricature. On the contrary, there was always "something to them".

So there was an element of truth in what the Swabian Liberal Karl Friedrich Moser wrote in 1758: *"Each nation has its main characteristic. In Germany it is obedience; in England liberty; in Holland trade; in France the gloire of the King."* And Henry of Huntingdon's 12th century portrayal of Britain seems just as apposite 800 years later: *"England is full of merriment, the people free-spirited and inclined to jest."*

"Each nation has its main characteristic" - one could write reams on the subject. But this book cannot close without examining at least some of these main and subsidiary characteristics of the British and the Germans, some of their idiosyncrasies, some of their curious and less curious differences.

It was Heinrich von Kleist (1777-1811) who recounted a delightful anecdote about two English boxers - one from Portsmouth, the other from Plymouth - who held a public exhibition bout to determine once and for all which of them was the best in the land. Every successful blow brought words of praise from the man on the receiving end. They beat each other to a pulp (boxing rules were slightly different in those days) yet neither of them forgot to compliment his opponent on the quality of his punches. This continued until the man from Plymouth suffered a final blow and, rolling his eyes, keeled over and died - but not before exclaiming "that was not a bad one either!"

The image of the British sportsman: an old characteristic which this anecdote takes to absurd extremes. Kleist implicitly distinguishes between "fighting" and "sport" - the former excessively rough, the latter taken to excesses of politeness and fairplay. But the two are obviously not mutually exclusive. The opponent's roughness does not preclude appreciation of his ability, even in defeat.

Fairplay - a "main characteristic" of the British? But one must not forget that there is another side to the coin: the British fighting spirit. How else could one explain the British reaction to the EU export ban on beef and beef byproducts...

Of course, fairplay is still the guiding principle of everyday life in the United Kingdom. If one accidentally treads on an Englishman's toes, he will mumble an apology, as if it were *his* fault ... Fairplay goes hand in hand with a highly developed sense of embarrassing situations. It might be embarrassing for someone accidentally to be placed in the situation of having to apologise. So the best thing is to anticipate this by saying "sorry" first...

This reflex action is accompanied by a preference for speaking softly, for understatement and an aversion to any outward display or preaching of beliefs - it might embarrass someone.

Fairplay is therefore allied to restraint, a traditionally Roman trait. "Spare the vanquished" was the call to the successful commander in the field. Losing is humiliating enough... Let us apply this to the everyday situation of the traffic chaos on our roads. It is bad enough to be at a disadvantage: the smaller versus the bigger engine, the slower versus the faster, the car versus the bus or lorry, the car on the slip road trying to filter into the main stream of traffic, not to mention the pedestrian versus the motor vehicle. Nowhere is one freed from all these situations in such an uncomplicated manner, nowhere is one liberated so quickly from such embarrassment as in the British Isles.

Sadly, one cannot be sure how long this blissful state of affairs will last. Even Her Majesty's subjects are no longer immune to the infectious disease spreading through all modern societies - inconsiderate and rude behaviour.

But every virtue has its price. Being naturally restrained, the British find it difficult to articulate their feelings. Apart from sporting events, where passionate commitment is permitted, the British tend to treat the world of emotions like Euro-sceptics treat Brussels - as far as possible, they avoid it like the plague. Feelings are the most powerful force on the Continent situated just off the English coast; they must be held in check at all cost. The balance of power must be maintained...

By the same token, the British never lose their composure (cf. "SPOTLIGHT 51"). This is a reflex reaction allied to restraint - a "main characteristic" which can be traced back to an ancient Roman precept: stoicism. The British have virtually been weaned on this idea, witness Alexander Pope's famous dictum in his "Essay on Criticism" (1711): *"Avoid extremes. (...) Let not each gay turn thy rapture move. / For fools admire, but men of sense approve."* The stoic, the gentleman and the dandy all have their roots here.

And when the chips are down, this is also how John Bull reacts. His outward composure belies the strength of his inner determination. After Dunkerque, it was Churchill's voice which kept the spirit of resistance alive in the darkest hours.

To return to Heinrich von Kleist. He is also the author of a famous novella entitled "Michael Kohlhaas", whose main protagonist displays something of what the Germans themselves have come to regard as one of their "main characteristics". The book is about pig-headed righteousness and the extremes to which someone will go to obtain justice, even at the cost of setting the whole world on fire. Kohlhaas pursues his point of view with single-minded disregard for the real world around him. Reality does not interest him. He is prepared to ignore it to the point of total destruction, even total self-destruction. This is the final consequence of his "konsequent" behaviour.

"*Konsequent*" is a virtually untranslatable German word, containing elements of "logical", "consistent" and "uncompromising". It presupposes an unwavering stance, sometimes bordering on the ruthless. A person is "*konsequent*" if his face remains expressionless because the occasion may be sad and laughter may therefore not be appropriate. Shakespeare, on the other hand, is completely "inkonsequent" because his tragedies are interspersed with what English drama tradition calls "comic relief". With his witty jests, the fool provides relief from the oppressive force of destiny and makes it bearable. Humour is a temporary means of evading the bitter certainty, the inevitable "*Konsequenz*", of death. It is an opt-out, a deep-seated reservation...

Often the British cannot be serious because they are afraid of making fools of themselves. In actual fact, they have a major problem with "*Konsequenz*". They know and accept the rules of the game, but otherwise nothing is sacred. Nor do they draw the line at self-irony. That is why they are predestined to make compromises, the pre-condition for a life without absolute truths.

As well as being "*konsequent*", Germans are also "*gründlich*" ("thorough") - another virtue which demands its price. An overall concept for restructuring the welfare state would be thorough - but unfeasible. The way Alexander the Great cut the Gordian knot was thorough. However, today's knots tend to be made of concrete and thus less easy to sever.

But never say die. At a symposium in Vail, Colorado in autumn 1995 (cf. p. 191) Margaret Thatcher said: *"Political leaders are not there to accept realities. We are there to change the inevitable."* That was the uncompromising nature of Margaret Thatcher's character, her Teutonic legacy as it were, her "Konsequenz", her thoroughness. For those qualities she was both much-admired and much-maligned. In the political arena, her determination seemed like a reversal of roles between British and German characteristics. She had an overall concept, an all-embracing view which she upheld to her own bitter end.

Heathrow Airport, by contrast, does not seem to work to any overall concept. But no society can be reduced to a single denominator. Margaret Thatcher was certainly not "typically English", if one is to believe an expert in this field, Hans-Dieter Gelfert (*"Typisch englisch - Wie die Briten wurden, was sie sind"*, 1995). Gelfert writes: *"Over the centuries, the English have learned that solutions are not all 'do or die' situations, that they prefer ad hoc solutions to a systematic approach, compromise to rigorous principle."* German thinking, on the other hand, is determined *"in politics by the concept of State, in philosophy by the principle of totality, in aesthetics by the sublime and in literature by the tragic."*

When it comes to defining the word "State", our two cousins are worlds apart. For the Germans, the word has mystical connotations. To British ears it sounds rather suspicious, almost as suspicious as the term "big government" to the Americans. It has been claimed that the differences in mentality between France, Britain and Germany are due to the different circumstances under which the Enlightenment reached these countries. In Britain, the Enlightenment was preceded by political and social upheavals, the "Glorious Revolution" of 1688/9 and the resulting reforms which strengthened Parliament. Consequently, English philosophers were empiricists who described an existing condition as they perceived it.

In France, the social, political and intellectual revolutions arrived virtually simultaneously so that the philosophers of the Enlightenment were in the vanguard of change. In Germany, however, the ideas of the Enlightenment were in place long before political liberation, so that "progress" could only serve the philosophers as material for speculation (cf. Chapter II, 6, "SPOTLIGHT 26"). A large gulf opened up between political emancipation and philosophy, leaving the middle ground for the abstract idea of the State to develop as an all-encompassing body, for the powerful and the ordinary citizen alike, eventually assuming total responsibility to dispense and regulate.

The British treat such notions with utmost scepticism. They still have no Residents' Registration Office, no identity cards and the British police are unarmed. (Although this no longer applies to the special services. Terrorism exacts its price.) In addition, the Army - unlike the Navy - has to be approved each year by Parliament. A standing army, you see, could rebel and jeopardise national liberty. Scepticism goes deep. The British expect much less of the State than the Germans do. They swear by private organisations for public welfare, such as Oxfam, Amnesty International, Friends of the Earth, World Wildlife Fund, Save the Children. Similar organisations have been established in Germany along these lines (SOS Kinderdorf etc.).

The British view is that the State must be deregulated - until a scandal like Mad Cow Disease comes along, a problem which was not taken seriously in Britain for a long time. In cases like that, the general public is liable to ask whether the principle of "restrained authority" may not have been taken too far. The downside of our national virtues...

One is tempted to conclude that the British do not recognise the concept of "the State" since they regard themselves more as one large family. This is indeed what sets them apart historically from their German cousin. The patchwork of territories that used to be Germany somehow never grew together as a people. Even when the Reich was united in 1871, the various German tribes still clung obstinately to their separate identities. Nowhere was this more acutely felt than in the country concerned. "The Germans really don't like each other very much", was the gist of Bismarck's thinking on the subject. Goethe also often dwelt on it:

"We are all very different: agreement is inconceivable: Everybody upholds the viewpoint of his respective province, his town, indeed his own self. We may have to wait a long time before we achieve any kind of homogeneity." (to Eckermann, 3.10.1828)

The British experience was altogether different. There was always a strong dose of individualism, but it never prevented a high degree of homogeneity among the people. London called the tune and the Monarch was the central figurehead to symbolise both tradition and familiarity. Visitors from the Continent, especially Germans, never failed to comment on this phenomenon. It was perhaps most lovingly described in the following excerpt from Heinrich Heine's *"English Fragments"* of 1828:

"Notwithstanding (...) opposing life styles and ways of thinking, the English display a unity of mind which clearly demonstrates that they feel themselves to be one people, (...) like plants which have blossomed forth from the same soil and live in miraculous harmony with it. In England, everything is discreetly interwoven with everything else, like in a network of correspondences. Hence the secret harmony of all life and activities in England, in contrast to one's first impression of total confusion and contradictions."

If the notion of "family", of feeling closely interwoven as a people, is one counterpoint to the concept of "the State", then "ground rules" provide the other. Such rules - the mortar between the bricks of a society which has no written constitution - may also succeed in holding a society together irrespective of its inequalities. Take school uniforms as a case in point. By donning school uniforms, British children literally leave their social differences at home: *this* uniform does not impose uniformity, it merely neutralises the natural lack of uniformity, thereby focusing attention on each child's true potential individuality. An interesting paradox.

A uniform, without uniformity

Ground rules. When an Englishman stands in a queue, he is no more virtuous than those who do not queue. He is simply restraining the chaos which would automatically erupt if such discipline did not exist. Anyone who has experienced the jostling at buffets on the Continent or the pushing and shoving on German stations as people try to board Intercity trains, appreciates the advantages of a calm and composed approach.

Germans are carefree where their British cousins are reticent; and reticent where the British are more carefree. German car owners vigorously uphold their freedom to drive as fast as they wish on their motorways, yet German pedestrians will wait patiently at a red light even if there is no traffic in sight. Don't even try to "understand" other countries, just look at their paradoxes. Germany is full of signposts explaining what is permitted and what is *"verboten"* - the legalistic expression of the underlying written constitution. The British, with no such formal constitution, are totally at the mercy of case law and tradition. For the British, a red light at a pedestrian crossing is merely an invitation to wait, not a mandatory legal requirement.

A love of the unregulated on the one hand and a highly developed sense of discipline, rules of the game and rituals on the other - that is one of many British paradoxes. There is an overwhelming desire not to be "typecast". This can sometimes take on curious forms. You will virtually never see an Englishman standing at a supermarket checkout with a purse in his hand like his German counterpart. It is inconceivable that he would produce small change from the compartments of a well-guarded receptacle and carefully count out the coins. The done thing in England is to carry loose change in one's pocket where it clinks away until casually produced in the manner of a *grand seigneur*. Many aspects of the British way of life reflect the attitudes of the old landed gentry, the lesser nobility.

Comparing the Germans and the British: Two voices.

One of the best comparisons of the more systematic Germans and the more pragmatically inclined British can be found in the writings of Ernst Jünger - an author who is actually more at home in the French aesthetic tradition than the Anglo-Saxon democratic world. The following is an extract from his "Paris Diary" dated 16.8.1942 (it is interesting to note that, typical of his generation (b. 1895), Jünger still refers to the Germans as "Prussians"):

"Anglo-Saxon constancy in deteriorating circumstances - a puzzling and surprising feature, which one would rather have expected of the Prussians. However, the difference lies in the fact that the Englishman can take a considerably greater portion of anarchy. If both were pub landlords in run-down areas, the Prussian would insist on the rules being strictly observed in each room. This would enable him to maintain a certain superficial degree of order while the entire sub-structure was eaten away by nihilism. The Englishman, on the other hand, would initially tolerate the growing disorder, continue serving ale and taking money until he could stand no more - at which point he would go upstairs with some of his customers and beat up the others.

In terms of character, the Englishman has the advantage over the Prussian of the phlegmatic over the highly-strung disposition, in practical terms that of the seafarer *over the landlubber. Seafaring folk are used to greater ebb and flow..."*

The following comment by an old lady in a London underground station in October 1940, after a large bomb had just exploded above ground, would seem to confirm Jünger's hypothesis:

"That Hitler - he is a fidget!"

(taken from a BBC live recording)

Not wishing to make a fool of oneself, not wanting to appear bourgeois and not succumbing to hypochondria - it is all part of the same secret *comment*. The nonchalant approach to money or the serious aspects of life may prepare the observer for another British oddity - the aversion to wearing warm clothes in winter. Men's overcoats are virtually out, unless we are talking about the professional man in the City and the dress code of his milieu - where scarf-wearing is frowned upon.

This is because it is the done thing to be freezing cold. It is "good form". Just look at the blue-lipped British students, how they brave the winter with open-neck shirts and only the scantiest protection against the cold, and you will know that snobbery, too, has its masochistic side...

Well, every society cuts its coat according to its cloth. The country with no written constitution prefers roundabouts at its traffic junctions. The country of mandatory and prohibitory regulations swears by the crossroad as the most reliable form of traffic control. The argument being that an uncontrolled flow of traffic increases the risk, also for insurances and their legal experts who would face a collision of judicial opinions about the rights and wrongs of every minor roundabout accident. Red and green lights are better suited to the "regulated" mentality, the roundabout better suited to voluntary restraint and "deregulated" thinking, risks included. Moreover, traffic flows at roundabouts and does not leave the driver time to dream, whereas a traffic light can be switched to red until the driver virtually falls asleep. Major annoyance potential, low risk - the secret of all bureaucracies.

"Each nation has its main characteristic. In Germany it is obedience, in England it is liberty...", Karl Friedrich Moser wrote in 1758. That begs the question as to what conclusions we can draw under the present-day conditions of free and democratic societies as we peruse the treasure trove of British-German differences, with all their charming, but sometimes disturbing peculiarities? Are they more than just details to enliven the small talk at cocktail parties the world over?

Comparative studies of this kind usually suffer from one serious shortcoming: they do not go beyond their own suppositions. They ignore the possibility of opposites being complementary, of extremes being convergent, of absolutes becoming co-operation, of incompatibilities turning into compromises, of exclusive positions generating synergy (cf. Chapter III, 1). They often fail to pose the question: what happens when differing attitudes are brought together and allowed to cross-fertilise?

The answer is not too difficult. Are contradictions not simply two sides of the same coin? In philosophy, "theory" and "practice" are not just opposites. They are also crucially important as complementary factors. In science, "experiment" and "experience" are equally fundamental to the acquisition and expansion of knowledge. Modern society, the very idea of the *contrat social*, would be inconceivable without both "law-abiding" and "free" citizens, just as every administration requires the simultaneous application of "precision" and "flexibility".

Is it not a fact that modern traffic systems need both crossroads and roundabouts, rigorous and flexible principles? And where would politics be without visions which can lend wings to experience, just as experience can pull visions back down to earth?

In other words: if one regards the British and the Germans as two archetypal counterpoles, the resolution of this tense relationship is of no less archetypal significance. At the point of synthesis, these two opposites meet in inseparable fellowship. That is also the underlying theme of this book.

In fact, this is one of the secrets of post-modernist politics, which cost endless effort and even greater suffering before it was discovered: European States which once sought their *raison d'être* in conflict and rivalry, now serve their own best interests by pursuing co-operation, trade and peaceful competition (cf. also *"En passant"*, p. 161ff.).

That is also why German-British relations have a depth and intensity which are now virtually taken for granted - perhaps not on all political issues, but otherwise across the entire spectrum of what we call culture and way of life, including academic and artistic exchange.

It is precisely the geographical and historical dissimilarities which ensure that this exchange does not lead to excessive standardisation. Over-zealous harmonisers would do well to heed Tocqueville's warning: *"The more alike people become, the more sensitively they react to differences"*. It is the differences which make us mutually interesting. But to ensure that these differences do not touch raw nerves, it is essential to preserve the natural dissimilarities from which they evolved.

Fortunately, there is little likelihood of the German and British cousins becoming identical twins. They are extremely compatible, without being interchangeable and derive their particularly close relations from some classic contrasts.

What greater compliment could one pay to the quality of a relationship?

THE END

4. A German in England: Prince Albert

SPOTLIGHT 15 (P. 50-51)

Queen Victoria was also of pure German stock. But how did Germans accede to the British throne in the first place?

SPOTLIGHT 16 (P. 53-54)

Prince Albert: Patron of the Arts, social reformer, open to technical innovations.

SPOTLIGHT 17 (P. 56-57)

In Albert's day, the Germans and the British were also linked by technology, transport and tourism.

5. An Englishman in Germany: Shakespeare

SPOTLIGHT 18 (P. 60)

Leo Tolstoy quipped: "Shakespeare is a German invention". How right he was...

SPOTLIGHT 19 (P. 62)

Shakespeare's early days in Germany: harmless, silly - but "typically English".

SPOTLIGHT 20 (P. 64-65)

Shakespeare: yes, but in moderation - said Goethe, who himself constantly returned to the Bard for inspiration.

6. Jewish Émigrés or the Continent comes to Great Britain

SPOTLIGHT 21 (P. 68)

In 1848/49, London was already the capital of a united Europe of the persecuted.

SPOTLIGHT 22 (P. 70-71)

How Marx and Engels hoped in vain for the revolution in Great Britain.

SPOTLIGHT 23 (P. 74-77)

Germany: Where political reforms were lacking, intellectuals soon sought refuge in theory and speculation... but also soon learned to joke about it.

SPOTLIGHT 24 (P. 79-81)

The books they write about one another have often been cultural "eye-openers" for the British and the Germans.

7. Educational exchange across the Channel today

SPOTLIGHT 25 (P. 83-84)

"That is what pleases our womenfolk!" What the ageing Goethe thought about the young British...

SPOTLIGHT 26 (P. 86)

Vocational training: A German-British joint venture.

SPOTLIGHT 27 (P. 88-89)

How Prince Pückler went to England in search of a bride.

8. Songs without words: German-British relations are alive with the sound of music

SPOTLIGHT 28 (P. 92)

The "Philharmonic Society" and Beethoven: A great symphony - and much warmth of feeling...

SPOTLIGHT 29 (P. 95)

Great Britain, a "country with no musical tradition": one of the oldest clichés around.

ANNEX II

Selected Bibliography

ATTALI, Jacques:
Verbatim III. Paris 1995.
In: MÜNCHHAUSEN, Tankmar von:
"Wir können Deutschland schließlich
nicht den Krieg erklären." Frankreich
und die deutsche Einheit. Mitterrand
distanziert sich.
In: *Frankfurter Allgemeine Zeitung*,
12.10.1995.

BIRKE, Adolf:
*Vom Mißtrauen zur Partnerschaft.
Aspekte deutsch-britischer Beziehungen seit
dem 18. Jahrhundert.*
In: Niedersächsische Landeszentrale für
politische Bildung (ed.), Großbritannien
und Deutschland. Nachbarn in Europa.
Hanover 1988.
and KLUXEN, Kurt (ed.): *Viktorianisches
England in deutscher Perspektive.*
Prinz-Albert-Studien Vol. 1.
Munich 1983.
ibid.: *England und Hannover.*
Prinz-Albert-Studien Vol. 4.
Munich 1992.

BREITENSTEIN, Rolf (ed.):
Those Germans ... and how we see them.
London 1973.
(ed.): *Twinning - Deutsch-britische
Partnerschaften.* London 1974.
(ed.): *Total War to Total Trust. Personal
Accounts of 30 Years of Anglo-German
Relations - The Vital Role of Non-
Governmental Organisations.*
London 1976.

BRINITZER, Carl:
*Hier spricht London. Von einem der dabei
war.* Hamburg 1969.

BROCK, George:
Why We Keep Getting It "Wrong".
Lecture to the Deutsch-Englische
Gesellschaft, January 1996. Typescript.

BUCHSTAB, Günther:
*Adenauer: "Es mußte alles neu gemacht
werden."* Die Protokolle des CDU-
Bundesvorstandes 1950-1953.
Stuttgart 1986.

COOPER, Robert:
German-British Relations.
Speech at the British-Bavarian seminar
in Hohenkammer, 24 July 1996.
Typescript.

CRAIG, Gordon A.:
The Germans. New York 1982.

DAHRENDORF, Ralf:
Die Bismarcks mit der Bundesbank.
Opening lecture at the Königswinter
Conference 1995.
In: *Die ZEIT*, 7.4.1995.
*A History of the London School of Economics
and Political Science 1895-1995.*
Oxford 1995.
in: HERZ, Dietmar: Spagat zwischen
*Theorie und Praxis. Ralf Dahrendorf erzählt
die Geschichte der London School of
Economics.*
In: *Die ZEIT* 15.9.1995.
WERBKE, Hans Joachim: *Ticket zum
Höhenflug. London School of Economics.*
In: Rheinischer Merkur, 13.10.1995.

DIERS, Michael:
*Dem guten Europäer gewidmet. Das
wiedergewonnene Warburg-Haus in
Hamburg.*
In: *Neue Zürcher Zeitung*, International
Edition, 16./17.9.1995.

FINSTERBUSCH, Stephan:
Aus dem Umerziehungslager für deutsche Kriegsgefangene ist ein internationales Konferenzzentrum geworden. Vor 50 Jahren wurde Wilton Park Conferences gegründet.
Frankfurter Allgemeine Zeitung, 30.7.1996.

FIRCHOW, Peter Edgerly:
The Death of the German Cousin. Variations on a Literary Stereotype, 1890-1920.
Bucknell University Press, Lewisburg 1986.

FISCHER, Manfred:
Belegte Brote. Die Gegend um Newcastle symbolisiert das Comeback des Landes.
In: *Wirtschaftswoche* No. 33, 10.8.1995.

FONTANE, Theodor:
Der englische Charakter heute wie gestern.
Collection of writings on contemporary history. Berlin 1916.

FOSTER, Norman:
At the democratic heart of the new Germany.
Sir Norman Foster in an interview with the *Financial Times*, 22.8.1994.

FRÄNKEL, Heinrich:
Deutschland im Urteil des Auslandes, früher und - jetzt. Munich 1916.

FULFORD, Roger:
The Prince Consort. London 1949.
Hanover to Windsor. London 1960 (Fontana Paperback 1966).
(ed.): *Dearest Child. Letters Between Queen Victoria and the Princess Royal 1858-1861.* London 1964.

GALL, Lothar:
Bismarck und England. In: Aspekte der deutsch-britischen Beziehungen im Laufe der Jahrhunderte. Stuttgart 1978 (see under Schlenke, Manfred).

GARTON ASH, Timothy:
In Europe's Name. Germany and the Divided Continent. London 1993
Security is the vital issue in Europe. Misunderstandings between Britain and Germany detract from the two nations' common interests. Abridged version of the concluding speech at the 1995 Königswinter Conference.
In: *Times*, 18.4.1995.

GELFERT, Hans-Dieter:
Typisch englisch. Wie die Briten wurden, was sie sind. Beck'sche Reihe Vol. 1088, Munich 1995.

GENSCHER, Hans-Dietrich:
Erinnerungen. Berlin 1995

GILLESPIE, George T.:
Prinzgemahl Albert - Ein Überblick.
In: Jahrbuch der Coburger Landesstiftung, 1971.
Das Englandbild bei Fontane, Moltke und Engels.
In: Viktorianisches England in deutscher Perspektive. Munich 1983 (see under Birke, Adolf).

GOETHE-Kalender auf das Jahr 1911
(*Urteile Goethe's über deutsche und Engländer*, pp. 50-82). Leipzig 1910.

GUNDOLF, Friedrich:
Shakespeare und der deutsche Geist.
Berlin 1920.

HAMANN, Christoph:
Michel und John Bull auf neuen Wegen. Jugendliche aus Deutschland und Großbritannien diskutieren in Berlin über die Zukunft Europas.
In: *Süddeutsche Zeitung*, 10.8.1995.

HAMBURGER, Michael:
Zwischen den Sprachen.
Essays. Frankfurt 1996.

HEAD, David:
Made in Germany. The Corporate Identity of a Nation. London 1992.

HEARNDEN, Arthur:
Red Robert - A Life of Robert Birley.
London 1984.

HEIMRICH, Bernhard:
Beim Wettlauf der guten Vorsätze sehen sich die Briten in bester Position. Klimaschutz und Umweltpolitik in Großbritannien.
In: *Frankfurter Allgemeine Zeitung,*
20 June 1995.

HERWARTH, Hans von:
Von Adenauer zu Brandt. Erinnerungen.
Berlin 1990.

HEYDEMANN, Günther:
Großbritannien und Deutschland. Probleme einer "Stillen Allianz" in Europa.
In: KASTENDIEK, Hans / ROHE, Karl / VOLLE, Angelika (eds.),
Länderbericht Großbritannien.
Geschichte - Politik - Wirtschaft -
Gesellschaft. Bundeszentrale für
Politische Bildung. Bonn 1994.

HILDEBRAND, Klaus:
Die britische Europapolitik zwischen imperialem Mandat und innerer Reform 1856-1876. Rheinisch-Westfälische
Akademie der Wissenschaften, Lectures
(G322). Opladen 1993.

HOWARD, Michael:
A Love-Hate Relationship: Anglo-German Relations in the 20th Century. Lecture
delivered in Berlin, Munich and Bonn,
autumn 1994. Typescript.

HUNDT, Josef:
Das Menschenbild der Demokratie.
Published by the Staatsbürgerliche
Bildungsstelle der Landesregierung
Nordrhein-Westfalen, Vol. 6.
Hamm 1947.

HUSEMANN, Harald:
I think, therefore I stereotype, therefore I caricature, therefore I am.
In: HERRMANN, Karin/HUSEMANN,
Harald/MOYLE, Lachlan (eds.),
Coping With the Relations - Anglo-German Cartoons from the Fifties to the Nineties.
Osnabrück 1993.
In: HUGHES, Terence (ed.): *The Image Makers.* National Stereotypes and the
Media. Transcript of a seminar at the
Goethe-Institut in London,
21.-22. 1. 1994.
Media response to the Cartoon
Exhibition "Coping With the Relations"
and the accompanying seminar "The
Image Makers", London, January 1994.
Facsimilie copies from the Goethe
Institut.

HUTTON, Will:
The State We're In. London 1994.

JENKINS OF HILLHEAD, Lord, i.a.:
Anglo-German Relations. Debate in the
House of Lords, 22.5.1996. Hansard
House of Lords, pp. 854-896.

JENNER, Michael:
Scenes from a Relationship. Britain's
German Heritage. Foreign and
Commonwealth Office, London 1996.

JOFFE, Josef:
Britain - Looking From the Outside In.
Speech at a conference organised by the
Foreign and Commonwealth Office,
London, 29.3.1995. Typescript.
Europa braucht Albion.
In: *Süddeutsche Zeitung,* 11.6.1996.

JOHNSON, Paul:
Hitler's Gift to Britain.
In: *Sunday Telegraph*, 29.1.1995.

JOLL, James:
War Guilt 1914. A Continuing Controversy.
In: Aspekte der deutsch-britischen
Beziehungen im Laufe der
Jahrhunderte. Stuttgart 1978 (for
further details see under Schlenke,
Manfred).

JONES, Rick:
Sing if you're glad to be Brits.
In: *Evening Standard*, 15.9.1995.

JUST, Klaus Günther:
Fürst Hermann von Pückler-Muskau.
In: JUST, K.G., Übergänge, Probleme
und Gestalten der Literatur.
Berne/Munich 1966.

KAELBLE, Hartmut:
*Nachbarn am Rhein. Entfremdung und
Annäherung der französischen und
deutschen Gesellschaft seit 1880.*
Munich 1991.

KAISER, Karl / ROPER, John (eds.):
*Die Stille Alliance - Deutsch-Britische
Sicherheitskooperation.* Bonn 1987.

KANT, Immanuel:
Der Charakter des Volks. In: Werke XII,
Schriften zur Anthropologie,
Geschichtsphilosophie, Politik und
Pädagogik 2. Frankfurt 1964.

KEEZER, Dexter M.:
*A Unique Contribution to International
Relations - The Story of Wilton Park.*
Foreword by Sir Robert Birley.
London/New York 1973.

KERSTING, Ann:
*Carl Halle - Sir Charles Hallé. Ein
europaischer Musiker. Beiträge zur
westfälischen Musikgeschichte,* hrsg. vom
Westfälischen Musikarchiv.
Hagen 1986.

KIELINGER, Thomas:
*Anglo-German Relations Within Wider
Partnerships.* Opening lecture at a
symposium of the Royal United Services
Institute and the Stiftung Wissenschaft
und Politik, Ebenhausen, 28.6.1996.
Typescript.
*Deutsch-britische Unterschiede - real,
altvertraut und doch überbrückbar.*
In: KAISER, Karl and KRAUSE,
Joachim, Deutschlands neue
Außenpolitik, Vol. 3: Interessen und
Strategien. Schriften der Deutschen
Gesellschaft für Auswärtige Politik und
Wirtschaft. Vol. 62, Munich 1996.

KONIGS, Philip:
*The Hanoverian Kings and their Homeland.
A study of the Personal Union (1714-1837).*
Lewes (Sussex) 1993.

KOPPENFELS, Werner von:
*Orwell auf dem großdeutschen Trümmerfeld.
Ein vergessener Augenzeugenbericht über das
Kriegsende.* In: *Neue Zürcher Zeitung*,
International edition, 6./7. 5.1995.

KUROPKA, Joachim:
*Britische Besatzungspolitik und Neubeginn
des öffentlichen Lebens. Probleme des
Wiederaufbaus in der britischen
Besatzungszone.*
In: ECKERMANN, Willigis and
KUROPKA, J., Neubeginn 1945.
Zwischen Kontinuität und Wandel.
Vechtaer Universitätsschriften, Vol. 4.
Cloppenburg 1988.

LAUFENBERG, Frank (in collaboration with Ingrid Hake):
Rock- und Pop-Lexikon, in 2 vols.
Düsseldorf 1994.

LEINS, Hermann (ed.):
Deutschland und England. Dokumente zu einem Staatsbesuch im Oktober 1958.
Tübingen.

LEONHARDT, Rudolf Walter:
77mal England. Panorama einer Insel.
Munich 1965.
Die beste Journalistenschule der Welt. Der German Service des Londoner Rundfunks.
Die ZEIT, 9.5.1975.
Engländer und Deutsche, die Vettern - vor Jahrhunderten und heute und überhaupt.
In: HILL, Roland i.a. (eds.),
Großbritannien: England, Wales
Schottland und Nordirland.
Munich/Lucerne 1981.

LLOYD, John:
Soll Schottland unabhängig werden?
In: Der kranke Mann am Ärmelkanal.
"Freibeuter" No. 54, Quarterly Journal
for Culture and Politics, Klaus
Wagenbach, Berlin 1992. (Contains i.a.
also: Marilyn Strathern: *Die Entsorgung
der englischen Gesellschaft;* Ian Aitken:
Fleet Street und die englische Privatsphäre;
Peter Scott: *Über die Zukunft der
englischen Hochschulen;* Patrick Wright:
*Großbritanniens Niedergang und der
deutsche Wald.*)

MACMURRAY, John:
*England - Wegbereiter der kommenden
Weltkultur? (The philosophical Pattern of
Our Time).* Essay with a Foreword by
Werner Milch. Deutsch-Englische
Gesellschaft e.V., Hann. Münden.
Series A, vol. 2. Hann. Münden 1950.

MAJOR, John:
Es geht auch um die Seele unseres Volkes.
Signed article on the BSE crisis. In:
Frankfurter Allgemeine Zeitung, 21.6.1995.

MANDER, John:
*Our German Cousins. Anglo-German
Relations In the 19th and 20th Centuries.*
London 1974.

MANSFIELD, Katherine:
In a German Pension. Penguin Twentieth-
Century Classics. London 1964.

MANZ, Gustav (ed.):
*Das Englandbuch der Täglichen Rundschau.
Ein Zeit- und Kulturspiegel.* Berlin 1915.

MARSH, David:
Deutschland im Umbruch.
Vienna/Darmstadt 1990.
*Die Bundesbank - Die Bank, die Europa
beherrscht.* Munich 1992.
*Der zaudernde Riese. Deutschland in
Europa.* Munich 1994.
*Contact between cultures. How UK
companies have benefited from a
German management perspective. Financial
Times*, 29.5.1995.
*Away with Kaiser Kohl. Britain must
conquer its fear of Germany if we are to
understand the problems facing Europe's
giant. New Statesman*, 21 June 1996.

MASSIE, Robert M.:
*Dreadnought. Britain, Germany and the
Coming of the Great War.* 1993.

MICHAELIS, Rolf:
*Eine Engländerin in Halle. Penelope
Willard, Geschäftsführerin der Franckeschen
Stiftungen und verantwortlich für ein
europäisches Kulturprogramm.*
Die ZEIT, 21.6.1996.

MOMMSEN, Wolfgang J.:
Vom Kriegsgegner zum Partner.
Die deutsch-britischen Beziehungen seit dem
Zweiten Weltkrieg.
In: 40 Jahre Deutsch-Englische
Gesellschaft e.V. 1949-1989.
Festveranstaltung 7. Juni Industrieclub
Düsseldorf. Bonn 1989.

MORGAN, Roger:
The History of Königswinter.
In: GILES, Frank (ed.), 40 Years On.
Four decades of the Königwinter
Conference. BPCC Blackpool Ltd. 1990.

NEILL, A.S.:
Theorie und praxis der anti-autoritären
erziehung. das beispiel summerhill.
Reinbek 1969.

NETZER, Hans-Joachim:
Ein deutscher Prinz in England. Albert von
Sachsen-Coburg und Gotha, Gemahl der
Königin Victoria. Munich 1988 (special
edition Deutscher Taschenbuch Verlag
1992).

NIEDHART, Gottfried:
Britische Deutschlandpolitik und Adenauers
Englandpolitik 1949-1956. In: ROHE,
Karl/SCHMIDT, Gustav/POGGE VON
STRANDMANN, Hartmann (eds.):
Deutschland - Großbritannien - Europa.
Arbeitskreis Deutsche England-
Forschung, Vol. 20. Bochum 1992.

OPPEL, Horst:
Englisch-deutsche Literaturbeziehungen.
Vol. I: Von den Anfängen bis zum Ausgang
des 18. Jahrhunderts. Vol II: Von der
Romantik bis zur Gegenwart.
Berlin 1971.

PIGOTT, Stuart:
Warum wird der Riesling wieder ein
Kultwein, Herr Pigott?
Interview with the *Frankfurter Allgemeine*
Zeitung, 10.11.1995.

PÜCKLER, Carl-Erdmann:
Einflußreiche Engländer. Porträtskizzen
englischer Politiker. Berlin 1938.

RADICE, Giles:
Offshore. Britain and the European Idea.
London 1992
The New Germans. London 1995.
In: POWELL, Charles: Germany
through rose-tinted glasses.
Review of Giles Radice "The New
Germans". *Financial Times,* 27.4.1995.

READING, Brian:
The Fourth Reich. London 1995.

RENTOUL, John:
Tony Blair. London 1995.

ROMBECK, Hans/ NEUMANN,
Wolfgang:
Die Beatles - Ihre Karriere, ihre Erfolge.
Revised and updated by Robert Lyng
and Andreas Schaffer (Bastei-Lübbe-
Taschenbuch Vol. 61318).
Bergisch Gladbach 1995.

SALCHOW, Burkhart:
Vom Main an die Themse. Deutsche Banken
werden britischer. Rheinischer Merkur,
3.11.1995.
In: hjf (initials): *Morgan Grenfell: Bulliger*
Auftritt in der City.
Die Investmentabteilung der Deutschen Bank
ist aufgewühlt - und verärgert die
Konkurrenz.
Welt am Sonntag, 22.10.1995.

In: LEGNER, Alfred: *In London schlägt das Herz von Europas Wertpapierhandel. Welt am Sonntag,* 17.12.1995. In: KÖLLE, Hans Martin: *Finanzplatz London - Warum es deutsche Banken über den Kanal zieht. Rheinischer Merkur,* 21.6.1996.

SCHARF, Claus and SCHRÖDER, Hans-Jürgen (eds.):
Die Deutschlandpolitik Großbritanniens und die britische Zone 1945-1949. Wiesbaden 1979.

SCHEUNER, Ulrich:
Das Europäische Gleichgewicht und die britische Seeherrschaft. Hamburg 1943.

SCHIRMER, Walter F.:
Der Einfluß der deutschen Literatur auf die englische im 19. Jahrhundert. Halle/Saale 1947.

SCHLAES, Amity:
Germany's Chained Economy. In: *Foreign Affairs,* September/ October 1995.

SCHLENKE, Manfred:
England blickt nach Europa. Das konfessionelle Argument in der englischen Politik um die Mitte des 18. Jahrhunderts. In: KLUKE, Paul and ALTER, Peter (eds.), *Aspekte der deutsch-britischen Beziehungen im Laufe der Jahrhunderte.* Speeches and lectures on the opening of the German Historical Institute in London. Stuttgart 1978.

SCHMIDT, Doris:
Realität der Natur als Vision. "William Turner in Deutschland" - Eine Ausstellung in der Kunsthalle Mannheim. Süddeutsche Zeitung. 4./5.11.1995.

SCHULZ, Bettina:
Ich hasse es, Geld zu verschwenden. Die Privatbankiers in der City müssen sich umstellen. Frankfurter Allgemeine Zeitung, 4.4.1995.

SCHWARZ, Hans-Peter:
Vom Reich zur Bundesrepublik Deutschland im Widerstreit der außenpolitischen Konzeptionen in den Jahren der Besatzungsherrschaft 1945-1949. Neuwied 1966.
Adenauer. Der Aufstieg: 1876-1952. Stuttgart 1986.
Adenauer. Der Staatsmann: 1952-1967. Stuttgart 1986.
Begegnungen an der Seine. Deutsche Kanzler in Paris. Zürich 1993.

SMITH, Thomas F.A.:
The Soul of Germany. A Twelve Years Study of the People From Within 1902-1914. New York 1915.

SÖSEMANN, Bernd:
Die sog. Hunnenrede Wilhelms II. Textkritische und interpretatorische Bemerkungen zur Ansprache des Kaisers vom 27. Juli 1900 in Bremerhaven. In: *Historische Zeitschrift,* 222/2, 1976.
"Pardon wird nicht gegeben; Gefangene nicht gemacht". Zeugnisse und Wirkungen einer rhetorischen Mobilmachung. In: WILDEROTTER, Hans and POHL, Klaus-D. (eds.), *Der letzte Kaiser /Wilhelm II. im Exil.* Bertelsmann Lexikon Verlag / Deutsches Historisches Museum Berlin 1991.

SPENDER, Stephen:
European Witness. Hamish Hamilton Ltd. London 1946

STEINBERG, Jonathan:
Monster im Märchenwald. Wie uns die Engländer sehen.
In: Evangelische Kommentare, Heft 1/1995.
In: BARING, Arnulf: *Im Märchenwald der deutschen Politik. Aus politischen Zeitschriften - Vorbehalte gegen eine Achse Bonn-London. Frankfurter Allgemeine Zeitung,* 8.3.1995.

THACKERAY, William Makepeace:
Vanity Fair. Penguin paperback.

THATCHER, Margaret:
Wozu haben wir den Kalten Krieg beendet? Die Nationalstaaten brauchen Autonomie, die Welt braucht Zusammenhalt.
Symposium in Vail, Colorado, October 1995, attended by Margaret Thatcher, George Bush, François Mitterrand, Mikhail Gorbachev. *Die ZEIT,* 8.3.1996.

THOMAS, Michael:
Deutschland, England über alles. Rückkehr als englischer Besatzungsoffizier.
Munich 1987.

TOYNBEE, Arnold J.:
Acquaintances. (Bonn in Nazi-Time and A Lecture by Hitler, pp. 262-295) London/ New York 1967.

TRAUTMANN, Günther (ed.):
Die häßlichen Deutschen? Deutschland im Spiegel der westlichen und östlichen Nachbarn. Wissenschaftliche Buchgesellschaft, Darmstadt 1991.

TURNER, George:
The Anglo-German Association.
In: Total War to Total Trust
(cf. also BREITENSTEIN, Rolf).

UHLIG, Ralph:
Die Deutsch-Englische Gesellschaft 1949-1983. Göttingen 1986.

VOLLE, Angelika:
Deutsch-Britische Beziehungen. Geschichte und Gegenwart.
Landeszentrale für politische Bildung Berlin, series II "Politik - kurz und aktuell", Vol. 43, 1985.
Der mühsame Weg Großbritanniens nach Europa. In: Länderbricht Großbritannien. Bonn 1994 (cf. also HEYDERMANN, Günther).

WATSON, Alan:
The Germans - Who Are They Now?
London 1995 (Mandarin Paperback Edition).
Thatcher and Kohl - Old Rivalries Revisited.
In: BOND, Martin/SMITH, Julie/ WALLACE, Williams (ed.), *Eminent Europeans.* London 1996.

WELCH, David:
British Political Re-Education and its Impact on German Political Culture.
In: Deutschland - Großbritannien - Europa. Bochum 1992. (cf. also NIEDHART, Gottfried)

ZEIDENITZ, Stefan/BARKOW; Ben:
The Xenophobe's Guide to the Germans.
Ravette Books, London 1993.